ADVANCE PRAISE FOR

WHAT WOMEN LOSE

"This book offers fascinating and vivid details about Caribbean migrant women's writing. María Cristina Rodríguez has analyzed a considerable amount of novels that focus on the energy and expectations involved in these personal and professional enterprises. She especially addresses the tensions between key issues such as the adaptation to the global cities and the memories from the Caribbean in the past and present.

This is certainly one of the broadest presentations of literature by Caribbean women who write about migrating from the Caribbean to the United States, Canada, and Europe. The author gives a vivid picture of the diversity of cultural encounters from the perspectives of these female citizens in the effort to improve their professional and personal lifestyles."

Ineke Phaf-Rheinberger, Professor and Critic of Caribbean Literature,
Free University of Berlin and University of Maryland

"In an age of travel, exile, and human displacement of all sorts, how have marginalized women undergone the trials of the migrant experience? María Cristina Rodríguez's book brilliantly answers this question by examining the works of a well-known constellation of women writers from the francophone, hispanophone, and anglophone Caribbean, among them Maryse Condé, Edwidge Dandicat, Julia Álvarez, Esmeralda Santiago, Michelle Cliff, and Jamaica Kincaid. Their narratives, shaped out of their own lives and different backgrounds, are analyzed through a rich array of readings, from the historical to the sociological, from the anthropological and cultural to the geographic. Moreover, this groundbreaking work not only represents the three major linguistic areas of the Antilles, but also proves that Caribbean women, while re-inventing themselves in their new socio-cultural environments, are able to preserve their Caribbean cultural origins."

Antonio Benítez-Rojo, Writer and Critic, Amherst College

WHAT
WOMEN
LOSE

Tamara Alvarez-Detrell and Michael G. Paulson
General Editors

Vol. 6

PETER LANG
New York • Washington, D.C./Baltimore • Bern
Frankfurt am Main • Berlin • Brussels • Vienna • Oxford

MARÍA CRISTINA RODRÍGUEZ

WHAT WOMEN LOSE

Exile and the Construction of Imaginary Homelands in Novels by Caribbean Writers

PETER LANG
New York • Washington, D.C./Baltimore • Bern
Frankfurt am Main • Berlin • Brussels • Vienna • Oxford

Library of Congress Cataloging-in-Publication Data

Rodríguez, María Cristina.
What women lose: exile and the construction of imaginary homelands
in novels by Caribbean writers / María Cristina Rodríguez.
p. cm. — (Caribbean studies; v. 6)
Includes bibliographical references.
1. Caribbean fiction—Women authors—20th century—History and criticism.
2. Women in literature. 3. Emigration and immigration in literature.
4. Marginality, Social, in literature. I. Title.
II. Series: Caribbean studies (Peter Lang Publishing); v. 6.
PN849.C3R74   809.3'0082'09729—dc22   2004018817
ISBN 0-8204-5675-6
ISSN 1098-4186

Bibliographic information published by **Die Deutsche Bibliothek**.
Die Deutsche Bibliothek lists this publication in the "Deutsche
Nationalbibliografie"; detailed bibliographic data is available
on the Internet at http://dnb.ddb.de/.

Cover design by Iván Figueroa
Interior text layout by Marcos Pastrana

© 2005 Peter Lang Publishing, Inc., New York
275 Seventh Avenue, 28th Floor, New York, NY 10001
www.peterlangusa.com

Printed in the United States of America

To my *compañero* Lowell Fiet,
my sister friend Brenda Alejandro,
my goddaughter Marzo and Arenys del Mar,
the child I saw being born, for their presence
and unconditional love. *Gracias*.

Puerto Rican women in the 1930s in New York City
(family photo: Aída and Lina Pagán).

Contents

Acknowledgments

The Universidad de Puerto Rico, Río Piedras Campus, granted me a one-year sabbatical leave (2000–01) which allowed me to set up the foundations for this book. Librarians at The Graduate Center (City University of New York), Medgar Evers College (CUNY), The Center for Puerto Rican Studies (Hunter-CUNY), The Research Institute for the Study of Man in New York, The University of the West Indies, Mona Campus, The University of Miami, Biblioteca del Caribe y Estudios Latinoamericanos (UPR/RRP), and the Office of Interlibrary Loan at the Universidad de Puerto Rico were essential for the research phase of this book. Lowell Fiet's readings and revisions of each chapter are responsible for diction, fluidity, and a sharper critical content.

Preface

> We can only retell and live by the stories we have read or heard. We live
> our lives through texts. They may be read, or chanted, or experienced
> electronically, or come to us, like the murmurings of our mothers, telling
> us what conventions demand. Whatever their form or medium, these
> stories have formed us all; they are what we must use to make new
> fictions, new narratives.
>
> (Carolyn Heilbrun, Writing a Woman's Life)

If I were to enumerate the "pleasures of exile" (George Lamming's
term) for the women characters in novels by Caribbean women
writers, I would not be able to include a sense of sisterhood, of
belonging, of being loved and cared for. The "pleasures" would be
largely economic: an opportunity to study, to work, to shape one's
own life without social or family pressures, and in the eyes of the
people back home, to be successful. Puerto Ricans, Dominicans,
Haitians, Jamaicans, Trinidadians, Barbadians, Antiguans,
Guadeloupeans converge in metropolitan centers as they seek jobs
that will allow them a space they can begin to define. According to
the feminist critic Chandra Talpade Mohanty, women who share a
location away from home/nation are held together by "imagined
communities of women with divergent histories and social locations,
woven together by the political threads of opposition to forms of
domination that are not only pervasive but also systemic" (4).

Caribbean novelists writing in the 1950s and 60s, with only a
handful of exceptions, were able to publish their works because they
emigrated to London, New York, Toronto, or in the case of the
francophone Caribbean, to Paris. Their self-exile was usually

promoted by a college scholarship, a job opportunity, or the adventure of daring to go to the metropole and trying their luck. The experience has been recorded in fiction in V.S. Naipaul's *The Mimic Men*, Samuel Selvon's *Ways of Sunlight* and *The Lonely Londoners*, and in George Lamming's collection of essays, *The Pleasures of Exile*, just to cite several better known examples. James Clifford has called this metropolitan exile "elsewhere": "a different place of inauthenticity, exile, transcience, rootlessness" ("Traveling Cultures," 96).

Women sometimes left the Caribbean region for the same reasons as men, but more frequently they left either because they were sent for, or the entire family decided to emigrate to metropolitan communities where other Caribbean peoples had already settled, because they married men who, in turn, emigrated and took them with them, or as single women or mothers who left their children behind with surrogate mothers, because they decided "to try their fortune" in the big city. Thus, it is not surprising that most women in exile perceive their experiences differently than men. To describe the differences, Clifford develops the term "traveler," even though it tends to imply the security and privilege to move about with a certain degree of freedom. He realizes that whereas "good travel" (heroic, educational, scientific, adventurous) is limited to men, "women are impeded from serious travel. Some of them go to distant places, but they do so largely as companions or as 'exceptions'" (105). In the fiction written by women from the anglophone, francophone, and hispanophone Caribbean, living "elsewhere"—in New York, London, Toronto, Paris—becomes a process of growing up away from home, surrounded by strangers and social tension, usually treated as inferiors, sex objects or possessions, and forced to become overly assertive and aggressive in order to survive and progress in a hostile environment.

This study critically examines the narrative works of women novelists from the anglophone, francophone and hispanophone Caribbean who focus on marginalized female characters who have migrated to metropolitan centers and attempt to hold on to an acceptable reality by assuming the appropriate interpersonal, social and cultural masks that allow them to find a sense of significance in their interior and domestic lives as well as in the at-large community.

When and if this project fails, they choose isolation either through death, madness, the obliteration of their past, or the re-creation of the location of that past. The novels studied narrate the experience of migration and diaspora in the lives of Caribbean women. The study does not include intra-Caribbean migration—although it is referred to when another island is used as a transitory place—because the characters do not sufficiently distance themselves from the familiar; links are stretched but never severed. Women can be maids and nannies in Jamaica or Barbados, but they cannot readily go to night school to acquire an education that will allow them to seek a better job and have more mobility to change,sometimes radically, their external and internal circumstances. Overall, intra-Caribbean migration benefits mostly men while it maintains women in the same low income and dependent position.

Caribbean women writers present a world in which women are ever present. They are the mothers, grandmothers, and aunts back home; they are the occasional friends and distant parents and relatives in the metropole. Men enter the lives of these women and sometimes bring moments of happiness, but mostly they deceive, abuse, and abandon them. In the novels studied, men are distant, incapable of commitment, selfish, and unwilling to listen to a woman's voice. In Jamaica Kincaid's *Lucy*, Paule Marshall's *Brown Girl, Brownstones*, Joan Riley's *The Unbelonging* and *Waiting in the Twilight*, Gisèle Pineau's *Exile According to Julia*, Maryse Condé's *Heremakhonon*, *A Season in Rihata*, *Tree of Life* and *Desirada*, Edwidge Danticat's *Breath, Eyes, Memory*, Myriam Warner-Vieyra's *As the Sorcerer Said...* and *Juletane*, Cristina García's *Dreaming in Cuban* and *The Agüero Sisters*, Esmeralda Santiago's *When I Was Puerto Rican*, *Almost a Woman*, and *América's Dream*, Dionne Brand's *In Another Place, Not Here*, Zee Edgell's *In Times Like These*, and Loida Maritza Pérez's *Geographies of Home*, women characters refer to men as insensitive, as strangers who, in the long run, only care for their own welfare. Thus, Caribbean women are twice marginalized. At home they are relegated to the fringes of the economy and represent what Samuel Myers refers to as persons either out of the labor force altogether because of the high unemployment in the region or not in the path that is likely to lead to productive participation. Yet women turn to exile as a way of escaping this deadened situation; they find themselves marginalized once more because they are foreigners (even if they have the "same" citizenship or the appropriate visas) and female, in a metropolitan society that will not accept them as equals.

The approach of women writers who have experienced this double marginality and set out to record in fiction the experience of women in exile differs significantly from that of their male counterparts. Fiction, especially the novel, is a dynamic process, and the possibility of change is always present. According to Barbara Harlow, "The use by Third World resistance writers of the novel form as it has developed within the western literary tradition both appropriates and challenges the historical and historicizing presuppositions, the narrative conclusions implicated within the western tradition and its development" (78). Caribbean women novelists incorporate into their fiction memoirs; stories handed down by mothers and grandmothers; folk tales; remembrances; testimonies; diary entries; letters received, reclaimed or never sent; notes on shared experiences; and the canonical readings that most impressed them. In the stories told by Santiago and Danticat about growing up in New York, fiction and memoir become indistinguishable, as characters struggle to articulate the fear of unknown cold and voices, or recall how to eat a guayaba, or relive how a young woman's virginity is "tested." These experiences respond not only to a notion of cultural hybridity but also to a literary hybridity in which Caribbean women writers' use of forms of writing become entangled in the orality of voices recalled, recreated, and renamed.

Although there are many short stories by Caribbean women that express this dislocation—Michelle Cliff', Aida Ambert, Lorna Goodison, Amryl Johnson—I have chosen the novel as a synchretic form that goes through a long process of conceptualization, gathering of materials, and collecting experiences and requires a continuity that incorporates periods of gestation, changes in location, and a mobility that can withstand abrupt changes. The novel, as conceived by these Caribbean women, is a project that aims is to gather voices to tell a life-long story at the same time distant and familiar. The novel re-creates women in a Caribbean ambiance that merges the real and the imaginary. Gina Canepa points out how traditional class analysis cannot fully explain the tensions that exist between races, generations, castes, religions, and, above all, genders. Women, the repressed sex, overlap these divisions. They are treated differently, as subordinates, in all societies, social classes, religions, and races. This marginality affects all cultural structures but especially the emotional one through the thinking process and language. This is why the female text can only exist on the margins. This other space, as Marta Traba calls it, is different but not apart or autonomous, since women writers are also confronted with the texts, traditions, techniques, styles, and trends that belong to a cultural center. However, within this other space created by the movement between the margins of being female and the center, women appropriate creative options. In the hands of women writers, the novel has become a hybrid narrative form. Their narratives include an inexhaustible list of memoirs, diaries, anecdotes, travel writings, chronicles, family albums, letters, autobiographies, personal essays, stories, and folk tales. Mohanty considers that "one of the most significant aspects of writing against the grain...is the invention of spaces, texts, and images for encoding the history of resistance....This history and memory are woven through numerous genres: fictional texts, oral history, poetry, as well as testimonial narratives" (35-36). Clifford refers to this abundant and rich material as travel stories, oral histories of immigrant women. I choose to refer to these writings as hybrid narratives, a term used by the Puerto Rican writer Ana Lydia Vega in her very inclusive book of essays, *El tramo ancla*.

In the novels to be studied here, the female characters or their parents were born in the Caribbean, most spent part of their childhood and adolescence there, and then they traveled to New York, London, Toronto, or Paris for various reasons: Juletane (*Juletane*) was left an orphan, Hyacinth's father (*The Unbelonging*) reclaimed her, while Sophie (*Breath, Eyes, Memory*), Marie-Noëlle (*Desirada*) and Coco (*Tree of Life*) were claimed by the mother they barely knew. Veronica (*Heremakhonon*), Marie-Helene (*Season in Rihata*), Hélène (*Juletane*), and Pavana (*In Times Like These*) had money or a scholarship to pursue their careers. Zetou (*As the Sourcerer Said...*) left with her mother to pursue an education, whereas América (*América's Dream*) and Lucy (*Lucy*) were offered jobs that allowed them to nearly sever all ties to the homeland, and so on. The women from the hispanophone Caribbean only consider the United States as center and New York, or Miami, (or more recently Orlando) as the desired location to try a new life. Puerto Ricans take advantage of their U.S. citizenship (imposed by Congress in 1917) to travel back and forth from the island to metropole. This mobility, without the need of a visa or work permit, has allowed millions of islanders to settle mainly on the Eastern seaboard from Connecticut to Florida. Cubans, on the other hand, became privileged immigrants when the United States granted political asylum to everyone who denounced the Cuban Revolution. After the United States' invasion of the Dominican Republic in 1965, immigration laws became more flexible for Dominicans; when these laws tightened, illegality became a way of life.

These migrant narratives require cultural, historical, sociological, anthropological, and geographic readings. Theorists from a variety of disciplines are cited in this study to examine the texts and explore the complexity of women characters undergoing the trials of the migrant experience. Gordon Lewis, Roberto Fernández Retamar, Antonio Benítez Rojo, Stuart Hall, in their open-ended defining essays on the Caribbean, and James Clifford, when referring to the same space, insist on the geographical/historical uniqueness, hybridity, mestizaje, chaos, the sameness and difference in cultural identity, and the systematic and chaotic modernity of a region that seems to derive from so many sources—from as close as neighboring same-language islands to the coldness of a scattered United Kingdom. As criticism in the fields of literary and cultural studies have further explored these concepts, the diasporic communities in London, Toronto, New York, Miami, and Paris appear to redefine themselves in terms of these variegated lifelines/lifestyles. As pointed out by Benedict Anderson, Iain Chambers, Rosemary Marangoly George, Susan Stanford Friedman, Doreen Massey, Caren Kaplan, Néstor García Canclini, and Mary Louise Pratt, new geographies become possible by unhinging place. In migrant and diaspora studies, fields that seem to have a dynamic historical context, including sociology, ethnography, anthropology, history, demography, politics, law and economics in the writings of Bonham C. Richardson, Mary Chamberlain, Robin Cohen, Jorge Duany, Nancy Foner, Charles Green, Winston James, Alejandro Portes, Elizabeth Thomas-Hope, George Gmelch, Irma Watkins-Owens, Margaret Byron, Nicholas Van Hear inform this particular literary analysis of women's writings.

The wider picture, the interconnection, and the crisscrossing of ideas, grows out of the work of Raymond Williams, Edward Said, Stuart Hall, and James Clifford.

Chapter 1 deals with the theoretical framework and historical background. It looks at migration processes—laws and regulations, government policies—in the Caribbean, focusing on women's migratory patterns within each island and to Europe and North America, family as a term reconstituted by the shifting presence and relocation of migrant women, and explores how terms like homeland identity, imagined homelands, space-place and time, memory, nostalgia sites, diaspora, flow and fixity, acquire various meanings and undergo subsequent changes through the constant movement of Caribbean peoples from island nation to metropole.

Chapter 2 focuses on novels written in or translated into English by women writers from the francophone Caribbean. Even though this study deals mainly with works written in English, an exception is made for the francophone Caribbean. Only Haitian Edwidge Danticat writes originally in English, and her island experience is quite distinct from the Martinican or Guadeloupean reality. Their histories, relationships with metropolitan France, migration routes, intra-island movement, and use of creoles are so different that the study needs to include both experiences. The novels of migration of three Guadeloupean writers are thus included: Maryse Condé, a prolific writer whose novels are quickly translated into English and have found a wide audience specially in the United States; Myriam Warner-Vieyra, whose only two published novels have been widely distributed in their English translations; and Gisèle Pineau, whose award-winning novels are only recently being translated into English.

Chapter 3 focuses on the novels written in English by women from the hispanophone Caribbean: Dominicans Julia Alvarez and Loida Maritza Pérez, Puerto Ricans Esmeralda Santiago and Judith Ortiz Cofer, and Cuban Cristina García. Their novels collect and reinterpret remembrances from a very particular "way of seeing" (J. Berger) that involves class and generation differences, continuous and interrupted periods of residence on the island and the metropole. Chapter 4 focuses on the novels written by women from the anglophone Caribbean: Jamaicans Michelle Cliff and Joan Riley, Belizean Zee Edgell, Antiguan Jamaica Kincaid, Barbadian Paule

Marshall, and Trinidadian Dionne Brand. Questions of race identity with other marginal groups in the metropole, the centrality of location, and the negotiation of space are central issues in these texts.

Chapter 5 is a conclusion marked by the gathering of ideas and the possibilities of expanding the study and incorporating other issues and other ways of seeing travel, migration, and voyage. Although chapters seem to separate the Caribbean on the basis of language and culture, the discussion follows the same flow that migrant female characters cross, counter, and contrapuntuate (Said's term) as they locate and relocate in shifting centers and peripheries. The stories of women coming from island cultures insert themselves in metropolitan spaces, reconstruct communities, and share the particularities of unfamiliar languages and accents, gender, ethnicity, race, and place of origin.

The study includes twenty-four novels by fifteen women from the anglo-, franco-, and hispanophone Caribbean. All deal with the experience of migration from the island to the metropole, but each one includes details of the particular situations of complex characters from specific national cultures. When they come in contact with difference, they reshape and redefine the known and familiar. These writers are situated in metropolitan centers and rely on family connections, frequent or sporadic visits to the island homeland, first-hand knowledge of island history, and personal experience as migrants in North America and Europe to write and retell these stories about Caribbean women. The writers comprise two generations: those born in the 1930s, 40s, and 50s and the younger group, born in the 1960s, who published their first, and in some cases, only novel when they were in their early twenties. Some of the women have published extensively and received great praise from metropolitan critics; others are barely known outside very selective audiences. I have chosen to accentuate these writers' cultural nationality because wherever they are situated, it is precisely the experience back home that informs the creation of female characters in these novels of migration.

Works Cited

Alvarez, Julia. *How the García Girls Lost Their Accents.* New York: Plume. 1992.

———. *¡Yo!* New York: Plume, 1997.

Berger, John. *Ways of Seeing.* London: BBC and Penguin, 1985.

Brand, Dionne. *In Another Place, Not Here.* New York: Grove P, 1996.

Canepa, Gina. "Representatividad y marginalidad literarias y la historiografía de la literatura latinoamericana." In *Literatura más allá de la marginalidad.* Suiza: AELSAL, 1988. 114-129.

Cliff, Michelle. *No Telephone to Heaven.* New York: Plume, 1987.

Clifford, James. "Traveling Cultures." In *Cultural Studies.* Eds. Lawrence Grossberg, Cary Nelson, and Paula Treichier. New York: Routledge, 1992. 96-116.

Cofer, Judith Ortiz. *The Line of the Sun.* Athens: U Georgia P, 1989.

Condé, Maryse. *Desirada.* New York: Soho P, 2000 (originally published in 1997).

———. *Heremakhonon.* Washington DC: Three Continents P, 1982 (originally published in 1976).

———. *A Season in Rihata.* Oxford: Heinemann, 1988 (originally published in 1981).

———. *Tree of Life.* New York: Ballantine Books, 1992 (originally published in 1987).

Danticat, Edwidge. *Breath, Eyes, Memory.* New York: Vintage, 1995.

Edgell, Zee. *In Times Like These.* London: Heinemann, 1991.

García, Cristina. *The Agüero Sisters.* New York: Alfred A. Knopf, 1997.

———. *Dreaming in Cuban.* New York: Ballantine, 1992.

Harlow, Barbara. *Resistance Literature.* New York: Methuen, 1987.

Heilbrun, Carolyn G. *Writing a Woman's Life.* New York: Ballantine, 1988.

Kincaid, Jamaica. *Lucy.* New York: Plume, 1991 (originally published 1990).

Lamming, George. *The Pleasures of Exile.* London: Allison & Busby, 1984.

Marshall, Paule. *Brown Girl, Brownstones.* London: Virago P, 1982 (originally published in 1959).

Mohanty, Chandra Talpade. "Introduction: Cartographies of Struggle." In *Third World Women and the Politics of Feminism*. Bloomington: Indiana UP, 1991. 1-47.

Naipaul, V.S. *The Mimic Men*. Middlesex: Penguin, 1969.

Pérez, Loida Maritza. *Geographies of Home*. New York: Viking, 1999.

Pineau, Gisèle. *Exile According to Julia*. Charlottesville: U Virginia P, 2003 (originally published in 1996).

Riley, Joan. *The Unbelonging*. London: Women's Press, 1985.

———. *Waiting in the Twilight*. London: Women's Press, 1987.

Said, Edward. "Reflections on Exile." In *Reflections on Exile and Other Essays*. Cambridge: Harvard UP, 2000. 173-186.

Santiago, Esmeralda. *Almost a Woman*. Reading, MA: Perseus, 1998.

———. *América's Dream*. New York: HarperCollins, 1996.

———. *When I Was Puerto Rican*. New York: Vintage, 1993.

Selvon, Samuel. *The Lonely Londoners*. Longman: Three Continents P, 1979.

———. *Ways of Sunlight*. Longman: Three Continents P, 1979.

Traba, Marta. "Hipótesis sobre una escritura diferente." In *La sartén por el mango*. San Juan: Huracán, 1985. 21-26.

Vega, Ana Lydia, ed. *El tramo ancla: Ensayos puertorriqueños de hoy*. San Juan: Universidad de Puerto Rico, 1988.

Warner-Vieyra, Myriam. *As the Sorcerer Said....* Essex: Longman, 1982 (originally published in 1980).

———. *Juletane*. London: Heinemann, 1987 (originally published in 1982).

CHAPTER 1

Migration/Homeland/Identity

For surely it is one of the unhappiest characteristics of the age to have produced more refugees, migrants, displaced persons, and exiles than ever before in history, most of them as an accompaniment to and, ironically enough, as afterthoughts of great post-colonial and imperial conflicts. As the struggle for independence produced new states and new boundaries, it also produced homeless wanderers, nomads, and vagrants, unassimilated to the emerging structures of institutional power, rejected by the established order for their intransigence and obdurate rebelliousness. And insofar as these people exist between the old and the new, between the old empire and the new state, their condition articulates the tensions, irresolutions, and contradictions in the overlapping territories shown on the cultural map of imperialism.

(Edward Said, *Culture and Imperialism*).

One striking feature of Sebastião Salgado's *Migrations* 2000 photography exhibition in New York City (2002 in Puerto Rico) is the constant movement of the people he so dramatically photographed during a seven-year period. Whether on the road going or coming from somewhere, as part of masses of workers waiting around for job offers, or in makeshift housing outside of the cities, men, women, and children can never stop their search for work that will provide them with survival necessities: food, clothing, and shelter. Caribbean people have been migrating from countryside to city, from island to island, from island to metropole in search of a better life ever since sugar cane became the most marketable product in Europe and the Americas. But as peoples marked by migration, movement also meant that distance never entirely severed family ties or island communities. Caribbean migration patterns are circular—migrants earn their living abroad but maintain family, social ties, and residence in their country of origin (Labelle and Midy, 216), or on a permanent airbus—traveling back and forth and never establishing a permanent home on the island or in the urban center (Sánchez). Jorge Duany refers to migrants as borderless people, while Nina Glick Schiller calls them transnationals in her analysis of economic global changes. Don Hill and Elizabeth Thomas-Hope, among other researchers of migration, point out the shift from a predominantly male migration to the metropole in the first half of the twentieth century to a huge movement of women traveling alone to cities where jobs are abundant in the service sector from the 1960s forward to the beginning of this twenty-first century. This chapter explores the concepts of homeland and identity, migration processes in terms of the reformulation of family, migration and the relocation and negotiation of space, and the relation of memory and nostalgia in the lives of women who migrate from the Caribbean to the United Kingdom, France, the Netherlands, the United States, and Canada.

It is not possible to talk about migration without examining the political, economic, and social mechanisms that accompany women's movement into new homelands. Social scientists who have studied the phenomenon of migration as the relocation of masses of people to specific urban centers theorize on the causes for this displacement and the effects of this movement on the "donor"—sending society/place of origin/point of departure—and the "host"—receiving society/place of settlement/point of arrival. Both Stuart Hall and Zygmunt Bauman see migration as a condition of a modern/postmodern "new world" characterized by permanent uncertainty and, in the case of the Caribbean, a continuous movement between centre (the privileged space) and periphery (pocket/margin). In this study, centre, is the hegemonic, predominantly white space that imposes its language, culture, values, traditions, and mores as the norm; "center" (metropolitan/urban center), placed within the "centre," is a movable space that expands or shrinks according to its necessities. Permanence becomes a state of mind sustained by an imaginary homeland, and instability turns into a quotidian experience. Studies by Jorge Duany; George Gmelch; Charles Green; R.J. Johnston; Peter J. Taylor; Michael J. Watts; Nikos Papastergiadis; and Nicholas Van Hear attempt to develop some understanding for the migratory movements that characterize the twentieth and twenty-first centuries. The perspectives vary between anthropological, cultural, structural, historical, psychological, or economic, but their concern is always the human context and not simply statistical reporting (government agencies dealing with census, education, economic aid, employment, etc.) and measurability. In the case of the Caribbean region, Duany, who has done extensive field study on migrants from the hispanophone Caribbean, considers that the emphasis on demographic numbers presents migrants as "passive victims of historical or economic processes" instead of seeing them "as people of flesh and blood" (73). Bonham Richardson reminds us that a migration tradition characterizes these islands (204). Since emancipation—and before, when runaway slaves sought refuge elsewhere—Caribbean people have traveled to other islands for better wages: to Panama to build the transoceanic railroad and later to be part of the French-U.S. canal ventures; to Central America to the lands appropriated by the United Fruit Company; to Cuba and the Dominican Republic to work on sugar plantations; to New York as a job center; to Trinidad, Antigua, British Guiana, and St. Thomas to work on the construction of U.S. military bases in the 1940s. These migrants were mostly young men because of the type of work required and the sites of available employment. In all these instances, when the project ended or an economic crisis affected the country, Caribbean people had to return home or move on to another job site. Even though it seemed that the main reason for migration was economic survival or improvement, this constant movement also entailed the socio-political and economic conditions of the "donor" island of origin, migration laws in the host country, and personal reasons usually involving issues of family and community. Migration and diaspora studies recognize the particularities of this ever-growing group in today's global economy.

Most migration studies attempt to develop a structure where migration responds to specific causes no matter where or when it takes place. William Safran (as quoted by Van Hear) specifies six conditions of diaspora: 1) dispersal from an original center to two or more peripheral regions, 2) retention of collective memory of the homeland, 3) partial alienation from the host society, 4) aspiration to return to an ancestral homeland, 5) commitment to the maintenance and restoration of that homeland, and 6) derivation of collective consciousness and solidarity (5). Van Hear drops many of these characteristics but keeps the first condition, makes the presence abroad enduring but not necessarily permanent, and maintains an open exchange between the immigrant populations in the diaspora (6). In his study of "mass exodus, dispersal and regrouping of migrant communities," Van Hear rejects the binary economic theory of push/pull (poverty at home and wealth in the metropole), the center-periphery models that privilege the West, and the shift from an agricultural peasantry movement to an industrial workforce and urban manufacturing. He always presents migrations as communities of people and not as faceless masses. Van Hear mentions technological change as loosening of the constraints of the movement and the resurgence of ethnic, religious, and nationalist aspirations and tensions among the many possible causes for migration not linked to economic factors (3). Instead of dealing with crises that provoke mass exodus, the author asserts that the conditions for migration precede the crisis. Papastergiadis is suspicious of using the term "waves" to describe migrations because of its linearity and prefers to consider rips and crosscurrents within them (24). He states that "migration is never a spontaneous gesture. It presupposes some knowledge of the other side, a guide, a map or, at least, a rumour" (25). Mary Chamberlain sees migration "as a continuing historical event which has been informed by, and continues to inform, a vibrant culture of transnational and circular migration, in the 'home' and in the 'host' countries" (10). Most of these studies stress the ample network that has been established through the years to facilitate the trip abroad whether for a short visit, long stay, or a lifetime. Van Hear asserts that kinship, friendship, neighborhood, and other types of community and affinity are primarily responsible for this continuous movement (15).

Since Caribbean islands were exploited for agricultural purposes, most of the population settled in plantation centers after emancipation. For the peasant population, the acquisition of a plot of land became an attainable goal, and people worked the land while others went off to island cities, other islands, and metropoles to secure the money needed to purchase land and build a home. Sooner or later, many of these migrant men and women would return to the place they never stopped calling home. This constant travel made people aware of the limited conditions at home, dramatized by the quick and chaotic expansion of island cities. As agricultural production declined, rural populations moved to centers ill prepared to absorb them: plagued by high unemployment, insufficient housing facilities, weak infrastructure, polarized class/race division—the very wealthy, educated, and professionals, and the very poor, uneducated, and unskilled—unavailable commodities, and highly politicized societies. In many instances, the island city was used as a buffer zone or a transitory place where rurality finds its binary, where there is little or no land to claim as one's own, where dwellings for recent migrants are frequently temporary, fragile, or dilapidated—lodgings used by strangers, then emptied, to be used again by other newcomers. The urban is perceived as a fast-paced space where people profess indifference, hostility, and mistrust. There seems to be no wholeness: family members go different ways, are attracted by easy money; authority is continuously challenged; ghetto life pulsates with its own local rules. As its binary, rurality means claiming of land, extended family, networking, geographical separation, knowledge of rules—respected, followed, and undermined—and sense of place and location.

These island cities are capitals, seats of government, and centralized places that attract a migrant population. Yet a move to the city is dangerous in part because it seems so familiar—the same people, language, culture—and deceiving and shocking because of failed personal expectations. Kingston, Port of Spain, Bridgetown, Belmopan, St. John's, Santo Domingo, San Juan, Havana, Miami, Basse-Terre, Port-au-Prince, Point-a-Pitre, Fort-de-France are centers of economic and trade transactions, tourism, newer shopping developments (malls), and entertainment (theatres, coliseums, convention centers)—the spaces of (post)modernity. The city is the closest point to the metropole with its proliferation of all kinds of vehicles and mass transportation and a variety of housing from plantation-like mansions to slums and extended barrack yards. It is also the site of employment, subemployment, marginal jobs, underground economies—contraband, drug traffic, prostitution, etc.—and transitoriness. Depending on "rumors" as well as publicized job recruitment, moving populations stay for shorter or longer periods in each island city, usually to move on when they have secured the money and documentation to reach the urban center/seat of power, and for many, the "nation," whose citizenship they claim. For women, island cities seem more menacing than the faraway, unknown metropole. These huge spaces occupied by people speaking the same language and sharing a similar culture offer little protection beyond their dependency on relatives, unfamiliarity with neighborhood and government bureaucracy, and acceptance of demeaning jobs for irregular wages. Migration to the distant metropole represents more apprehension but less fear. The anonymity of the big city favors single women: failure, shame, rejection become individual experiences that are rarely heard of back home. The worst seems left behind in the island city once they move on to the metropole. There, one expects discrimination; there, one becomes a minority in terms of race, class, and ethnicity. A second skin grows to facilitate the embattlement.

Caribbean people who migrate to London, Paris, Amsterdam, New York, and Toronto have to immediately deal with a harsh climate, a white society that manages every facet of daily living, strong prejudices and hostility, ghettoized housing, and close scrutiny by law enforcement agencies. Gmelch, who studies cases of West Indians who migrated and then returned, states that "being abroad serves to remind them of the drawbacks of life in the metropolitan society: the impersonality, not feeling safe on the streets at night, racial prejudice, the 'rat race'" (297). Winston James in his study of the Caribbean diasporic community in Britain discusses the "suffocating consequences of racism in their everyday life" and the position the great majority occupies on the "lowest rung of the social hierarchy in Britain" (245). The one problem they did not encounter was unemployment: they had been recruited or could easily find jobs as bus conductor trainees, nursing trainees, hotel maids, house servants, street sweepers, nannies, factory workers, seamstresses, and all conceivable jobs in the service sector. These jobs held little attraction for the existing urban population because of the low wages, instability, zero fringe benefits, and poor or, in many instances, deplorable working conditions. But still they came in the hundreds and thousands. The recruitment of cheap labor in times of reconstruction—especially after the war that devastated London and much of the rest of Europe—took place through the existent colonial relation that established these European cities as centers of power. Later,

New York, Miami, and Toronto provided the difficult-to-refuse opportunity for employment and social improvement. However, to be more precise, the political relations between colonial powers and colonies, more often than not, legislated the migration policies—plantation system, post-emancipation, labor movements, self-government, confederation, départements d'outre-mer (DOM), independence/commonwealth—that set people in motion. The 1948 Nationality Act allowed all West Indians vested with British colonial citizenship as citizens of British colonies to enter with no restrictions and stay in Britain indefinitely. That same year, the *SS Empire Windrush* brought the first wave of post-war Caribbean migrants to Britain (James, 286). London Transport, the British Hotels and Restaurants Association, and the National Health Service were the main employers. The Immigration and Nationality Act of 1952 in the United States established quotas for each region, thus limiting the number of people coming from the Caribbean. In 1962, Canada adopted a "universalist policy" with restrictions based on individuals instead of nationality (Gmelch, 53).

Travel/migration in the 1960s to metropolitan France by citizens of the country's overseas departments—Guadeloupe, Martinique, French Guiana, and the island of Réunion in the Indian Ocean—was facilitated by a quasi-governmental travel agency that also placed new arrivals in working-class jobs (Grosfoguel, 607). Illegal migration from the Caribbean has always been an alternative for anyone determined to enter any of these countries. Tourist or student visas lapse into permanent residence, and work permits are unnecessary when the salaries are under minimum wage. Of course, the most dramatic and dangerous illegal entry takes place in rickety boats (*yolas/balsas*) by Haitians and Dominicans, who have been denied entrance to the world's richest country that prides itself on being a nation of migrants. The women characters in this study travel to New York, London, or Paris legally by being citizens, having work or study visas, or being admitted as political refugees.

What seemed a feasible, logical, advantageous, and economically sound program allowing particular groups to enter the Euro-American countries and to fill certain jobs proved to be surprisingly attractive as unexpected numbers took advantage of the relatively open migration policies. These countries made ample use of their power to exclude and include through their immigration laws. For example, the Commonwealth Immigrants Act of April 1962 specified that those West Indians already residing in the United Kingdom on July 1, 1962, could thereafter bring only wives, husbands, or children under 18 from abroad to live with them. All others were essentially barred from living in England. This brought over 100,000 new immigrants to beat the ban. Hyacinth in *The Unbelonging* and Adella and her children in *Waiting in the Twilight* in Joan Riley's novels settle in the United Kingdom under this reunification exception. To extend even further the racial/ethnic divide, in 1981 the British Nationality Act decreed that children born in Britain of West Indian parents would no longer qualify for British citizenship. A similar act was passed in France in the 1990s. More recently, the European Union, having collapsed its borders and established a common currency and "unrestricted" migration across all its member nations, has increased restrictions for new "others" from South Asia, North Africa, the Philippines, Latin America, and the Caribbean— the migrants who would normally settle in these countries to do the menial jobs. In a more tragic sense, as a result of the terrorist attacks of September 11, 2001, profiling has become the guideline to determine who enters, stays in, or leaves the United States, regardless of citizenship, naturalization, green cards, or visas. This return to the open categorization of people by race and ethnicity and the imposition of new laws that violate human and civil rights— Ashcroft's Patriot Act and the more recent Homestead Program under the direct supervision of the Immigration and Naturalization Service—tend to collapse the foundation of the multicultural society that the United States advertises as a unified America. Once more, "other" is defined as non-white, coming from elsewhere, descendant from another country or ethnic group, not a native speaker of English, and culturally different.

Even for those who carry passports as proof of citizenship, relocation to the metropole is often a short-term enterprise. According to Abenaty, Byron, Chamberlain, Colen, Gmelch, Hill, Thomas-Hope, most migrants speak about the need of a five-year period to accomplish their goals: get or claim a job, secure safe housing, and save enough money for the return. What they found when they arrived confirmed their decision to return: an England, France, or

United States with strong prejudices and a hostile attitude, housing difficulties because of high rents or refusal to allow them to locate in certain buildings and sectors and confinement to special ghettoized sectors or government housing, job immobility, difficulty saving money because of the high cost of living, and unequal medical services and education opportunities. Sarah Lawson Welsh describes postwar Britain as "a society with racial prejudice of endemic proportions, riddled with social and economic inequalities. The new immigrants often found themselves at the bottom of the pile, subject to the worst working conditions, the most overcrowded and unsatisfactory housing, and denied full access to a range of rights many believed were theirs by right as British nationals" (45). In these urban centers, immigrants were quickly categorized as an urban underclass, a problematic term frequently used by social scientists to "define" such large groups of blacks and Hispanics as long-term welfare recipients, unwed teen mothers, the homeless, the surplus labor force, school dropouts, street criminals, hustlers, and participants in the drug subculture—lacking skills, education, technical preparation, and other job-market prerequisites of post-modern society (Green, 114). Terms such as "urban underclass" to describe migrants and their offspring who live at the margins of the city— Hyacinth in Riley's *The Unbelonging*, Kitty and Clare in Michelle Cliff's *No Telephone to Heaven*, Martine and Sophie in Edwidge Danticat's *Breath, Eyes, Memory*, Reynalda and Marie-Noëlle in *Desirada*, Silla and Selina in Paule Marshall's *Brown Girl, Brownstones*, Marina, Rebecca, and Iliana in Loida Maritza Pérez's *Geographies of Home*, and Monín in Esmeralda Santiago's *When I Was Puerto Rican* and *Almost a Woman*—attempt to explain from the authority-invented centre the behavior of unbelonging and dislocation of the different other. Their behavior is unacceptable because of their inability to represent normative behavior—something that the centre denies the migrant for reasons of race, ethnicity, and class. In a no-win situation for the immigrant, the centre creates the conditions of marginalization and then blames the marginalized for not functioning inside the centre itself. Terms like "urban underclass" are a convenient way to explain by categorization so that the margin remains in its place and does not threaten the established categories. This urban underclass is seen as powerless, a burden on the centre, which never acknowledges the role it plays in creating the need for immigrant workers to fill the menial jobs left open because of their low wages, poor and dangerous working conditions, and demeaning status.

The jobs usually available to immigrant laborers, and especially to women, include cleaning jobs in offices, homes, hospitals, or schools; homecare as nannies, maids, caretakers of the elderly, the sick and bedridden, and the disabled; and jobs dependent on private industry or the whole gamut of subcontract employment by small or large companies that are cost efficient because of short-term contracts that are non-union and offer no medical plan or sick leave. Martine in *Breath, Eyes, Memory* works as a nurse in a home for the elderly; Monín in Santiago's fictional memoirs, Rebecca in *Geographies of Home*, and Adella in *Waiting in the Twilight* work in the garment industry; Silla in *Brown Girl, Brownstones* works in an ammunition factory during World War II; and Lucy in Kincaid's novel, Reynalda in *Desirada*, and América in Santiago's *América's Dream* are employed as nannies. Once the job is done, hourly contracters pay employees off until the next contract. In her study of global cities, Saskia Sassen sees "the massive expansion of a new high-income stratum alongside growing urban poverty" (337). Not having technical skills immediately pushes these immigrants to the lower echelon of the job market, which Sassen refers to as "the downgrading of jobs" (10). What is conveniently ignored is that people grouped as urban underclass come from societies in which they have always been able to make a living, never going hungry or being idle. They are multiskilled without formal training; men learn a craft—plumbing, carpentry, electrical work, construction—from parents, relatives, older members of the community back home just as women learn their imposed gender skills from mothers, grandmothers, elderly women—cooking, sewing, homecaring, caretaking. Although women on the island do not earn money for this kind of work, in the urban center they are able to sell these skills at bargain wages that are still far higher than their earning potential back home. And so they stay, some of them for ten-, twenty-, or thirty-year periods. They settle on the margins, creating their own centre in communities that sustain homelands as sites of nostalgia but also of shared memories, as places to converge and blur national differences and thus transform the margins set up by the centre. According to Chambers, migrancy "involves a movement in which neither the points of departure nor those of arrival are immutable or certain" (5).

Although there is always an attempt by the center of power to fix the centre, economic changes and developments, open markets, job opportunities, migration policies, and improvised alternatives make this impossible. Both homelands and centers can be imagined and restructured according to people's needs. For those who migrate from the countryside in Puerto Rico, Cuba, Dominican Republic, Jamaica, Trinidad, Guadeloupe, and Haiti, island centers like San Juan, Havana, Santo Domingo, Kingston, Port of Spain, Point-a-Pitre, Port-au-Prince become the center. Other larger, more populated, or wealthier islands can also become centers: Puerto Rico to the Dominicans, the Dominican Republic to Haitians and Antiguans, St. Thomas to St. Vincentians, St. Croix to Viequenses. Shalini Puri and other scholars explore in *Marginal Migrations: The Circulation of Cultures within the Caribbean* some of these intra-island migrations. But all these centers are continuously shifting as people move from place to place in search of a better life. While the host societies are characterized by fixity—the rules, the institutions, the forms, the laws, and patterns of organization to bring and keep the established order—Caribbean people who migrate are perceived as fluid, able to adapt to but not assimilate to the structures of the host countries because they are the ones in need and are willing to work at any job and comply with almost all requirements in order to participate, although never under the same conditions, in what the host country offers. Although Clifford differentiates between immigrants and diasporic populations in terms of their willingness to integrate into the dominant society (250), Alejandro Portes argues that this compliance depends on how the centre reacts to these new groups. The more they are treated as outsiders, the less their readiness to relinquish or subordinate their home culture (465–466). Migrants know they can find jobs, training and education, healthcare, and basic housing because of the existing surplus in metropolitan centers. They understand that things run differently than in their homeland, but they can bend as long as they know that the situation is temporary. They remain "in-between," living the intersection of histories and memories. Even when it seems the stay may be permanent, the imaginary homeland reminds them of the possible return. It is precisely this fluidity that forces the center to expand and the borders to stretch.

Contrary to their male counterparts, no matter where they come from or are going to or the migration waves they are part of, Caribbean women always migrate to acquire some degree of independence—even when traveling with family. Most women do not just take off (the exception being some of the women in the novels of the francophone Caribbean); they plan their departures very carefully, making sure that children, mothers, and other dependent relatives are taken care of; they give loved ones a sense of security while they travel to precarious places where the family/kinship network is non-existent or fragmented (as illustrated by Esmeralda Santiago's Monín and América). No matter how many friends or relatives have already settled in the metropolitan center, women cannot take too much for granted. Immigrant women leave behind the security of home—a roof/shelter, regular meals, parents' protection and unsolicited supervision, known space, family and kinship, knowledge of culture—to embark on an adventure that entails fear because of the place's newness and foreignness and of having to be on their own with no direct help from known and familiar social props. But taking this risk also means correcting the errors back home, keeping the favorable—openness, expression of feelings, non-confrontational attitudes and mediating voices, extended family ties, sense of space/ home, concept of time, choice of food, clothing, and language— and rejecting or reorganizing negative gender assumptions: a woman's "place" in island society as sex object, a faithful, passive, and subservient wife, or the sacrificing mother of baby boys. This female resolve is basic for Chicana writer Gloria Anzaldúa for whom "the process of remembering is inseparable from the process of selecting: she must pick and choose from among the cultural models she has inherited in order to reconstruct her own identity" (Browdy de Hernández, 45). She will work in whatever jobs she gets that will allow her to generate her own income: maid, nanny, caretaker, cleaning woman, bar attendant, waitress, or sex worker. She will seek and get better training and education—usually night school or special training offered free by the city or special projects sponsored by private enterprise—that will give her mobility to get a better-paying job. By earning her own money, she will be able to get her own place—even if it is in a ghettoized area of the city—where she can buy things according to her taste and needs. If she left children back home, she will be able to send money and perhaps, in time, send for them or provide for them through the parents or relatives in charge of their care. She will send remittances that will allow her family back home to live better or mail clothing, accessories, small appliances, and other items for their own use or to be sold or traded. She will also serve as host for family, relatives, and friends who decide to emigrate for short–or long–term stays. What women will rarely do is sever all ties with the island or country (the exceptions being Reynalda in Condé's *Desirada*, Verlia in Brand's *In another Place, Not Here*, and Lucy in Kincaid's novel). According to Van Hear and Douglas Massey's theories of international migration (as cited by Van Hear), these women migrants can be placed in two categories: migrant networks and institutions, and migration order shaped by the macro-political economy. Women establish relationships that link former, current, and potential migrants and those who do not migrate in countries of origin and destination. Even if they do not travel back and forth, write, call, or send tapes and photos frequently, they will still be tied to the people and land back home because of the constant travel of others and the dream of going back to settle or re-tire—when there is less need to make good money or when they are sufficiently stable economically to return successfully. This may never happen, but what distinguishes Caribbean people—the perennial travelers according to scholars and researchers of migrant studies—is that the idea of return is always tied to the migration plan.

Caribbean women often find in the metropole a freedom they never experienced at home. The expected roles of daughter, wife/companion, and especially mother, are overturned by the needs, fragmentation, strangeness, and mobility in metropolitan urban centers. These women, who leave behind children and loved ones, travel with damaged lives. Their decision to break away is made with a sense of guilt: some occurrence or unbearable emotional and/or economic condition has forced them to migrate. As they accommodate themselves in the new location, race and ethnicity become issues as they are placed on the margins, looked at as other and inferior, and labeled as minority. In spite of their legal dependence on men, they gain a measure of autonomy almost immediately when they secure a job and receive their own paycheck. For women, according to Clifford, life "in diasporic situations can be doubly painful—struggling with the material and spiritual insecurities of exile, with the demands of family and work, and with the chains of old and new patriarchies. But despite these hardships, they may refuse the option of return home when it presents itself, especially when the terms are dictated by men" (259). After a number of years, a working-class woman like Adelle in Joan Riley's *Waiting in the Twilight* is able to buy a rundown house in one of the outcast edges of London. This new positioning and self-assurance of Caribbean women also provokes domestic violence as men feel threatened by women's mobility.

In their studies of migrant women, Oliva Espín and Carol Boyce Davies agree that even if the loss experienced by these women can never be compensated, there are decisive advantages in living outside the homeland. A woman in the big city is expected to move around on her own in search of a job and a living space. There is no one to take her under her or his wing and provide for her as long as she is a wife, daughter, mother. These roles are redefined so that they become secondary: without a job that brings in money she cannot provide for her children or family in the new place or back home. She learns that everything is negotiated, and these skills will assure her survival in this initially hostile environment. She will take advantage of night school, second and third jobs, special or new training, facilities such as daycare centers and health services. This new world that suddenly opens up for women, according to Espín, will directly affect their sexuality:

> Frequently, newly encountered sex-role patterns in the "host culture" combined with greater access to paid employment, create for women the possibility to live a new way of life. Some women become employed outside the home for the first time after the migration. Many of them encounter new opportunities for education. All of them are confronted with the alternative meanings of womanhood provided by observing the lives of women in the host country. (4)

In her study on violence against women in London's black communities, Amina Mama concludes that the main factor that triggers a man's aggression against his spouse is "that when women have even a limited material advantage over the men they have relationships with, this in itself may in fact provoke those men to assert their male authority literally with a vengeance, through violence"(134). Adella's husband, in Riley's *Waiting in the Twilight*, becomes more abusive as she becomes more economically independent.

Holding a job and earning a salary immediately make women take control of their lives and see themselves as persons with rights—even if they are not certified citizens: the right to work, to choose a place to live, to marry or live with the man or woman of her choice, to acquire commodities, to travel, to spend her money, to seek a better job, to take advantage of educational and training opportunities, to move around. Women can claim their own space, something very difficult to do even if you are professional and middle class in most Caribbean island societies. Women gain freedom in the private space even if in the public one they are exploited and discriminated against. It is precisely their new location, the metropolitan/modern city, that allows these changes to take place. These women are poised between modernity and postmodernity. They are part of the displacements created by the global economy, the flow of goods, but at the same time, they are intensely individual, relinquishing the collective sense of community, embracing alienation and anonymity in an urban center that seems so different and distant from home. Their jobs respond to the needs created by expanding cities and the need for cheap labor. Iain Chambers describes this location with its centre and margins as the

> gendered city, the city of ethnicities, the territories of different social groups, shifting centres and peripheries—the city that is a fixed object of design (architecture, commerce, urban planning, state administration) and yet simultaneously plastic and mutable: the site of transitory events, movements, memories. (93)

These women characters have no urge to trace their roots. They go to cities to free themselves from the class/race/family stronghold of the island culture. Place becomes an "intersection," where there is a constant sense of becoming (Cresswell, 26). Their choice of place is characterized by centres of power—large populations; access to first-world commodities at bargain prices; access to training, education, jobs; ethnic communities in constantly redefined margins; and self-distancing from the island country. In fact, the modern city exerts such an attraction for Caribbean peoples, especially women, that the examination of the source of attraction becomes an obligatory point of departure. London, Paris, and New York seem fairytales come true when the migrants first arrive. The massiveness, velocity, and hustle and bustle of swarms of people frighten, threaten, and challenge the newcomers as a space of unimagined possibilities. For Mary Louise Pratt, this is the space of colonial encounters—the contact zone— "in which peoples geographically and historically separated come into contact with each other and establish ongoing relations, usually involving conditions of coercion, radical inequality, and intractable conflict" (6). Raymond Williams describes the metropolitan societies of Western Europe and North America as "the 'advanced,' 'developed' industrialized states; centres of economic, political and cultural power" (279). The impression of the modern city as order, futuristic planning, multiplicity of resources and commodities, flexibility to absorb variety and difference, imagination to create new concepts is demystified by Walter Benjamin's description in *The Arcades Project* of the transformation of space by the needs of all those who converge in the center. Néstor García Canclini emphasizes the bewildered and overpowering effect the city has after many decades of modernity: massiveness of housing and building structures, public and private transportation, limitless possibilities of communication, multiplicity of consumer-goods stores/malls, educational and medical services. Edward Said in *Culture and Imperialism* looks at the city in the modern age as the place and time "To have produced more refugees, migrants, displaced persons, and exiles than ever before in history" (332). Caren Kaplan in *Questions of Travel* concurs with Sebastião Salgado that "displacement" refers to mass migrations produced by modernity which include troop deployment, refugees from famine, genocide, incarceration, guest workers, illegal aliens, poor people in search of work (3–5). This study focuses on women who move to cities and, by so doing, put their bodies in harm's way in order to get jobs to feed, clothe, and shelter themselves and their families.

After a prolonged stay in the urban center, without ever dismissing the possibility of return, citizenship becomes an important issue for both men and women. Caribbean people usually see themselves as belonging to an island nation: they have a citizenship "by virtue of which they enjoy a set of rights and obligations within a given nation state" (Labelle and Midy, 214). Citizenship always implies exclusion, and when people move from an island to a metropolitan center, they face their own nonacceptance in the Otherland. Labelle and Midy point out that "these populations are carriers of a new difference, being ethnically, phenotypically or religiously distinct" (215). Martinicans and Guadeloupeans, who are legally French citizens, and Puerto Ricans, who are U.S. citizens, are as foreign to the metropolitan center as Haitians, Dominicans, or Jamaicans. Becoming a naturalized citizen of the United Kingdom, Canada, the United States, or France entitles Caribbean people to a passport and equal rights with all other citizens, but in reality, they continue to be seen and treated as foreigners or second-class citizens. New temporal and spatial maps are drawn that contest "the axes upon which British citizenship had formerly rested" (Welsh, 45). For Caribbean women, citizenship can be a step toward securing better working conditions and the right to bring their children to the metropole. However, becoming legal can also mean being policed, incarcerated, and possibly deported by being more visible and, thus, vulnerable to the agencies that wield power.

Quoting Brubacker, Micheline Labelle and Franklin Midy present the classic liberal model of citizenship, where belonging is egalitarian, sacred, nationalist, democratic, unique, and socially consistent (215). Migrants know that, whether at home or abroad, the rights of a citizen depend on class, place, race, and gender. By moving to England, the United States, or France, it did not take very long for West Indians, Puerto Ricans, Martinicans, and Guadeloupeans to realize they were second-class citizens. They were quickly relegated to the margins with non-citizens—U.S./U.K./French—who entered the country illegally or with temporary work visas. They understood then what now is so prevalent: exclusive citizenship is very seldom an advantage when you are labeled as part of the invisible moving work force that is so easily replaced by incoming migrants. Instead, it can become an impediment in today's global economic instability, where jobs emerge or disappear in a relatively short period. The most important right for the migrant is to move freely, with few or no restrictions, and to go where the jobs are. In today's reality, permanence and exclusivity are words of the past.

According to Stephen Castles and Alastair Davidson, there is "a new layer of citizenship above that of the nation—the citizen who does not belong" (157). On the one hand, Dennis Conway and others who study the relationship of Caribbean migrants and citizenship see the possibility to sponsor further family migrations, the right to receive Social Security benefits in their new homeland, and the right to vote as the only advantages of becoming a citizen of the host country. On the other hand, island nations have conveniently liberalized their laws so their citizens can travel back and forth, maintain dual citizenship, participate in home elections, contribute to the national economy through their remittances and buying power. Metropolitan centers and island nations both profit from this "liberalization": islanders pay taxes, buy insurance and commodities, serve in the armed forces of the host country, while in the Caribbean they can enter and leave with few restrictions, bring in taxable merchandise, and purchase property and build residences with dollars, pounds, or Euros.

For women migrants, even with its restrictions, citizenship can be a desirable objective because it means the right to bring one's family to the host country (Rebecca in Pérez's *Geographies of Home* manages to bring her parents and siblings to the United States) and to ensure that children will "enjoy" the advantages of having been born in the United States, the United Kingdom, or Canada. But they are also aware that citizenship does not guarantee equality or better treatment for the second or subsequent generations. Although being born in the United States automatically makes you a citizen (as of 2004, at least), despite the parents' place of origin, the rights granted or taken away can be based on other factors (the U.S. citizen, born of Puerto Rican parents, José Padilla, can be incarcerated without access to a lawyer because of his suspected connections to Al Qaeda). In the case of the United Kingdom or Canada, birth does not immediately make island people citizens, and so they are always liable to extradition according to the continuous changes in the law. Migrants who maintain their link to the homeland can, according to Conway, "achieve the best of both worlds—culture and identity in the former; money, wealth, and skills in the latter" (341).

This geographical and emotional journeying from the homeland to the metropolitan city relies on memory to reconstruct the lost world (Said), to look back at the past, "retrospection to gain a vision for the future" (Fischer, 198). In that past, the sense of community and the importance of kinship are always recalled precisely because women migrants have a sense of loss when they relocate by themselves or a limited number of family members. Even if the immediate aim of the temporary or semi-permanent relocation is to find a job that renders a salary they can live on and that also allows them to send remittances back home, the rest of their time is spent constructing a home away from home. Women are always embarking in both activities: there is no time to sit and romanticize the past because landlords will evict if the rent is late, electricity and phone services will be cut off when the bills are not paid, and there is only so much credit that they can get at the neighborhood store. Women in the novels in this study are always employed or seeking employment regardless of being pregnant, ill, or disabled. So the very limited spaces of leisure that women have can only be used to recall a sense of community and reproduce in the city the distant remembrance of the way things were back home. Clifford explains that the homeland is "a place of attachment and not something simply left behind" (256). And this past "is always constructed through memory, fantasy, narrative and myth" (Hall, 395).

According to Gayle Greene, "whereas 'nostalgia' is the desire to return home, 'to remember' is 'to bring to mind' or 'think again,' 'to be mindful of,' 'to recollect'" (297). Even if women become nostalgic, what they recall and recreate are usually the good memories: love and sharing in a familiar place. But they also remember clearly the problematic situations back home—poverty, loss of land, kinship abuse, gender oppression, sexual repression, violence—reasons why they moved away and became migrants in unwelcoming places. However, memory is the link of being/belonging to land, people, culture; it is stable and solid because of its distance; it is the dream of the return; it is family in its ample and inclusive sense, which includes immediate and outer members, relatives, neighbors, community; it is the one thing they can claim as their own. For women it is a selective process of remembrance. The women in the novels included here recall repressive and controlling fathers and mothers, abusing husbands, neglecting and mentally ill mothers, the burden of domestic work, the absence of male breadwinners, the barrenness of the land, the shantytowns, and gender fixity. Because of their positions in the island of origin, women tend not to identify "home" as a site of nostalgia: "place as bounded, a site of an authenticity, as singular, fixed and unproblematic as identity" (Doreen Massey, 5). According to Isabel Hoving, for women, relocation is "a sign of change" and a "potential for transformation, an opportunity to choose new subject positions" (14). No matter how overburdened women may be or how lonely or distant from their ethnic community, they always remember the space of silence, obedience, and restriction where they were situated back home. The identity of that place called home is "forever open for contestation" (Massey, 169). Some women characters might duplicate the accepted behavior back home—Riley's Adella in *Waiting in the Twilight*, Brand's Elizete in *In Another Place, Not Here*, Santiago's América in *América's Dream*, Pérez's Rebecca in *Geographies of Home*, Myriam Warner-Vieyra's Zetou in *As the Sorcerer Said*—but their contact with the general society will make them question their position and challenge the imposed roles.

   Throughout this chapter, I have established the historical basis of Caribbean migration particularly as it has affected women from the franco-, hispano-, and anglophone Caribbean. By looking at theoretical studies of migration and diaspora, the patterns and exceptions of Caribbean migration have been established in order to study the women in the novels of the fifteen writers who have chosen to write about this particular experience. These women writers selected narrative to recollect, remember, and repeat "in order for there to be an escape from repetition, in order for there to be change or progress" (Greene, 291). Place has acquired multiple meanings so that home, homeland, otherland, host and donor countries are no longer spaces with fixed meanings, nor are they empty containers to be filled in with any substance or locations to be classified, marked, and labeled. These places are spaces inherently movable and dynamic, where women have the opportunity to reshape, revise, and construct better places, where home becomes their own site of possibilities and change.

Works Cited

Abenaty, Kenton. "Intergenerational 'Return' Migration to St. Lucia: A Comparative Analysis." (Eastern Caribbean Island Cultures Conference-St. Lucia. November 2001).

Bauman, Zygmunt. "The Making and Unmaking of Strangers." In *Debating Cultural Hybridity: Multi-Cultural Identities and the Politics of Anti-Racism*. Eds. Pnina Werbner and Tariq Modood. London: Zed Books, 2000. 46-57.

Benjamin, Walter. *The Arcades Project*. Cambridge: Harvard UP, 1999.

Brand, Dionne. *In Another Place, Not Here*. New York: Grove P, 1996.

Browdy de Hernández, Jennifer. "The Plural Self: The Politicization of Memory and Form in Three American Ethnic Autobiographies." In *Memory and Cultural Politics: New Approaches to American Ethnic Literatures*. Eds. Amritjit Singh, Joseph T. Skerrett, Jr., and Robert G. Hogan. Boston: Northeastern UP, 1996. 41-59.

Byron, Margaret. *Post-War Caribbean Migration to Britain: The Unfinished Cycle*. Aldershot: Ashgate, 1994.

Castles, Stephen and Alastair Davidson. *Citizenship and Migration: Globalization and the Politics of Belonging*. New York: Routledge, 2000.

Chamberlain, Mary, ed. *Caribbean Migration: Globalised Identities*. London and New York: Routledge, 1998. 1-17.

Chambers, Iain. *Migrancy, Culture, Identity*. London: Routledge, 1994.

Cliff, Michelle. *No Telephone to Heaven*. New York: Plume, 1987.

Clifford, James. "Diasporas." In *Routes: Travel and Translation in the Late Twentieth Century*. Cambridge: Harvard UP, 1997. 244-277.

Colen, Shellee. "'Just a Little Respect': West Indian Domestic Workers in New York City." In *Muchachas No More: Household Workers in Latin America and the Caribbean*. Eds. Elsa M. Chaney and Mary García Castro. Philadelphia: Temple UP, 1989. 171-194.

Condé, Maryse. *Desirada*. New York: Soho P, 2000 (originally published in 1997).

_____. *Heremakhonon*. Washington DC: Three Continents P, 1982 (originally published in 1976).

————. *A Season in Rihata*. Oxford: Heinemann, 1988 (originally published in 1981).

————. *Tree of Life*. New York: Ballantine Books, 1992 (originally published in 1987).

Conway, Dennis. "The Caribbean Diaspora." In *Understanding the Contemporary Caribbean*. Eds. Richard S. Hillman and Thomas J. D'Agostino. Boulder: Lynne Rienner, 2003. 333-353.

Cresswell, Tim. "Introduction: Theorizing Place." In *Mobilizing Place, Placing Mobility: The Politics of Representation in a Globalized World*. Eds. Ginette Verstraete and Tim Cresswell. Amsterdam: Rodopi, 2002. 11-31.

Danticat, Edwidge. *Breath, Eyes, Memory*. New York: Vintage, 1995.

Davies, Carol Boyce. "'Writing Home': Gender, Heritage and Identity in Afro-Caribbean Women's Writing in the United States."In *Black Women, Writing and Identity: Migrations of the Subject*. London: Routledge, 1994. 113-129.

Duany, Jorge. "The Creation of a Transnational Caribbean Identity: Dominican Immigrants in San Juan and New York City." In *Ethnicity, Race and Nationality in the Caribbean*. Ed. Juan Manuel Carrión. San Juan: Institute of Caribbean Studies, 1997. 195-232.

Espín, Oliva M. *Women Crossing Boundaries: A Psychology of Immigration and Transformations of Sexuality*. New York: Routledge, 1999.

Fischer, Michael M.J. "Ethnicity and the Post-Modern Arts of Memory." In *Writing Culture: The Poetics and Politics of Ethnography*. Eds. James Clifford and George E. Marcus. Berkeley: U California P, 1986, 194-233.

García Canclini, Néstor. *Consumers: Globalization and Multicultural Conflicts*. Minneapolis: U Minnesota P, 2001.

Gmelch, George. *Double Passage: The Lives of Caribbean Migrants Abroad and Back Home*. Ann Arbor: U Michigan P, 1992.

Green, Charles. "Identity and Adaptation in the 1990s: Caribbean Immigrant Youth in New York City." *Wadabagei* 1, 1 (Winter/ Spring 1998): 111-139.

Greene, Gayle. "Feminist Fiction and the Uses of Memory." *Journal of Women in Culture and Society* 16.2 (1991): 290-321.

Grosfoguel, Ramón. "Colonial Caribbean Migrations to France, The Netherlands, Great Britain and the United States."*Ethnic and Racial Studies* 20. 3 (July 1997): 594-612.

Hall, Stuart. "Cultural Identity and Diaspora." In *Colonial Discourse and Post-Colonial Theory: A Reader*. Eds. Patrick Williams and Laura Chrisman. New York: Columbia UP, 1994. 392-403.

Hill, Donald R. "The Impact of Migration on the Metropolitan and Folk Society of Carriacou, Grenada." *Anthropological Papers of the American Museum of Natural History* 54.2 (1977): 189-391.

Hoving, Isabel. *In Praise of New Travelers: Reading Caribbean Migrant Women's Writing*. Stanford: Stanford UP, 2001.

James, Winston. "Migration, Racism and Identity Formation: The Caribbean Experience in Britain." In *Inside Babylon: The Caribbean Diaspora in Britain*. Eds. Winston James and Clive Harris. London: Verso, 1993. 231-287.

Johnston, R.J., Peter J. Taylor, and Michael J. Watts, eds. *Geographies of Global Change*. Oxford: Blackwell, 1995.

Kaplan, Caren. *Questions of Travel: Postmodern Discourses of Displacement*. Durham: Duke UP, 2000.

Kincaid, Jamaica. *Lucy*. New York: Plume, 1991 (originally published 1990).

Labelle, Micheline and Franklin Midy. "Re-reading Citizenship and the Transnational Practices of Immigrants." *Journal of Ethnic and Migration Studies* 25. 2 (April 1999): 213-232.

Mama, Amina. "Women Abuse in London's Black Communities." In *Inside Babylon: The Caribbean Diaspora in Britain*. London: Verso, 1993. 97-134.

Marshall, Paule. *Brown Girl, Brownstones*. London: Virago P, 1982 (originally published in 1959).

Massey, Doreen. *Space, Place, and Gender*. Minneapolis: U Minnesota P, 1994.

Papastergiadis, Nikos. *The Turbulence of Migration: Globalization, Deteritorialization and Hybridity*. Cambridge: Polity P, 2000.

Pérez, Loida Maritza. *Geographies of Home*. New York: Viking, 1999.

Portes, Alejandro. "Conclusion: Towards a New World—the Origins and Effects of Transnational Activities." *Ethnic and Racial Studies* 22. 2 (March 1999): 463-477.

Pratt, Mary Louise. *Imperial Eyes: Travel Writing and Transculturation.* London: Routledge, 1992.

Puri, Shalini. "Introduction, Theorizing Diasporic Cultures: The Quiet Migrations." In *Marginal Migrations: The Circulation of Cultures within the Caribbean.* Oxford: Macmillan, 2003. 1-16.

Richardson, Bonham C. "Caribbean Migrations, 1838-1985." In *The Modern Caribbean.* Eds. Franklin W. Knight and Colin A. Palmer. Chapel Hill: U North Carolina P, 1989. 203-28.

Riley, Joan. *The Unbelonging.* London: Women's Press, 1985.

———. *Waiting in the Twilight.* London: Women's Press, 1987.

Said, Edward. "Movements and Migrations." In *Culture and Imperialism.* New York: Vintage, 1993. 326-336.

Sánchez, Luis Rafael. "La guagua aérea." In *La guagua aérea.* Río Piedras: Cultural, 1994. 11-22.

Santiago, Esmeralda. *Almost a Woman.* Reading, MA: Perseus, 1998.

———. *América's Dream.* New York: HarperCollins, 1996.

———. *When I Was Puerto Rican.* New York: Vintage, 1993.

Sassen, Saskia. *The Global City: New York, London, Tokyo.* Princeton: Princeton UP, 1991.

Thomas-Hope, Elizabeth. "Emigration Dynamics in the Anglophone Caribbean." In *Emigration Dynamics in Developing Countries. Vol. III: Mexico, Central America and the Caribbean.* Ed. Reginald Appleyard. Aldershot: Ashgate, 1999. 232-284.

Warner-Vieyra, Myriam. *As the Sorcerer Said...* Essex: Longman, 1982 (originally published in 1980).

———. *Juletane.* London: Heinemann, 1987 (originally published in 1982).

Welsh, Sarah Lawson. "(Un)belonging Citizens, Unmapped Territory: Black Immigration and British Identity in the Post-1945 Period." In *Not on Any Map: Essays on Postcoloniality and Cultural Nationalism.* Exeter, Devon: U Exeter P, 1997. 43-66.

Williams, Raymond. "The New Metropolis." In *The Country & the City.* New York: Oxford UP, 1973. 279-288.

CHAPTER 2

Francophone Caribbean Dismemberment: Life without Links

> Since my father was a former civil servant and my mother was still working as a teacher, they were regularly entitled to a paid vacation from their home in Guadeloupe to the *métropole* with their children. For them France was in no way the seat of colonial power. It was truly the Mother Country and Paris, the City of Light that lit up their lives.
>
> (Maryse Condé, *Tales from the Heart*)

Similar to women writers from the anglo and hispanophone Caribbean, Maryse Condé, Myriam Warner Vieyra, Gisèle Pineau, and Edwidge Danticat concern themselves with the plight of women who migrate to metropolitan centers to seek a different life. Many of these women characters enter this new space with notions of an imaginary, almost magical, place that offers possibilities unforeseen in their Caribbean society. Once in the metropolitan center, they discover that they are voiceless and invisible, only recognized as disposable workers located at the margin/border. Living elsewhere, in New York or Paris, becomes a process of growth and adaptation, surrounded by strangers and social tension, where different usually means inferior, sex object, possession, or exotic woman. They, in turn, become overly assertive and aggressive so as to survive and progress in a hostile environment.

Haiti, Martinique, and Guadeloupe have maintained different relations with the former colonial power. While Haiti seemed to have severed ties with France after the Haitian Revolution of 1804, Martinique and Guadeloupe have been part of that country's extended empire, creating a new map with a direct connection with metropolitan France and its colonies, whether in the Caribbean,

Africa, Asia, or the Indian Ocean. While Haiti officially rejected white France, its leaders and the established mulatto elite continue to see France as the center of culture and advanced civilization. In the twentieth and twenty-first centuries, Haitian migrant routes depend on class: the mulatto bourgeoisie has the money to travel and live in France while the black peasants and working class set their eyes closer to home in North America (Richardson, 218). By relocating in New York, for example, where *jus soli* (citizenship by virtue of birth in the territory resided) dictates migration policies, Haitians are able to become residents and later claim equal privileges for children and parents. If they were guest workers in France, the *jus sanguinis* (citizenship by descent) would not allow them to claim citizenship for their children (Heisler, 85). For Martinicans and Guadeloupeans, France is the place to travel: no visas or work permits are needed to enter the country, and job opportunities and training are available for the working class through the *Bureau pour lr Développement des Migration des Départements d'Outre-Mer* (BUMIDOM), the state-funded employment aid program (Richardson, 217; Murdoch "Negotiating," 131). According to Ramón Grosfoguel, this agency covers all or part of the transportation costs and provided training for most of these unskilled migrants. "The dominant policy was to incorporate them within the French public administration" (607). The four francophone women writers discussed in this chapter—Edwidge Danticat, Gisèle Pineau, Myriam Warner-Vieyra and Maryse Condé—insert their female characters in the migration realities of each island and its relation to the metropole. Betty Wilson points out that "Whether she is in the Caribbean, in France, or in Africa, the situation of the black *Antillaise* woman is portrayed as one of confinement and frustration. Her life is depicted as tragically limited and her efforts at resistance doomed to failure" (*Voyage*, 47). Martine and Sophie in Danticat's *Breath, Eyes, Memory*, Julia in *Exile According to Julia*, Helene and Juletane in Myriam Warner-Vieyra's *Juletane* and Zetou in *As the Sourcerer Said...* by Warner-Vieyra, Veronica in *Hermakhonon*, Marie-Hélène in *A Season in Rihata*, Thécla and Claude Elaïse/Coco in *Tree of Life*, and Reynalda and Marie-Noëlle in *Desirada* by Maryse Condé travel from island to metropole, a journey that totally changes their lives and forces them to see the world differently. These women will leave the homeland to relocate in the metropole, rethink their past while adapting to a new way of life, and deal with nostalgia for an imaginary home.

The past has consistently determined the present relations of these Caribbean islands with the metropole, and these events—invasion, foreign occupation, imposed forms of government—have marked Caribbean people. The United States's invasion and occupation from 1915 to 1934 (Castor), and the double reign of the Duvalier family (François 1957-1971 and Jean Claude "Baby Doc" 1971–1986) maintained Haiti in a state of poverty and political and economic instability. The intra-island migration of Haitians took them to seek work in the Dominican Republic, where, in 1937, 15,000 were massacred. Danticat has recorded this experience in her 2001 novel, *The Farming of Bones*. Although a percentage of the Harlem population in New York in the early part of the twentieth century was Haitian, it is not until repression became the way of life in Haiti that the numbers of legal and illegal migrants increased significantly (Richardson, 220–221). Some came with the proper student, work, or tourist visas like Sophie, Martine, and Marc in *Breath, Eyes, Memory*, but many others, especially in the 1990s, risked their lives to reach the waters of Florida in rickety boats as documented in Danticat's 1996 book of stories, *Krik? Krak!* France, on the other hand, continues to be the place to travel, live, and retire for wealthy Haitians like Duvalier and his family. Paris also becomes the meeting place of the francophone Caribbean as captured in the novels of Maryse Condé. While in France, Haitians, Guadeloupeans, and Martinicans assert their nationality even if they bond with other blacks from Africa and various former colonies. In New York, they are immediately seen as part of the larger black American community, and, thus, their nationality is not a marker. (I use black American instead of African American following Stuart Hall's political definition of "black" as a unifying element in the diaspora.) Yet, just like anglo West Indians, the majority of Haitians, older and younger generations, in spite of the stigma of AIDS, accentuate their country of origin "as a way to claim a particular space where they belong; alone they were labeled but together they become a force in a 'multicultural society'" (Fouron and Schiller, 63). In *Breath, Eyes, Memory*, Sophie assumes the opposite attitude by trying to erase any foreign accent so no one can trace her ancestry: "After seven years in this country, I was tired of having people detect my accent. I wanted to sound completely American..." (69). Danticat's protagonist/narrator, Sophie, begins her story as a child in Haiti's countryside under the warm care of her grandmother and her aunt. The mother figure is the long-distant provider who allows her to have nice clothes and go to private school. This family unit is disrupted when Martine, the mother, sends money to buy Sophie clothes and a ticket to New York. Albeit at the beginning she is leery of the new place and of her mother, Sophie, as the obedient child she was raised to be, works very hard at becoming what Martine envisions. Although Sophie is an ardent defender of Haitian culture, she cannot help but be influenced by her mother, who from the moment of her arrival in New York, stresses that the only way to make it in this country is to learn English as quickly and perfectly as possible so that she can secure a good education (51). Political changes in Haiti with the flight of the Duvaliers and the groundswell of Jean-Bertrand Aristide's Lavalas movement created a stronger sense of belonging within the concept of "overseas Haitians as the Tenth Department" and the formation of the "Ministry of Haitians Living Abroad Within the Haitian Cabinet" (Foner, "Transnationalism," 46). When Sophie returns to Haiti after almost ten years, her grandmother speaks about hope returning to their country when she refers to the young priest they call Lavalas (167). The Sophie who has now come to terms with her mother, said farewell to Grandmé and Atie, challenged the stigmatization of women by women, will teach her daughter Brigitte that Haiti is her place of origin no matter where she may choose to locate as an adult.

The affirmation of African roots in the African/francophone Caribbean movement of Negritude provided a distinct element in the formation of Martinique and Guadeloupe as *Départements d'Outre Mer* (DOM). These islands could continue to trace their ancestors to Africa, but from 1946 on, they were officially departments of France, with political representatives and French passports. Jacky Dahomay, Fred Constant, Justin Daniel, and Randolph Hezekiah refer in various essays to the apparent contradiction of an affirmation of African ancestry and the championing of the Law of Assimilation to become politically part of the French Republic. Edouard Glissant, Patrick Chamoiseau, Jean Bernabé, and Raphaël Confiänt have dealt with this ambiguity by focusing on the notions of *créolité* as the manifestation of cultural identity. Maryse Condé includes this political and ideological debate in all the novels that deal with contemporary issues. She uses fiction as a space to question such issues as assimilation, independence, nationalism, internationalism, and globalization. This divide between cultural and national identity is also debated within the political reality of Puerto Rico and its more-than-100-year-old colonial relationship with the United States. The questions of language, political allegiances, roots, and routes are also part of the migration experiences in the narratives of Caribbean women writers. Even if Guadeloupeans and Martinicans enjoy the same rights, are ruled by the same laws, and hold the same responsibilities as citizens in the European metropole, in everyday affairs islanders are different. In the European Union, for example, Martinique and Guadeloupe are referred to as "ultra-peripheral regions": they are "territories of member states that suffer from structural handicaps" (Daniel, 70). The term *négropolitain,* used by islanders and residents of France to refer to French blacks living in the metropole who have Parisian attitudes, aspirations, values, and lifestyles and who do not speak Creole or do so with a Parisian accent (Burton, 12) is already a verbal differentiation that sets skin color as a sign of other. According to Stephen Castles and Alastair Davidson, phenotypical characteristics such as skin color and other physical features that denote race, cultural expressions such as dress and language, and national origin are "markers constructed by dominant groups to differentiate minorities" (62-63). Alec Hargreaves explains that young people of Caribbean descent "encounter widespread discrimination in the search for jobs and housing as well as in gaining access to leisure facilities such as nightclubs. The color of their skin, the spelling of their names, or simply a reference to their address is often sufficient to disqualify them in the eyes of an employer" (13).

Instead of settling in the center, working-class and sometimes professional Guadeloupeans and Martinicans in the metropole are relegated to social margins and live in proximity to foreign workers and illegal migrants (*sans-papiers*). It is easier for them to live in intensely urbanized areas on the social margins of French cities such as the *Banlieue* ("suburban neighborhoods characterized by low-quality social housing and high-level of unemployment," Hargreaves, 13) around Paris, *Bidonvilles* (shantytowns), and the *zones d'urbanization prioritaire* (ZUOs). As Mark McKinney points out, these settlements duplicate "the territorial divisions of colonial space" (Majumdar, 148). As we see in the families that reside in the city of Le Pointe in Guadeloupe in Condé's novels, the town center is populated by the wealthy French, other Europeans, and the mulatto middle class. The periphery of restricted and rundown self-made dwellings is populated by the black peasants and the working class. In *Tree of Life*, a particular racial class group of the francophone Caribbean is introduced: the black bourgeoisie which Régine Altagrâce Latortue particularizes as the source of class and color conflict in the francophone Antilles (55). It is this group that is prominent in Condé's novels.

Contrary to the anglo and hispanophone Caribbean narrative, francophone Caribbean women writers frequently present antagonistic mother-daughter relationships. Surrogate mothers fill the space of the absent mother in *Breath, Eyes, Memory*, *As the Sorcerer Said...*, *Tree of Life*, and *Desirada*. The mothers who for diverse reasons claim their daughters after seven to ten years of separation can never establish a bond that resembles the relationship that the daughters knew as children with surrogate mothers. Pamela Mordecai and Betty Wilson state that this contrast also exists in male writing: "in male writing the portrayal [of the mother] is almost always positive, whereas in female writing there are ambivalent and on occasion—as often in the francophone contribution—negative portraits" (xiv). These ruptures are the result of migration with the clear exception of Jamaica Kincaid from the anglophone Caribbean.

The other distinct quality of the francophone Caribbean is the African connection, which, in the novels of Condé and Warner-Vieyra, becomes a demystification of Africa as source of origin. In *Juletane, Hermakhonon*, and *A Season in Rihata*, African culture is so patrilineal that women can only occupy the roles of wives, mothers, and caretakers of the home and the sick and elderly. The cultural shock is based on the upbringing and westernized cultural values that Guadeloupeans have learned from France. Condé's narrator/protagonist in *Hermakhonon* was forced out of her island home when she disgraced her family by crossing class and racial barriers when she became the lover of a mulatto. Once this relationship is hurriedly ended by the affected families, Veronica is sent to Paris with a generous allowance. After awhile she chooses to "trace her roots" by securing a job contract in Africa, but at the end of her story, she has decided to leave Africa and settle once again in Paris where she will have the space to participate or not in local politics, to denounce repressive governments, to join the *sans-papiers* movement, to have a white lover. In a sense, Paris allows Veronica the freedom to be herself that she can never have in Guadeloupe or Africa. Warner-Vieyra's Juletane keeps a diary that allows her not to forget where she came from or who she was before settling in Africa with her husband. It is a painful story of displacement and alienation after leaving her island home, moving to Paris, and severing all family ties when her father, grandmother, and godmother die. Zetou in Warner-Vieyra's *As the Sorcerer Said...* continually strives to preserve some notion of family unity when her mother first neglects and later abandons her. This is the motivation behind Zetou's arguments to convince her mother—during one of Rosamond's rare visits to the island—to take her to Paris, never realizing that no one else was interested in bringing together fragments of the past. If Juletane and Zetou had the economic means to choose, the former would return to Paris and the latter to the island of Karura and the fishing village of Cocotier. Although Pineau's Julia is very different from Condé's and Warner-Vieyra's characters because she is an uneducated, spouse-abused older woman, they all undergo forced or voluntary journeys because the place of arrival is seen as transitory: they come to study like Marie-Hélène, live with a relative like Juletane and Zetou, distance themselves from "shameful" situations like Veronica, or are integrated into another family away from home like Julia. Pineau's Julia is rescued by her son's family when her husband, Asdrubal, increases his physical abuse and puts her life at risk. She is secretly removed from her home and shipped to France to live with her daughter-in-law and grandchildren in Aubigné as kin to active-duty soldiers. She remains with them in this southern region and later in Paris for five years but returns eventually home as a woman who, although she still loves her husband, no longer tolerates his abuse. Marie-Denise Shelton describes these stories by francophone Caribbean women writers as "somber tales of disconnection, loneliness, alienation, and resentment" (718).

Once living in the metropole, these women readjust their notions of home. Castles and Davidson explore the process of community formation, whether it is a short or prolonged stay, by emphasiz-
ing home-building and place-making. According to them, home-building implies closure, which brings security, familiarity, community,
and a sense of possibility (131). Place-making is "a spatial extension
of home-building through which ethnic groups partially reshape their
neighborhoods to correspond to their needs and values" (131). In
the francophone novels mentioned in this chapter, the women characters seem determined to obliterate their island past. Martine and
Sophie, who are continuously connected to Croix-des-Rosets keep
their apartment and, later on, their one-family house as bare as possible. The only different aspect here is the color red: "We decorated
our new living room in red, everything from the carpet to the plas-
tic roses on the coffee table" (*Eyes*, 65). Red represents an act of
transgression, and this is why Sophie buries her mother in a red
dress. Although in *Breath, Eyes, Memory* there is no home-building,
there is plenty of place-making as the characters live in Haitian communities, attend Haitian churches and schools, sponsor Haitian restaurants, and engage in discussions about politics back home. From
the moment that her daughter arrives in New York, Martine insists
that Sophie become as American as possible in terms of language
and education ("Your schooling is the only thing that will make people respect you" 43) but warns her of being disrespectful to family
and adults and especially to not allow American boys (which includes whites and black Americans) to get close to her body. Martine's discourse on a young woman's proper behavior is very similar
to the one used by the mother in *Annie John* and especially in Jamaica Kincaid's early story "Girl." When Sophie falls in love with Joseph, a paternal figure because of his age, Martine becomes the
guardian of her daughter's virginity by establishing the ritual "test-
ing" and increasing her vigilance. Once Sophie devalues the meaning of the hymen, then Martine has no role in her daughter's life
and asks her to leave. The irony here is that the lessons taught and
upheld by Martine are totally severed from her own reality of rape
and madness. *Breath, Eyes, Memory* is centered on the mother-daughter relationship—first as a distant memory while Sophie lived in
Haiti and Martine in New York; second, when the mother claims

her daughter and Sophie must now relocate; third as an apparent inreconcilable rupture when Sophie mutilates herself to stop her mother's "tests"; and last when Sophie and Martine communicate once more when they meet in Haiti and discover each other as traumatized women who share a common culture no matter where they now live.

Evelyn O'Callaghan's description of female adolescents in Caribbean novels by Jean Rhys, Myriam Warner-Vieyra, and Zee Edgell can be used very effectively when referring to most of the women characters in the francophone Caribbean. They are insecure and helpless with vulnerable personalities, have histories of rejection by one or both parents, little physical affection in childhood, and experience loneliness and depression, feelings that are exacerbated by physical displacement (90). Both Juletane and Zetou arrive in Paris to live with people who had settled there before. They have no input on how the space they inhabit will be decorated, and Juletane's godmother lives in very frugal conditions where the apartment is only a place to rest her tired bones. Zetou's mother does not want anything to remind her of Karura; she wants everything to be as French as possible. Since her only reminder of her origin is Zetou, she will try to get rid of her daughter as quickly as possible, first by marrying her off and later by giving up her maternal rights and turning her into a ward of the state. In the case of Helene, her journey to Paris was to be transitory since she went there to become a social worker and then to return. But as she continues to postpone her return, she then attempts to become a Parisian by getting a better apartment, securing a higher-paying job, and visiting Guadeloupe as a tourist. There is, of course, some kind of long-range plan to return, perhaps when she retires and can guarantee a generous pension. Meanwhile, she has built a house next to her parents, which is now occupied by her widowed sister.

Even if they live in ethnic neighborhoods, these women characters avoid place-making no matter how many years they remain abroad. They first attempt to erase the country of origin, even if they still keep in contact by distant communication: letters, photos, audiotapes, home videos, telephone calls, and remittances. Invoking an array of reasons, Danticat's Martine, Warner-Vieyra's Helene, and Condé's Reynalda and Thécla choose to disassociate from the ever-pressing island life. Reynalda in *Desirada* and Thécla in *Tree of Life* live on two opposing sides of Guadeloupean society—the former is a servant's daughter while the latter comes from a wealthy family—but they both see France as the only place where they can restart their lives on their own terms. While Reynalda will deliberately take each step necessary to achieve what she considers success, Thécla will travel to distant places, attach herself to men with challenging ideas, and never think of making herself part of a larger society. For both of these women, migration becomes an escape from provinciality and ingrained prejudice. When the past—embodied by Guadeloupe—intrudes in their lives, their resentment is so great that they become as hostile to their people as the host country has been to them. Even though they chose to leave the homeland, they remain antagonistic to the new environment, never integrating and just surviving in order to achieve specific goals. There is no sense of collectivity or of belonging. The island home is far away with only family ties, friends barely remembered, and with just a handful of agreeable recollections. The only way to survive in the alienating city is by concentrating on the self, rejecting all attempts at bonding, setting an individualistic goal for betterment, or escaping into madness. Their relation to the exile community varies with Danticat's Martine choosing the Haitian middle-class sectors, which in New York are seen as another ghetto; Warner-Vieyra's Helene and Juletane living in non-ethnically defined structures; Condé's Veronica and Marie-Hélène occupying student housing specially chosen because it has a tradition of well-off African and Caribbean student populations; and Reynalda living first in the Jean Mermoz housing projects at Savigny-sur-Orge and later "moving up" to an ethnically undefined sector for professionals so that she is not stigmatized by place of residence. Hargreaves observes that "the *banlieue* now functions as a synonym for ethnic alterity, social disadvantage, drugs and crime" (13).

All these women barely decorate their apartments and houses; they perceive their stay as transitory. In a way, having no reminders of back home forces them to look forward; Helene expresses this attitude as "She never took the time to dream or even to just think about the past. She ordered her life 'watch in hand.' She was very immersed in the present and deliberately focused on the future"

(18). Danticat's Martine maintains closer connections to the family back home, uses tapes, letters, and remittances but has not returned to Haiti in ten years. It is only when she feels that she is about to lose her daughter and granddaughter—her only connection away from home—that she decides to make the dreaded trip back home after so many years away. Even though there was no circular migration, Martine worked to support her family in Haiti, provided the best for her daughter, brought her to New York, and gave her the best education she could afford to ensure that she could lead a different life. Martine always saw the possibility of change for her daughter in the metropole, yet she still viewed Sophie as a gendered body whose virginity had to be preserved. Pineau's Julia feels estranged even if her son Maréchal and his family try to provide a home away from home for her. She only comes out of her cocoon when the sun warms up and she can plant the lot behind the family's house. Lucía Suárez confirms that the grandmother "brings another rhythm and language (Creole), and other scents and flavors, thus rendering the private space of the home into a reproduction of the island" (16). However, temporality and transience are the only assurances that a soldier and his family have, since he is assigned to different places for long or short periods while the family lives in reserved soldiers' compounds. This is why Julia always has her things packed just in case Guadeloupe is the next post. Warner-Vieyra's Helene in *Juletane*, who makes yearly visits to Guadeloupe and has saved enough money to have her own place back home, is totally situated in Paris where her life revolves around work and the enjoyment of having no restraints on her behavior. She sees herself as a liberated woman who smokes, drinks, has sex with as many men as she chooses, moves to various places to work, and has decided to marry because she wants to have a child. Still the circuit is never broken, even when her engagement at twenty with a childhood friend did not culminate in marriage as everyone back home had expected. She writes, phones, and sends remittances to her parents and other relatives.

Even Condé's Reynalda, who has methodically severed all her ties to Guadeloupe, sends postcards with large pictures and little writing, money remittances, and no return address. Never asking about her daughter's welfare, never telling about her own whereabouts, Reynalda remains a distant figure, just a memory of a pregnant fourteen-year-old who tried to drown herself. Her migration to Paris was made possible precisely by official and informal circuits like the BLUMIDOM and ecclesiastical referrals. She was assured a job placement that would provide room and board, wages, and travel expenses for four years. Once the contract is terminated, Reynalda has no intention of looking back at what she had left behind. It is only because of her companion's insistence and perhaps a sense of guilt, that Reynalda reestablishes the network by contacting Ranelise, the surrogate mother, and sending for Marie-Noëlle, a decision that she regrets from the moment her daughter arrives in Paris. Reynalda had hoped that if no one heard from her, if she became as anonymous as her postcards, she would be forgotten at home, and once Ranelise and her own mother, Nina, had died, she would be erased. When she sees her daughter after ten years, everything Reynalda had wanted to forget—who she was, where she came from, how her daughter was born—is brought back. The erased past is once more legible. Danticat's Martine reacts differently to her daughter's presence, even though it also signified a rape, shame, the ever-present memory of violence, and a life filled with nightmares and mental health problems. She incorporates Sophie into her daily life by taking her to her work places—both the day and night jobs—introducing her to friends and acquaintances, and securing a space/room that she call her own.

While Condé's Thécla in *Tree of Life* is the privileged daughter of a very wealthy black bourgeois family, Reynalda in *Desirada*, the young adolescent who was saved from committing suicide, secretly makes all the arrangements to leave her island and become an au pair in Paris once her daughter is born. She waited four years to be emancipated from this job commitment, while Thécla traveled throughout Europe, the United States, and the Caribbean once she places her daughter, Coco, in a hospice. There was never a maternal connection that could change their attitude toward what they considered the right choices and life for them; neither woman should have claimed her daughter ten years later. Both daughters are "adopted" by strangers from whom they will receive some kind of love and acceptance, even if it doesn't last very long: Ludovic (the stepfather), Madame Esmondas (a neighbor), Natasha (her mother's friend) with Marie-Noëlle, and Madame Bonoeil (foster mother), Jacob (grandfather),

Patience and Terence (relatives) with Coco. Thécla not only gave up her daughter to total strangers but again was persuaded to face her past by her French husband who thought that she was hurting because of this shameful deed. And just like Reynalda and Marie-Noëlle, the moment Thécla meets Coco, she recognizes that they have nothing in common, and no love can ever spring from this reunion.

This rejection of the child by her mother has been internalized in the case of Juletane because when orphaned at birth, there is no hope of recuperating the loss. She creates very dangerous dependency links that will eventually drive her to total isolation and madness. She is ten years old when her father dies and is claimed by her godmother who has lived in Paris for some time. Juletane describes her as a "strict, devout, old maid," (7) who took her surrogate mother role very seriously by overprotecting her goddaughter. When her godmother dies, Juletane is helpless, for she knows no one else and has no idea what Paris is all about. When she meets and very quickly falls in love with the African student Mamadou, he comes to represent all the loved ones who have died—the mother, father, and godmother: "For my part, I loved him with all the ardour and intensity of a first and only love. In my eyes he was perfect. I had no relatives, few friends, so Mamadou became my whole world" (12). Undoubtedly, Warner-Vieyra's Zetou is the child most traumatized by this separation of mother and daughter. Rosamond, who rationed her affection to her four children, depending on how dark or light they were, runs off with a very light-skinned creole (considered white in the village). Zetou is precisely ten years old when her mother abandons her family to go to Paris. Her paternal grandmother becomes her surrogate mother, but after six years—just when she was preparing for the primary certificate exams—her mother comes back to town. Although Rosamond never thought of taking any of her children to Paris, Zetou persuades her to do so. In her dreamlike vision of Paris and in her assurance that she is equal to any French citizen, Zetou believes that only in Paris can she continue her studies and become educated: "What danger could I run? None at all. In Paris my future was assured; all I had to do was to settle down seriously to my school work; my future depended on myself, and so it was quite assured" (41). The mother's betrayal goes from denying her the opportunity to enroll in school, introducing her as a cousin, using

her as a cook and servant, and the last deed, marrying her off to
Joseph de la Pierre, an "old white man" (59). Like Juletane, Zetou
has no family in Paris, and as a sixteen-year-old girl she cannot return to Cocotier, for she has no authority to decide what to do with
her life. Once the maternal claim is made, there is no going back.
Jacob, the grandfather in *Tree of Life*, may want to keep Coco with
him since it is impossible to pin down Thécla, but she will not agree
even if she never pays attention to her daughter and lets her run
wild wherever they settle. Ranielise's (*Desirada*) and Atie's (*Breath,
Eyes, Memory*) petition to again take care of Marie-Noëlle, and Sophie will simply be dismissed, just as Rosamond (*As the Sorcerer Said...*)
would rather give her daughter up to the state than send her back to
Cocotier. Whether they say they care or not about what people say
back home, returning the child claimed after so many years would
be a sign of failure in the eyes of the community of origin.

As in the case of almost every immigrant coming from countries
considered non-Western, immigrants and former colonial subjects
from Guadeloupe, Martinique, or Haiti are rarely placed in the same
class or job structure unless they are members of the Antillaise bour-
goisie with businesses in Paris. But in Condé's novels, not even the
Haitian Olnel in *Season in Rihata*, Veronica in *Heremakhonon*, Thécla
in *Tree of Life*, or Juletane in Warner-Vierya's novel, are recognized
by the dominant society as competitive professionals. Juletane's family was part of the bourgeoisie, but when her godmother moved to
Paris, she worked as a highly skilled seamstress for a steady salary
that would allow her to live in the metropole in a two-room apartment. Juletane has already started a similar job when her godmother unexpectedly dies one afternoon. Those who come to Paris to
study and earn the same degrees as their French counterparts can
either go back home—which, of course, Veronica and Helene in
Juletane choose not to do—or easily find well-paying jobs abroad
(Africa) or state jobs created by the center to deal with the most
recent problems in the metropole: the communities of immigrants
and their adaptability problems. Veronica goes abroad but Helene
not only accepts "missions" to earn more money in a short time, but
she has her own Parisian job as a social worker, and this is why
Juletane's case is referred to her. Helene inquires back home to try
to find some family tie, but there is no trace. Helene is a social

worker whose patients/clients are people from the Caribbean and Africa. These groups of workers, set apart by their race, ethnicity, and place of origin, have adaptability problems. And who is best prepared to handle them than professionals from these same groups? Even with these concessions and restrictions, these women achieve in the metropole what would be almost impossible to do on the island nation or DOM. They take advantage of the openings created by the centre (the dominant culture) to dissolve any potential conflict. The centre allows them to move in the assigned spaces, which also means that the centre stretches so that it can continue to control and segment the population by maintaining cultural difference.

In *Desirada,* Reynalda's experience in seeking a job in the metropole is totally different from that of Marie-Helene in *Juletane* and Thécla in *Tree of Life*, who can afford an education in France or have access to the best schools on the island, where they will be tutored to pass the preparatory exams. Reynalda had no chance of this ever happening because she was extremely poor, a very young unwed mother, and had access to no more than a basic education. From the moment she is forcefully brought to La Pointe and put in the service of the Coppini family, she makes plans to leave but not to return to Desirada, perhaps the only place where she remembers once being happy. Reynalda seems to be duplicating her own mother's relationship with her. Poverty overwhelmed Nina, her mother, with no time for warmth, care, or comfort, since the only thought in her life was to survive in any way possible, including selling/lending her daughter to secure a job that would provide them with food and shelter. Although Reynalda has only disdain for her mother, she also survives any way she can when she first moves to Paris. Even if the centre—exemplified by the city—is fixed, rigid, immobile, the migrant's way of life is marked by mobility so as not to starve, be caught, or be fixed. So no matter where she or he moves to, she or he will continue to be transient. Women are more flexible and are not intimidated by distant, hostile, and unfamiliar spaces. They have learned to survive in the worst conditions imaginable; they have faced scarcity, discrimination, verbal and physical abuse, poverty, indifference, back home and in the city.

Isabel Hoving reminds us that, in postcolonial writing, the issue of place is often thematized as displacement, a sign of loss, a poten-

tial for personal transformation, an opportunity to choose new subject positions (14). This is Reynalda's situation when she secures a
job as an au pair in Paris. She can go to this distant place with a
guaranteed room and income. She will do her job well—efficiently
without ever being emotional— taking advantage of the opportunity to study and learn whatever she can from this culture. After earning a scholarship to become a social worker, a position created to
deal with the margins, she takes her leave without any appreciation
for the employers who facilitated her arrival in Paris and the opportunity to move on. Reynalda will use people along the way, just as
she feels she was used as an adolescent. Men who enter her life must
serve her purposes and never become obstacles, and children are
accidents of life that she refuses to deal with—she lets others take
care of those emotions. Her aim from the moment she decided to
leave her island was to enter the city, learn its labyrinthian structure,
play its power game, and always come out ahead. Every time she is
placed at the margin, she will push her way to the centre. The centre
will yield, even if only periodically and with extreme restrictions. But
Reynalda does not care; she now forms part of the city; she has erased
the island in her.

If Veronica and Marie-Hélène like Veronica's sisters, Aida and
Jalla had followed their family's plan of studying in Paris, finding a
good Guadeloupean suitor (meaning black and rich) whether in Paris
or on the island, marrying back home, and then settling wherever
their husbands' businesses would take them, these women would
not still be wondering where home is or why Africa does not even
partially seem to answer that question. For these two women, studying did not fulfill their lives; domesticity is always rejected, and place
has no name. How important is the job that draws Veronica to Africa and then later brings her back to Paris? For her, being a teacher
or a consultant seems to be a poor excuse to remain in a place.
Marie-Hélène is so enmeshed in the female roles of African culture
of wife and mother of many children that she can only put aside her
bad humor, discontent, and frequent despair by recalling her life in
Paris and snapshots from Guadeloupe. Sam Haigh believes that the
house in Rihata becomes "a refuge, a place of self-definition, even if
she [Marie-Hélène] has to define herself as mother in order to have
some independence of movement..." (79).

While Juletane in Warner-Vieyra's novel, has had an urban bourgeois upbringing with a more direct link to France (6), Helene
comes from the countryside where education is limited to primary
grades, unless there are family savings or a scholarship for private
schooling. Because as a feeble child she could not work in the fields,
she was sent to the best school in the region. She withstood the
white and mulatto children's mockery, the teachers' prejudice about
a black girl's intelligence, and passed her preparatory exams: "In
the classroom, the white children were in the first rows, then came
the mulattos and finally, the last bench, at the very back of the
class, was reserved for blacks. Helene's place was in the darkest
corner, at the end, against the wall" (18). She shields herself in the
same way in Paris until she finishes her degree. Both Reynalda and
Helene live in Paris and are very successful social workers who are
able to move up in their field. Yet, Reynalda chooses to do so by
positioning herself at the centre (pursuing a terminal degree, securing a government job as director/supervisor, publishing, and
being recognized in the field), while Helene takes what she wants
from that centre (job security, good salary, fringe benefits), remains connected to her island, and establishes a link with Africa
on her own terms by accepting work contracts when and where
she chooses. Reynalda decides that dealing with cases is only a
means to gather data to do research, earn a higher degree, and
write and publish books on the subject of immigrants. She has
separated herself even from those immigrants—from Africa and
the Maghreb—who had no relation to what and who she despised
in Guadeloupe. Even though these are the cases Reynalda has to
deal with in her job, she would rather distance herself from anyone marginal in this society. She wants no emotional link to these
immigrants who did not try hard enough, as she did, and now
struggle to survive in the centre. If Juletane's case would have been
brought to her attention, she would have probably reacted as if it
were one more case not worth her time. Perhaps because of the
proximity of her work to human beings who are closer in cultural
context and location to the centre, Helene does care about her
patients. She still has this feeling of impotence, of not being able
to extend lives, to find ways for families to be reunited, to deal with
generation gaps and pressures:

> She always had a feeling of powerless rebellion when a child died in her care. In spite of almost twenty years in her profession, she could not really get used to the suffering of others. The whisky, the cigarettes, the wild parties were a way of arming herself against pity, of doing her work without exposing her own feelings of compassion. (56)

Quite the contrary, Reynalda moves away from actual cases into the area of research and publication where she deals with statistics, and reality is shown through numbers and graphs: [her book] "was a well-documented essay—in which she dealt with migrant families from the Caribbean and sub-Saharan Africa, mainly migrant women, in fact, their social and family conditions, their traumas and—daringly enough—their sexual fantasies" (200).

Zetou in Warner-Vieyra's *As the Sorcerer Said...* is the saddest case because discrimination and exploitation come from her own family. She is so sure that if she does not leave Cocotier, she would continue the tradition of women in the village ("There were only two alternatives when you left primary school: either to stay at home and see to the housework till you got married, or else get a job as a maid-of-all-work in town...." 54) that she convinces her mother—the one who abandoned her and the other siblings, the one who reproached her own mother for marrying her off to a black man, the one who only showed affection for children who were light skinned—to take her to Paris where she could lead a different life. However, in Paris she was forced by her mother to be the maid and the cook, sex partner of her lover, and someone who could be married for profit. Zetou realizes that school is no longer an option and that she cannot return home even if she wants to: "My present situation was nothing but a bad dream; when I woke up I would be back in my village" (51). At sixteen, in Paris, Zetou can only be a maid or prostitute on her own or a state ward until she turns twenty-one.

Pineau's Julia also perceives France as an oppressive place that has no connection to her. Others decide what is best for her: her son Maréchal, who wants her as far away as possible from her husband; her daughter-in-law Daisy, who welcomes someone who can help her with the house and the young children; her granddaughter/narrator, who teaches her to write and is always eager to learn stories from Guadeloupe. Julia prefers to stay inside the house so she does not see the strange looks of the white people in the community. Julia's inability to speak proper French, and her insistence on dressing, speaking, and behaving as if she were in Guadeloupe, upsets the unshakable institutions of school, police, and army. When Julia decides to pick up her grandchildren at school and wears her son's army coat to protect herself from the rain, she is arrested by the police for desecrating the honor of the country and for not explaining her motives—she could only speak to them in Creole. "The entire school is there. The whole village is staring at us. Lots of eyes, alarmed. Why the police? Because of the army cap, the military overcoat? Why these solemn faces, these grand outraged airs? Man Ya [Julia] did not intend to insult France, only to keep off the rain" (50–51).

In Paris, she is less conspicuous because of the many immigrants who populate this space, especially the periphery where the families of the African and island soldiers reside. Her pilgrimage to the Basilica of Sacré-Coeur ("The belly of Paris does not frighten her any more than the little town of Capesterre. She sets off, her mind free, as if she knows the way." 62) could be very dangerous because she does not know her way around, does not speak French, did not tell anyone at home where she was going, and is accompanied by her seven-year-old grandson. But after walking almost the entire day, Julia succeeds in entering the church that was a mere tower from her kitchen's window. She has found God's house in this so-distant place.

Although there is a need for place-making in these women's lives, there is no sense of community in the diaspora in these novels. Even though defining a place is one of the first acts of an alien group to establish a point of arrival, these women characters use the communities merely as temporary steps before abandoning these ethnic niches where they were "protected" from the demands of the dominant society and breaking away from the familiar, and to them, suffocating environment. While men such as Marc, Martine's lover in *Breath, Eyes, Memory*, Ludovic, Reynalda's husband in *Desirada*, the Louis men, Thécla and Coco's male relatives in *Tree of Life* seem to be the seekers of this known space, women immediately associate these spaces of arrival and contact with the restraints put on women back home. They seek the anonymity of the city, where they are not observed, supervised, or advised. Within the student groups, there is no pressure because they are there specifically to escape the demanding environment back home, to which they will eventually return. They all play at being rebels within their family's structures, but they know that their future is dependent on the family. Olnel, the Haitian, and Zek, the African, in *Season in Rihata*, Hector, Helene's ex-boyfriend in *Juletane*, and Jean-Marie, Veronica's lover in Guadeloupe, in *Hermakhonon*—if he would have been in Paris at this time—see themselves as free, wealthy, intelligent representatives of their family's name abroad but also part of the westernized way of thinking, at least while they remain in Paris. In a different context, Maréchal in *Exile According to Julia* also considers himself superior to the men back home and knowledgeable about Western culture because he is a soldier in the French army and his family lives in France while he is on active duty. The women in these novels tend not to differentiate between loving temporarily or establishing lifelong attachments. For example, Marie-Hélène in *A Season of Rihata* experiences an emotional breakdown when, after her sister's suicide, Olnel, her brother-in-law, decides to return to Haiti without claiming his son; Hector in *Juletane* can return home with his pregnant French lover after canceling his official wedding to Helene a few days before. In these unsupervised student communities the only pressure for both men and women is to finish their degree within a certain reasonable time and return back home.

Reynalda in *Desirada* cannot afford this luxury. Each goal is set as if her life depended on it. She finishes her degree in record time. She lives in cheap housing around Paris, where she can move to her various jobs and have a space to study for her examinations. She does not socialize with her neighbors, some of whom, like Madame Esmondas, come from the same island. She leaves that to her lover Ludovic and her daughter Marie-Noëlle:

> ...hordes of brown-skinned children played, for the building housed a high percentage of Africans, West Indians, and Réunion islanders. The West Indians and Réunion islanders got along well together. They spoke Creole among themselves. They paraded together through the streets at Carnival time. They celebrated their weddings and christenings in the communal hall, whose walls were painted by frescoes by a Martinican who passed as an artist. (26–27)

As soon as she can afford to, Reynalda moves out of this ethnic neighborhood into what she understands is a more suburban but still Parisian housing complex: "a brand-new apartment house in the XIIIth arrondissement" (85). Still, she continues to furnish her space as a no-person's land:

> Around them the living room was poorly furnished. Four places were set at a trestle table, for despite their social rise Ludovic and Reynalda seemed no more interested in refinement and comfort than they had been in the past. The furnishings were hardly different from Savigny-sur-Orge. Old pieces mixed in with new ones, and she recognized them like familiar faces in a strange crowd. (85)

Contrary to her mother, Reynalda, Marie-Noëlle is always attempting to form communities ever since her first relocation from La Pointe to Paris. She roams around the buildings in Savigny-sur-Orge looking for the family warmth she cannot find at her mother's side. Her first home community is the sanatorium in Vance, where her co-patients become her friends, and later on family, as they make Nice a city they can belong to. Marie-Noëlle chooses not to finish her studies, and to go off wandering with Stanley, a friend who later becomes her lover. Her other alternative was to return home to Reynalda. This yearning to establish a family defined by true love and friendship and not family kin, is what motivates her to be part of a quasi-commune on the outskirts of Boston with people she knew very little about and did not have much in common with except having sex and talking about gigs and music: "...the chaos and discomfort of the house she lived in, the ugliness of Camden Town, the dismal façades of buildings destined for demolition but never demolished..." (100). In contraposition, Marie-Noëlle turns to Anthea and Molara's constructed household, where men are not a factor in any decision made, where learning is continuously stimulated, and where African Americans have re-written their history as one of success. But after a while, Marie-Noëlle sees this construction as another denial of reality: No matter how protective of the perils of prejudice and discrimination, they do live in a white racist society.

Marie-Noëlle's return to La Pointe seems to represent her obligation to pay her respects to the woman who was her surrogate

mother for ten years. But as is true for Coco in *Tree of Life*, it becomes
a search for roots, for the origin, one that can be approached because
the witnesses are still there to tell their stories. How fantastic or how
close to reality these stories are remains a matter for the listener to
decide according to her needs. When Marie-Noëlle returns home,
the picture of place frozen in her mind for twenty years is similar to
the village's picture of the little girl who left at age ten to join her
mother in Paris. It takes Marie-Noëlle eighteen years to return, and
very quickly, people started wondering how could she never have
returned at least once to see Ranèlise, the woman who raised her,
and how much she seemed to have changed now that she has lived
elsewhere:

> [she]was no bigger or taller than when she left. Not very well
> dressed or well kempt either, her hair cut any old way. Her eyes
> just as melancholy and languishing, set in large circles that looked
> as though they had been outlined with makeup. Her jeans and
> flowery shirts no different from any other "Negropolitan" or
> "white trash" you met thumbing a lift by the side of the road.
> She was awkward and spoke in monosyllables. She had not
> cried—everyone noticed it—when she knelt down beside
> Ranèlise's coffin. (122-123)

Her stay in La Pointe becomes a search for the people who were
part of her and her mother's childhood. She traces Reynalda's steps
in this place she so hated, where she attempted to put an end to her
and her unborn child's life, where she secretly planned her disap-
pearance leaving behind mother, daughter, friends, and a community that had opened its arms to protect her. Marie-Noëlle makes
her journey to her grandmother's shack—almost inaccessible by road
but connected to the outside world through cable TV (""Even those
peoples who have never migrated...do not live in the same 'local'
culture as before because of radio, television, film and the internet." Van Alphen, 55). Nina, the storyteller—the woman whom Reynalda vilified whenever she bothered to refer to her—is more than
eager to have an audience to listen to her and warns her granddaughter not to seek any other "truth": "Don't ask your maman for
anything more, she's a first-rate liar. Leave her be with her fairy
tales. In fact, don't ask anyone for anything more" (184). Now that

Marie-Noëlle has spoken to the witnesses, she can leave La Pointe, remember the stories, the hazy protagonists, and go back to Boston. She returns to the security and anonymity of her university job. This can only be achieved by crossing out Guadeloupe, Paris, Reynalda, Nina—the links that would draw her back, that would remind her of identity and place. She can now live in a city that is a buffer zone, a nameless and timeless space, a centre where she has positioned her re-constructed self. Still she is unable to erase all memory: the brightness of the sun, the richness of colors, and the distant voices muffled by time and distance.

Even though in Condé's *Tree of Life* the storytellers and life historians are men, since the women die young or cannot write, Coco becomes the self-appointed historian. She will enter her grandfather's library with a mission: to recover the history that her mother denied her. She will sift through piles of old photographs and meet her ancestors, ask everyone about their particular stories, fill the gaps with rumor and imagination, and recover lost links like Bert, Bébert, and later on, Aurélia.

> Still gasping, I opened the cardboard box. I had come to know them, the faces of all those dead long since returned to dust in the shadows of the family crypt....And I liked listing, arranging those ever-more-dated images that reduced these lives to a succession of ritual ceremonies—christenings, weddings, First Communions—and to mere entertainments—swimming in the creek, picnics at the seaside. (236)

In her case, Coco is filling the ten-year void when she was no one's child. And yet, going back to Guadeloupe for the first time felt like going back home, the one she had never heard of but knew she must be part of. When Thécla decides that her own search for roots leads to Jamaica, repeating Pastor's ideas, Coco wants to stay in Guadeloupe: "I was going, leaving the island that had already become my own, leaving those who had set me in affectionate ground, covering me with little words of tenderness" (237). Forced to move by her mother's authority to places more imaginary than real, Coco yearns for her roots, a place where she belongs, is loved and remembered, can trace her ancestors, and claim an extended family that includes the spirits that inhabit the old house as well as the cousins who attend the ceremonial weddings and funerals. When Thécla decides to leave again, Coco prays: "'You up there, Gawd or Jah, black or white, make her leave me here!' Guadeloupe, this was my land!" (298). Coco will have a third opportunity to explore her island, this time as part of the Louis—her ancestors—world without the disturbing presence of her mother.

For Reynalda in *Desirada*, Veronica in *Hermakhonon*, and Marie-Hélène in *A Season in Rihata*, there is no return. They chose to leave or were encouraged to stay away from the island because they did not conform to the standards of their class. The ties were severed apparently with no regrets because they all found spaces they could call their own. As members of the bourgeois both Veronica and Marie-Hélène were expected to do well at school and then go on to Paris to continue their studies. This emphasis on education is part of the marriage project: to secure a wealthy prospective husband within the local bourgeoisie. Both women sabotage these plans: Veronica by having an affair with a member of the mulatto elite and later taking a white French lover, and Marie-Hélène by falling in love with a member of the mulatto Haitian bourgeoisie and later marrying an African. They become estranged daughters back home. Pineau's Julia—a different generation and class—is forced to leave home but only yearns to return to her land and to the husband "God gave her." She always sees her stay in France as a brief vacation, so she never tries to make concessions and learn the language and ways of the French. While her son and his friends see themselves as French citizens, Julia finds no link to the white people in Aubigné or Paris. While the Guadeloupean soldiers' families have only disdain for the island they came from and continuously gloat on how superior they are to the people who still live there ("Long ago it was a land of slavery, which no longer has anything good in it. Don't ask about the past! Take advantage of France! Take advantage of the luck you have to be growing up here!" 16), Julia teaches the children Creole and tells them stories so they never forget where their ancestors come from. This is also Julia's way to preserve the memory of home. Meanwhile, Veronica in *Heremakhonon* attends carnival in Paris as a way of remembering and reconstructing the homeland she left nine years before. When she catches herself in this mood, she tries to immediately break away from any nostalgia:

"The Caribbean Festival. Chateau de Vincennes. Whatever came over me? Nine years. I'm telling you. Homesickness" (69). She does realize that she needs that homeland to hold on to when she sees the African streetcleaner in Paris. He becomes her reality check: no matter the social class she belongs to back home, in the metropole she is just a black woman visually catalogued for menial and service jobs in the big city. Vévé Clark sees the African streetcleaner as "doubly-exiled—from his point of origin and from the culture he serves" (312). On the other hand, Marie-Hélène's decision to marry Zek, adopt Delphine's baby, and move to Africa has blocked any possibility of a return to either Guadeloupe or Paris:

> Returning to Guadeloupe had meant little more for Marie-Hélène than going back to her mother. The island had symbolised one thing: her mother; a womb which she could retreat from her suffering, eyes closed, fists clenched, soothed by the throbbing blood circulating round her. But her mother was dead. The grief of having lost her for ever, of not having been near her at the last moment, had made her hate the island and it had become like a sterile womb, never to nurture a foetus again. So Africa, Mother Africa, had appealed to her imagination and raised her expectations. (63)

Yet after years of leading a life of privilege in an African community and having delivered six daughters and now pregnant with her seventh child, Marie-Hélène can only describe her life in Africa as an exile in total solitude (20). With no family left in Guadeloupe after her mother's death—her father is an object of derision and a representative of the poor black population she so hates—and Paris seen only as a dream that turned into a nightmare, Marie-Hélène can only hope that her brother-in-law and one-time lover Madou's connections will secure Zek some diplomatic post that will allow the family to live again in a metropole.

Pineau's Julia is housebound most of the time she lives in Aubigné and Paris. Everything outside these transitory homes is foreign and antagonistic, so Julia stays inside speaking Creole, trying to cook homestyle food, praying to God and her saints, healing colds and cuts with home remedies, and in the summer, attending to her garden: "In France, she prefers to stay in her Guadeloupe time, which swings between rain and sun, between going and coming" 73. Gardening and cooking during the very short French summer means transporting herself to the town of Routhiers and returning to her roots while residing elsewhere: "She is going back to her garden, which gives her food, herbs for healing, her road to Routhiers, her big woods at the foot of Soufrière, her house at the foot of the Carbet Falls..." 104. Her only concession to the dominant culture is her preference for French television, particularly the news with images of the outside world, including black people like Martin Luther King and Josephine Baker (who at that time resided in France). "Man Ya acquires a taste for the images, becomes interested in the newscasts, which take her to every continent and span oceans with supernatural ease, to show parts of the world, pieces of living history" 76.

James Clifford maintains that community can be a site both of support and oppression (260), which is exactly how someone like Danticat's Martine in *Breath, Eyes, Memory* views both the community back home and the artificially and conveniently formed communities of the metropole. When she is sent by her mother to New York after her brutal rape by a Ton Ton Macoute, geographical distance helped her get back on her feet; she studied, worked at various jobs, earned good wages, established herself as an independent woman, chose her friends and companion. Even though the violence perpetrated against her body and mind comes back almost every night in terrible nightmares, she found strength to send for the child whose mere presence made her see the face of her rapist over and over again. This is partly why Martine cannot embrace Sophie and treat her as a wanted child. Although she never considers returning, she remains emotionally tied to the homeland, and she has made arrangements to be buried in Haiti. She also makes the trip back home in an attempt to establish a link with Sophie who felt herself betrayed by a mother blinded by old customs who degraded her as a daughter and a woman. It is only in this "neutral" territory that Martine and Sophie can talk to each other again:

> "You and I, we started wrong," my mother said. "You are now a woman, with your own house. We are allowed to start again." (162)

My mother placed her hand on my grandmother's shoulder and signaled for her to wait. She turned back to me and said in English, "I want to be your friend, your very very good friend, because you saved my life many times when you woke me up from those nightmares.'" (170)

Haiti can never be a site of nostalgia because the remembrance of Grandmé, Atie, and the town of Croix-des-Rosets can never hide the violence of Martine's rape, the power of the Ton Ton Macoute, and the country ravaged by poverty. This is portrayed drastically in Port-au-Prince, the gateway through which Sophie leaves for the first time to meet her mother and to which she returns to receive her mother. Myriam Chancy describes the many valid reasons for leaving Haiti, even if something is irreplaceably lost: "Exile is what makes remaining in one's homeland unbearable or untenable: the threat of governmental/political persecution or state terrorism; poverty, enmeshed through exploitative labor practices that overwork and underpay..." (2).

Returning to Haiti is not an option for Martine or Sophie. Both have made their lives in New York. They have found there the anonymity they so desired. No one reminds Martine that she was raped and had a fatherless child when she was very young. In New York, she is known as a working woman who sends remittances to her family and who has saved enough money to send for her daughter and provide her with a private school education to assure that she becomes a professional. Sophie now has a husband and daughter whose world is New York and not Haiti. This new community within the metropole becomes a meeting place of difference. This way Joseph can also be family, just as Sophie's support group—women from different cultures who share a history of violence—can share this space where place/identity is being redefined. The homeland for both of them remains the place of the ancestors—both living and dead—the place where Martine will be buried next to her family. Sophie will be the family's memory who tells stories to her daughter Brigitte so that in time she can continue honoring their ancestors.

Coco and Aurélia in Condé's *Tree of Life* are very special cases because they were born in the metropole and learned about Guadeloupe through relatives who emphasized the negative aspects of that far-away place. According to these reports, the people there were so narrow–minded that they could not accept a woman with an independent mind who could have a life outside of marriage and the household and connect to people not directly linked to their family tree. Coco learns about her grandparents and other relatives from her mother, who like Maréchal's army buddies in Pineau's *Exile According to Julia*, is always putting down her family during the very infrequent times that she speaks about home. Visiting Guadeloupe for the first time should have meant that Coco would show no regard for these people who were so provincial that they only valued their family and their island. Yet, the moment Coco arrives in Guadeloupe, she knows that this is home, no matter if she is meeting her grandfather for the first time and listening to the stories of ancestors she never knew she was linked to. When Coco finally settles in Paris and goes back to boarding school, she has the security that she belongs somewhere, that there is a place where people care for her, where her ancestors are buried, and where she can reconstruct her life through family pictures and old story tales. Whether she will go back once she is independent of her mother is something not even Coco knows. But she will always have her imaginary country that no one can take away from her.

> My country? Now they were giving me the island! In gratitude I gave them dreams. We climbed up along the sides of a volcano whose gaping mouth swallowed clouds. We bathed in a too-blue sea that hid its icy heart, and netted giant crayfish in the crystal of its streams. (332)

Coco's chance meeting with Aurélia Louis when she comes to teach at the special school she is attending is the beginning of a lifelong friendship and collaboration. Coco will at last link Aurélia to her father's and grandfather's land by filling the empty spaces in the family tree and by returning to Guadeloupe with the story of the two relatives "lost in France." In France, Aurélia only heard the terrible accusations of her grandmother, Marie. For this white ancestor, the Louis family were just "niggers! Without us, you went around with your private parts showing! You ate each other raw. Cannibals!" (333). Bert, who when he first arrived in France was startled by its open hostility, "told himself that cities exist perhaps only in the subjective experiences of those who live them" (154). When he could not fulfill his father's expectations of pursuing studies in Angers and follow his convictions to "uphold the Negro race," Bert became despondent. Shunned by his father, living in poverty when his father stopped writing and sending money, married to a white woman he did not love, and father of a child he barely noticed, Bert died in an apparent accident and was heard of no more until his body was sent back to Guadeloupe, at his younger brother's insistence. Marie's resentment at never having been recognized by the Louis family as Bert's rightful wife and mother of his only son, Bébert, will translate into this prejudiced talk that fails to see that she is also insulting her granddaughter. Even when Aurélia is adopted by her mother's second husband, François Paoli, growing up was still very hard. Lucette, her mother, asks Coco, "Are they giving you a hard time at school because of your color?...Times change! They gave my Aurélia such a hard time!" Aurélia remembers the songs the other students made up to make her feel like an outsider, an inferior with no right to be there:

> A Negro girl was drinking milk
> Ah, she thought, if only I could
> Soak my face in the bowl of milk
> I'd be whiter than all the French-heh-hench! (328)

She made up her mind to prove them wrong and, with the same determination that Helene and Zetou in Warner-Vieyra's novels put into their education, Aurélia excelled in every single course she took throughout her years in school. But in the end, she chose to study special education "because I could not forget my childhood, my troubled adolescence, wordless, speechless, sightless and unsmiling, shut away behind its wall of solitude" (329).

When Coco is allowed to go back to Guadeloupe to visit her sick grandfather, Aurélia accompanies her vicariously by writing a long letter to Jacob and describing the photos that were sent to him through the years. She makes Coco promise to find the "tree of life" that joins their families. When Jacob takes Coco to the cemetery and the family pantheon and shows her the engraved names of Bert and Bébert Louis, Coco has fulfilled Aurélia's promise by securing a space for the names of her ancestors through the memory of all those that will come afterwards. Much as in Danticat's *Breath, Eyes, Memory*, home is the place where all family members return to, whether physically, like Martine, or spiritually, by inscribing the names of these two Louis men who were lost in metropolitan France. Now Aurélia has a place to return and claim her roots.

When Julia/Man Ya in Pineau's novel—a poetic narrative of re-membrance by a young narrator born in France of Guadeloupean parents—finally returns to Guadeloupe, there is no need to readapt after a five-year absence. She goes back to her little house in Routhiers, links once more with friends and neighbors, and awaits the return of her grandchildren to the place of origin, even if they were born elsewhere. Her abusive husband, Asdrubal, will no longer exert his authority over her: her absence and perceived loss made him distant and no longer interested in blaming her for the pain suffered in war. Julia's granddaughter, the narrator, summarizes what it means to leave home and move around, pretending that such a place can be reconstructed at will: "At each departure, you leave a little of yourself behind, even just the dust of dreams. They leave empty spaces in your heart, like those light-colored spots that are left on walls when pictures are taken down" (159). Julia understood from the moment that she departed Guadeloupe at her son's insistence that her stay in France was a temporary solution to rescue her from an abusing husband. She never has any desire to adapt, assimilate, insert, or integrate (Sourieau, 171) into the French culture. She sees no advantage in doing this because she has a home to return to, a culture she loves and respects, a land where her ancestors have lived through slavery and emancipation, a place of her own.

While Veronica, Marie-Hélène, Reynalda, and Thécla—all born in the Caribbean—made the mistake of looking at the homeland as "bounded, a site of authenticity, as singular, fixed, and unproblematic as identity" (Massey, 5), those not born there, Coco and Aurélia, see the Caribbean as a place where one lives "in the intersections of histories and memories" (Chambers), and where these women find a foundation/solid ground from which to contest the "identity of any place, including that place called home" (Massey, 169).

Works Cited

Burton, Richard. *French and West Indians: Martinique, Guadeloupe and French Guiana Today*. Charlottesville: UP Virginia, 1995.

Castles, Stephen and Alastair Davidson. *Citizenship and Migration: Globalization and the Politics of Belonging*. New York: Routledge, 2000.

Castor, Suzy. *La ocupación norteamericana de Haití y sus consecuencias (1915-1934)*. México: Siglo XXI, 1971.

Chambers, Iain. *Migrancy, Culture, Identity*. London: Routledge, 1994.

Chancy, Myriam J.A. *Searching for Safe Spaces: Afro-Caribbean Women Writers in Exile*. Philadelphia: Temple UP, 1997.

Clark, Vèvè A. "Developing Diaspora Literacy: Allusion in Maryse Condé's *Hérémakhonon*." In *Out of the Kumbla: Caribbean Women and Literature*. Eds. Carole Boyce Davies and Elaine Savory Fido. Trenton, NJ: Africa World P, 1990. 303–319.

Clifford, James. "Diasporas." In *Routes: Travel and Translation in the Late Twentieth Century*. Cambridge: Harvard, 1997. 244–277.

Condé, Maryse. *Desirada*. New York: Soho P, 2000 (originally published in 1997).

_____. *Heremakhonon*. Washington DC: Three Continents P, 1982 (originally published in 1976).

_____. *A Season in Rihata*. Oxford: Heinemann, 1988 (originally published in 1981).

_____. *Tales from the Heart*. New York: Soho P, 2001 (originally published in 1998).

_____. *Tree of Life*. New York: Ballantine Books, 1992 (originally published in 1987).

Constant, Fred. "The French Antilles in the 1990s: Between European Unification and Political Territorialisation." In *Islands at the Crossroads: Politics in the Non-Independent Caribbean*. Eds. Aaron Gamaliel Ramos and Angel Israel Rivera. Kingston and Boulder, CO: Ian Randle and Lynne Rienner, 2001. 80–94.

Dahomay, Jacky. "Cultural Identity versus Political Identity in the French West Indies." In *Modern Political Culture in the Caribbean*. Eds. Holger Henke and Fred Reno, Mona, Jamaica: U West Indies P, 2003. 90–108.

Daniel, Justin. "The Construction of Dependency: Economy and Politics in the French Antilles." In *Islands at the Crossroads: Politics in the Non-Independent Caribbean*. Eds. Aaron Gamaliel Ramos and Angel Israel Rivera. Kingston and Boulder, CO: Ian Randle and Lynne Rienner, 2001. 61–79.

Danticat, Edwidge. *Breath, Eyes, Memory*. New York: Vintage, 1995.

———. *The Farming of Bones*. New York: Soho, 1998.

———. *Krik? Krak!*. New York: Vintage, 1996.

Foner, Nancy. "Transnationalism Then and Now: New York Immigrants Today and at the Turn of the Twentieth Century." In *Migration, Transnationalization, and Race in a Changing New York*. Eds. Héctor R. Cordero-Guzmán et al. Philadelphia: Temple UP, 2001. 35–57.

Fouron, Georges E. and Nina Glick Schiller. "The Generation of Identity: Redefining the Second Generation within a Transnational Social Field." In *Migration, Transnationalization, and Race in a Changing New York*. Eds. Héctor R. Cordero-Guzmán et al. Philadelphia: Temple UP, 2001. 58–86.

Grosfoguel, Ramón. "Colonial Caribbean Migrations to France, The Netherlands, Great Britain and the United States." *Ethnic and Racial Studies* 20. 3 (July 1997): 594–612.

Haigh, Sam. *Mapping a Tradition: Francophone Women's Writing from Guadeloupe*. London: Modern Humanities Research Association, 2000.

Hargreaves, Alec G. "Perceptions of Ethnic Difference in Post-War France." In *Immigrant Narratives in Contemporary France*. Eds. Susan Ireland and Patrice J. Prouix. Westport: Greenwood P, 2001. 7–22.

Heisler, Barbara Schmitter. "The Sociology of Immigration: From Assimilation to Segmented Integration, from the American Experience to the Global Arena." In *Migration Theory: Talking Across Disciplines*. Eds. Caroline B. Brettell and James F. Hollifield. New York: Routledge, 2000. 77–96.

Hezekiah, Randolph. "Martinique and Guadeloupe: Time and Space." In *A History of Literature in the Caribbean. Vol. 1 Hispanic and Francophone Regions*. Ed. A. James Arnold. Amsterdam: John Benjamins, 1994. 379–387.

Hoving, Isabel. *In Praise of New Travelers: Reading Caribbean Migrant Women's Writing.* Stanford: Stanford UP, 2001.

Kincaid, Jamaica. "Girl." In *At the Bottom of the River.* New York: Plume, 1992.

Latortue, Régine Altagrâce. "Francophone Caribbean Women Writers and the Diasporic Quest for Identity: Marie Chauvet's *Amour* and Maryse Condé's *Hérémakhonon*." In *Winds of Change: The Transforming Voices of Caribbean Women Writers and Scholars.* New York: Peter Lang, 1998. 55–59.

Majumdar, Margaret A. *Francophone Studies: The Essential Glossary.* London: Arnold, 2002.

Massey, Doreen. *Space, Place, and Gender.* Minneapolis: U Minnesota P, 1994.

Mordecai, Pamela and Betty Wilson. "Introduction." In *Her True-True Name: An Anthology of Women's Writing from the Caribbean.* Oxford: Heinemann, 1989. ix–xx.

Murdoch, H. Adlai. "Divided Desire: Biculturality and the Representation of Identity in *En attendant le bonheur*." *Callaloo* 18. 3 (1995): 579–592.

————. "Negotiating the Metropole: Patterns of Exile and Cultural Survival in Gisèle Pineau and Suzanne Dracius-Pinalie." In *Immigrant Narratives in Contemporary France.* Eds. Susan Ireland and Patrice J. Prouix. Westport: Greenwood P, 2001. 129–139.

O'Callaghan, Evelyn. "Interior Schisms Dramatised: The Treatment of the 'Mad' Woman in the Work of Some Female Caribbean Novelists." In *Out of the Kumbla: Caribbean Women and Literature.* Eds. Carole Boyce Davies and Elaine Savory Fido. Trenton, NJ: Africa World P, 1990. 89–109.

Pineau, Gisèle. *Exile According to Julia.* Charlottesville: U Virginia P, 2003 (originally published in 1996).

Richardson, Bonham C. "Caribbean Migrations, 1838–1985." In *The Modern Caribbean.* Eds. Franklin W. Knight and Colin A. Palmer. Chapel Hill: U North Carolina P, 1989. 203–228.

Shelton, Marie-Denise. "Condé: The Politics of Gender and Identity." *World Literature Today* 64. 4 (autumn 1993): 717–722.

Sourieau, Marie-Agnès. "Afterword." In *Exile According to Julia.* Charlottesville: U Virginia P, 2003. 171–187.

Suárez, Lucía. "Gisèle Pineau: Writing the Dimensions of Migration." *World Literature Today* 75.3 (summer/autumn 2001): 9-21.

Van Alphen, Ernst. "Imagined Homelands." In *Mobilizing Place, Placing Mobility: The Politics of Representation in a Globalized World.* Eds. Ginette Verstraete and Tim Cresswell. Amsterdam: Rodopi, 2002. 53–69.

Warner-Vieyra, Myriam. *As the Sorcerer Said....* Essex: Longman, 1982 (originally published in 1980).

———. *Juletane.* London: Heinemann, 1987 (originally published in 1982).

Wilson, Betty. "Introduction." In *Juletane.* London: Heinemann, 1987. v–xv.

Wilson, Elizabeth. "'Le voyage et l'espace clos'–Island and Journey as Metaphor: Aspects of Woman's Experience in the Works of Francophone Caribbean Women Novelists." In *Out of the Kumbla: Caribbean Women and Literature.* Eds. Carole Boyce Davies and Elaine Savory Fido. Trenton, NJ: Africa World P, 1990. 45–57.

CHAPTER 3

Hispanophone Caribbean Language and Culture: Markers of Identity

[los emigrantes puertorriqueños] Tenían un imaginario, una memoria y una cultura que hacían casi imposible su 'asimilación'. Pero esa memoria también les permitía adaptarse- selectiva y conflictivamente- a las nuevas circunstancias en una sociedad que, en general, los despreciaba....Grabar, para que la imagen permanezca legible, es uno de los sentidos de la palabra memoria.

(Arcadio Díaz Quiñonez, *La memoria rota*)

The foreignness of language upon entering the United States immediately sets apart the women in the novels of Cristina García, Julia Alvarez, Loida Maritza Pérez, Judith Ortiz Cofer, and Esmeralda Santiago who migrate from Cuba, the Dominican Republic, and Puerto Rico. Although Haitians undergo a similar experience when first arriving in New York and Miami—their main ports of entry— they arrive better prepared to face the hostility they encounter. Cuban, Dominican, and Puerto Rican women have constructed their own myth of "this land of plenty" and often blindly believe in the Immigrant's Dream. Returning migrants uphold the myth and those who tell different stories are not heard. These women seek a life that they are convinced they can never achieve on the islands. They wish to remake their lives and leave behind poverty, oppression, and repressive patriarchal societies. They feel that nothing could be worse than the lives they lead in the present; their future must be shaped elsewhere.

Geographical proximity, direct military intervention, and their incorporation in the U.S. global economy have made the hispanophone Caribbean islands of Cuba, the Dominican Republic and Puerto Rico consider the United States as their principal metropolitan destination. While the francophone Caribbean looks to metropolitan France as the metropolitan center because of their history as former colonies who share an imposed language and culture, the link between the United States and the hispanophone Caribbean has more recent military implications and is rooted in today's global culture of marketable commodities throughout the world. Moreover, the image of the United States during the late nineteenth and mid-twentieth century was of a colossus that established policy in the western hemisphere through military and economic might without the consent of other nations. Yet, it is precisely this gigantic and powerful image with a new world order discourse that made it so attractive to newly-forming nations and revolutionary groups fighting for sovereignty and independence from the 1860s to the 1920s. Late-nineteenth-century Dominican political leaders who feared another invasion from Haiti and wanted to avoid a re-annexation to Spain began negotiating with the U.S. government for other alternatives (Bosch). Cuban rebels welcomed U.S. troops in 1898 as a way of accelerating their struggle to gain independence from Spain (Bosch; E. Williams). Puerto Ricans from various segments of society were encouraged by General Miles's speeches of bringing democracy and progress to an island that had only begun to acquire a degree of autonomy from various repressive Spanish governments (Lewis; Scarano). All soon realized that a military invasion is not a promise of democracy and that an invading army is not subject to local rule or requests to leave. For Dominicans, the United States stopped being a constant presence; in Cuba the new political groups had to accept the Platt Amendment and lose part of their territory, Guantánamo (Foner); the U.S. military never left Puerto Rico (although is now reduced by the closing down of the Vieques and Ceiba naval bases) but allowed a civil government to develop over a long period of time, culminating in 1948 with the island's first elected governor (Scarano, Delgado, Pasapera).

Increased political and, especially, economic instability on these islands in the twentieth century turned migration into a real choice, and the wealth and vastness of the United States made it the preferred destination for most immigrants. Most often, the first to migrate were men, who, if married, would most likely later send for their wives and children. The number of women from the hispanophone Caribbean migrating on their own became noticeable after 1960. This is the group of women who inhabit the shifting living and working spaces of the Cuban-born writer Cristina García, the Dominican-born novelists Julia Alvarez and Loida Maritza Pérez, and the Puerto Rican narrators Judith Ortiz Cofer and Esmeralda Santiago.

When Puerto Ricans became U.S. citizens in 1917, a door opened to the population to migrate freely, most often to New York City, where a community had existed for many years. In the nineteenth century, New York was the place for dissidents, political leaders, forced exiles, musicians, tobacco makers, and many others to meet and frequently conspire to liberate the island from Spanish rule. After 1917, the very harsh conditions in Puerto Rico because of the closing down of coffee and tobacco fields, the change from small landowners to American ownership of sugar cane fields, the slow recuperation from devastating hurricanes made the trip to "the unknown" a valid alternative (Scarano, Vega). By the late 1940s and 1950s, the government sponsored programs to stimulate migration as a way of "balancing the budget" back home (Scarano).

There was very little emigration from the Dominican Republic during the *Trujillato* (1930–1961), except by the upper classes—like García's grandparents and parents—who came to the United States as tourists, diplomats, or seekers of political asylum. After the 1965 U.S. invasion, the numbers soared dramatically and now included middle- and working-class immigrants (Pessar). Nowadays, the number of Dominicans willing to sell the little they have to pay a *yolero* to smuggle them into Puerto Rico or Miami is still undocumentable but probably soars into the thousands annually. Even though there were Cuban enclaves in Miami and Tampa, the Cuban presence in the United States was unnoticed until the Caribbean island 90 miles from the shores of this country declared itself economically independent and allied with the Cold War enemy of the United States, the former Soviet Union. When the Cuban Revolution succeeded, which meant that the privileged class no longer held power, thousands of upper- and middle-class Cubans left their homeland and were welcomed with open arms as political refugees by the United States (M.C. García, Grosfoguel, "Puerto Ricans").

Puerto Ricans believed that U.S. citizenship assured them of equality under the law and access to all the economic opportunities available to the population of the contiguous 48 continental states. Dominicans were made to believe that the United States was willing to open its borders for them after sending 14,000 marines to their country in 1965 to guarantee a government friendly to U.S. interests after 30 years of *Trujillato*. Cubans had no doubts that the United States would welcome them once they openly condemned the imposition of Communism on their island. Alejandro Portes states that immigrant groups almost immediately set up a particular relationship to the "host society" depending on the reception they receive. Because of their physiognomy and culture, Dominicans and Puerto Ricans "are uniformly rejected and confined to a permanently inferior status" (465). The first wave of Cubans arriving in Miami, because of their number, political situation, apparent whiteness, and class, were almost immediately accepted. Portes argues that the initial rejection, in the case of Puerto Ricans and Dominicans, made these groups "draw a protective boundary around the group, identifying it with traditions and interests rooted in the home country....Immigrants in these situations are *in* the country, but are certainly not *of* it, preferring to see themselves as belonging elsewhere both socially and economically" (465). When the opposite situation occurs, as in the Cuban case, "there are no grounds for reactive ethnicity and the array of transnational activities associated with it. Immigrants may seek to avoid whatever stigma is associated with their particular nationality by claiming membership in a different group or even 'passing' as part of the host population" (466). Even though the Cubans in Miami stressed their *cubanidad*, they were at the same time integrating themselves to the larger community, which their wealth, whiteness, and class made possible. This "passing" began to change with the three subsequent waves of Cuban immigrants (M.C. García).

Whether called ethnic enclaves, community-based neighborhoods, or ghettos (Brettell, Dávila, Turner), location is an essential component in the migration process for people coming from the hispanophone Caribbean. Women, in particular, depend on these support groups when they first arrive to secure an abode, even if temporary, and from there begin to plan their lives. Usually there is no husband present, and the woman is on her own to find her way around, get a job, establish a budget that will eventually allow her to get her own place, and start making arrangements to relocate some or all members of her family. If children accompany the woman, then this process of adaptation is even harder: childcare and schools must be provided for, and the budget might not have any surplus for remittances. To facilitate this always disruptive process, the destination chosen must not present insurmountable obstacles. Miami and New Jersey for Cubans, Manhattan's upper West Side for Dominicans, and designated neighborhoods in the Bronx, Brooklyn, Manhattan's El Barrio, and New Jersey for Puerto Ricans become "safe houses" for the new migrants.

The relationship established by the migrant and her chosen site is also closely related to class and race. In Julia Alvarez's *How the García Girls Lost Their Accents*, the family's first dwelling is in New York City close to where the father/sole provider has secured a job as doctor and professor of medicine. At the first opportunity, they move out of the city to the suburbs. In Cristina García's *The Agüero Sisters*, Constancia and her family reside immediately with same-class relatives when they first arrive in Miami. For the members of this economic class, migration is simply a transition in which they are never plunged into the terror of scarcity. It is merely a matter of time until they are able to secure equally stable or more positions than the ones they left behind. Some things change, and they do not have the same possessions as before—vast amounts of land, for example—but they never lack money, or feel treated like "foreigners" or face poverty. They build brick and cement walls to keep out the undesired elements and re-create their privileged lives in the Dominican Republic and Cuba. The members of this upper class trace their ancestors to the Spanish Conquistadores and proclaim European bloodlines uncontaminated by Indian or Ethiopian ancestry (Torres-Saillant, "Dominican"). Many times, these Dominican and Cuban whites cannot "pass" the white/black racial binary of the United States. This initial rejection will encourage them to try harder to assimilate to American culture and, at the same time, become leaders in their exclusive communities. Carlos García in Alvarez's novels moves to the suburbs, sends his daughters to expensive, private schools, establishes ties with other medical professionals, and celebrates when one of his daughters marries a white American or foreigner. García's Constancia Agüero lives a life of leisure in Key Biscayne, with only infrequent visits to Miami, where many of her relatives reside. She is a member of an exclusive marina club, dresses in 1940s American fashion, drives a Cadillac, and is totally immersed in the production of age-arresting potions.

New York, the global city, the immigrants' preferred port of entry, is "a unique place where racial, ethnic, and national diversities interact with a changing political economy to place groups in particular positions in economic and social hierarchies and structures" (Smith, Cordero, and Grosfoguel, 1). New York is a "contact zone" as Mary Louise Pratt redefines space in *Imperial Eyes*: it is a coming together "in terms of copresence, interaction, interlocking understandings and practices, often within radically asymmetrical relations of power" (7). Yolanda Martínez-San Miguel describes New York as a space of negotiation and transit of various cultures (388). In New York City, this convergence happens both in the center and on the periphery. In Puerto Rican and Dominican enclaves, people who were total strangers on the islands now blur regional differences to become part of an ethnic force of resistance. Washington Heights becomes the Dominican Republic as unity replaces territorial fragmentation. During ethnic and national celebrations, ethnonational meeting grounds, such as Fifth Avenue, become contact zones, spaces where everyone is welcome and, like Carnival, race, class, and ethnic barriers are lowered. Esmeralda Santiago's Monín and her family feel at home when they first arrive in New York because they immediately recognize the familiar: the relatives who pick them up at the airport, the warm place created inside the first apartment they live in with everyone caring for one another, the language they speak, and the food they prepare and eat. Later on, in the dancehall, they will meet people from other towns in Puerto Rico and make new friends.

Robert Smith, Héctor Cordero-Guzmán and Ramón Grosfoguel also caution that New York functions as a site

> for the development of a sophisticated stratification system where racial phenotype, immigrant status, and ethnicity and nationality all figured into creating racializing hierarchies, which evolved as

the definitions of whiteness and blackness, and other categories, have changed. These categories matter because once they are established, they influence life chances and future trajectories. (5)

Saskia Sassen in her study of New York, London, and Tokyo as global cities, points out how the cities' economic growth is not equivalent to a more democratic distribution of wealth. Quite the contrary, it creates and contributes to the growth

> of a high-income stratum and a low-income stratum of workers. It has done so directly through the organization of work and occupational structure of major growth sectors. And it has done so indirectly through the jobs needed to service the new high-income workers, both at work and at home, as well as the needs of the expanded low-wage work force. (13)

In his study on the Dominican community in New York, Jorge Duany finds that many "have been displaced from light manufacturing, especially the garment industry, to the low-wage and low-skilled sector, thus moving sideways or downwards in the labor market" ("Creation," 217). Esmeralda Santiago's Monín in *When I Was Puerto Rican* and *Almost a Woman*, América in *América's Dream*, and Loida Maritza Pérez's Rebecca in *Geographies of Home* occupy this low-income stratum where they service the upper stratum by cleaning homes and offices and working in factories and the garment industry. These women are unable to escape enduring poverty, but they provide their daughters with the chance to study and follow another path. Ortiz Cofer's Marisol in *The Line of the Sun*, Santiago's Negi and Rosalinda in the already mentioned novels, Alvarez's Sarita in *¡Yo!*, and Pérez's Iliana in *Geographies of Home* are convinced that a college education will allow them to leave behind—and if possible, forget—the difficult process of growing up in Hispanic communities encircled by poverty, patriarchal values, and the imposition of island cultures.

I agree with Ramón Grosfoguel's contention that since the 1960s, ethnicity has been turned into race in the North American society. "Ethnic" and "migrant" became part of the racial code and grouped together the separate groups that populate the periphery ("Puerto Ricans," 244). "Puerto Rican" has become a racial marker applied to the various New York City Hispanic communities. In the Euro-American imaginary this means someone dark skinned or of mixed race, foreign-born or non-American "ancestors," a non-native speaker of English, "with traits such as laziness, criminality, stupidity, and a tendency toward uncivilized behavior..." (Grosfoguel and Georas, 98). The results of a study made on Puerto Ricans in New York in the 1970s by Mary Powers and John J. Macisco, and Grosfoguel and Chloé Georas' study twenty-five years later shows very similar results: "Puerto Rican" signifies high unemployment rates, low labor force participation, less formal education, low-skilled jobs, living in economically depressed areas, a high percentage of single women with children as heads of households, and high poverty rates in the New York Metropolitan area (Powers; Grosfoguel and Georas, 99). Dominicans now fall into this racialized category as well.

In contrast, Puerto Ricans and Dominicans have constructed a racial imaginary to distinguish themselves from black Americans and West Indians in the United States. This forced distance translates into friction with and alienation from these two communities that have the advantage over Spanish-speaking islanders of being native speakers of English. By believing themselves racially different from African Americans, Dominicans and Puerto Ricans invent a non-existent superiority in a society that places a double burden on the migrants: language and foreignness. Dominicans never see themselves as "black" because this is an epithet reserved only for Haitians in their own country. So the great majority of dark-skinned Dominicans with African features trace their ancestry to the Taíno Indians without any link to Africanness (Torres-Saillant, "Dominican"; C. Williams; Baronov and Yelvington). The lighter they become through use of lightening beauty products and hair straightening, the more attractive and accepted they are in their community. Women tend to be the believers in and enforcers of these transformation effects. This reveals itself in the different treatment received by darker members of the Hispanic families in the novels studied: Negi in Santiago's stories—a nickname to mask *negrita*—Iliana, called "nigger" by her classmates in Perez's, and the servants—who are always black—in Alvarez's. Puerto Ricans might protest, go into denial every time they are marginalized, and claim their equality because of their U.S. citizenship, but "No matter how 'blond or blue-eyed' a person may be nor whether s/he can 'pass,' the moment that person identifies her/himself as Puerto Rican, s/he enters the labyrinth of racial Otherness" (Grosfoguel, "Puerto Ricans," 245).

In this chapter, the discussion of these and related issues is organized by nationality or point of origin of the writers and characters within the hispanophone Caribbean. The discussion of the Cuban-Miami experience is first treated in Cristina García's *The Agüero Sisters* then moves to New York to trace the migrant experience in García's *Dreaming in Cuban*. The analysis of the Dominican experience in Julia Alvarez's *How the García Girls Lost Their Accents* and *¡Yo!* starts in New York but has very little to do with the urban center itself. In Loida Maritza Pérez's *Geographies of Home*, the focus returns to the Dominican ethnic enclaves in New York City. The Puerto Rican experience begins not in New York but in "El Building" in New Jersey, where the family in Judith Ortiz Cofer's *The Line of the Sun* moves temporarily until they can go to a better place. Esmeralda Santiago's *When I Was Puerto Rican*, *Almost a Woman*, and *América's Dream* are situated in the traditional Puerto Rican ghettos, and Manhattan is seen as a contact zone and suburbia as a foreign space.

Although García's *The Agüero Sisters* tells the stories of two sisters, Constancia, the elder, exemplifies the migrant experience, while Reina moves to Miami as a mature woman with no political agenda. The story also includes Dulcita, Reina's only daughter, who first migrates to Madrid and then to Miami at her mother's insistence. Each chapter in the novel begins with the name of the third-person narrator, the place, and the year this particular event takes place. The stories of these women characters entwine until eventually the resentments that separated them are blurred, enabling them to create a home based on common threads among the women of the Agüero family. Constancia and Reina lose their mother at a very young age and are raised by their father, an admired ornithologist. Both were privileged children in Cuba because the family owned property and land and both parents were career professionals. The sisters did not grow up together because of sibling resentment: Constancia was sent to her grandfather's farm in Camagüey, while Reina stayed close to her mother in Havana. When the Revolution triumphed, Constancia, who had married twice into a very wealthy family—first to Gonzalo for less than a year and then, after her divorce, to Heberto, her brother-in-law—sends her young son along with other Cuban children to the United States (Operation Peter Pan) and later leaves for Miami with the rest of her family to settle in New York City. Although in Cuba she was exclusively a wealthy wife and mother, in the United States, now that the children are on their own, she has chosen to make herself useful by creating a line of beauty products ("Ojos de Cuba," "Pies de Cuba"). Reina remained in Cuba and became an accomplished master electrician, but after she has an almost fatal accident and her daughter leaves for Madrid, she decides to try her luck in Miami with her sister. Quite understandably, their outlooks on life are extremely different, which creates friction between them, even though Reina always softens critical situations.

Although there is always the mourning for the lost country, the adaptation of Constancia, husband Heberto, ex-husband Gonzalo, and son Silvestre to Miami and New York was quick and painless. Cubans, who left their island and arrived by the hundreds and then thousands in Miami, after relations between the United States and Cuba were first lacerated and then broken off, were given preferential treatment over not only any other refugee or migrant group but also over the white American working and lower-middle-class population (Grosfoguel and Georas, 112). The Centro Hispano-Católico, Voluntary Relief Agencies (VOLAGs), and the Cuban Refugee Emergency Center in downtown Miami were established very early on to provide immediate help to the Cubans (M.C. García, 19–21). Under the Kennedy Administration, the Cuban Refugee Program (CRP) was established under the umbrella of the Department of Health, Education, and Welfare (HEW). By doing this, all government agencies established the Cuban migrants as a political priority. "Cuban refugees received welfare payments, job training, bilingual-language programs, educational support, subsidized college loans, health care services, help in job search efforts, and money for resettling out of Miami..." (Grosfoguel, "Migration," 111–112). U.S. citizens, such as Puerto Ricans, working and middle-class white Americans, black Americans, and other refugees such as Haitians, were not given special aids to rise above poverty; no economic incentives were made available for middle-class U.S. citizens who wanted to set up businesses or become small investors; no special programs in schools and colleges guided them to better jobs and the acquisition of degrees and practicing licenses; no subsidized housing became available without a long waiting list; no training programs emerged to prepare them for jobs more suited to the present economy; no guaranteed jobs surfaced; no money was allotted for relocating. In contrast, Grosfoguel and Georas point out that through the Cuban Refugee Program, "Every city where Cubans settled received millions of dollars in government assistance to cover expenses in education, welfare, hospitals, and other public services for the refugees" (111). García's Constancia Agüero in *The Agüero Sisters* and Lourdes del Pino de Puente in *Dreaming in Cuban* chose to settle in New York.

María Cristina García divides the Cubans' arrival in the United States into three stages: the first between 1959 and 1962; the second, the "freedom flights" from 1965 to 1973; and the third in 1980 known as the "Mariel boatlift" (1). A fourth stage was added in the 1990s: the so-called "Balseros" (rafters) because of their very rustic and dangerous mode of transportation. Since the Cuban Refugee Program was phased out in the 1970s, these last two groups, who were mostly Afro-Caribbean and "from a more popular class background than the pre-1980s Cuban migrants" and who settled in Miami and New York, did not receive the same state assistance nor were they "cushioned against racial discrimination" (Grosfoguel and Georas, 113). The del Pino Puente and Agüero Cruz families in Cristina García's novels come to the United States in the first and second stages, while Reina Agüero enters with a tourist or visiting visa from the Bahamas and then stays on, and Dulcita enters through the family reunification program. No details are given on these legalities. None of them goes through the often long and tortuous process of most immigrants who enter and eventually settle in the United States.

It seems contradictory that Constancia Agüero wants to separate herself from the Miami Cuban community represented by her husband's relatives, and at the same time lead the lifestyle of the exiled Cuban upper classes. She once voted for the Democratic Party ticket (*Agüero Sisters*, 45) and rejects the accepted and celebrated Cuban nostalgia. After living in New York City, she has agreed, upon her husband's retirement, to live in Key Biscayne because Miami seems to have frozen in time and re-creates too closely the Cuba she once knew: "Miami is disconcerting to her, an inescapable culture shock, the air thickly charged with expiring dreams" (46). She is aware of the ridiculous suicide act that her father-in-law's wife puts on at the cemetery; she sees the fantasy created by her ex-husband and friends about forming an army to invade and liberate Cuba; and she refuses to sit down with friends or acquaintances to reminisce about life in Cuba in the 1950s. Nevertheless, Constancia is home-building and place-making (Castles and Davidson's terms) in numerous ways that she does not seem to be aware of. Every Friday she goes to a bodega in Little Havana to buy fruits that immediately remind her of her childhood in Cuba (46); her favorite radio show is *La hora de los milagros*, and she listens to the news on a Spanish-speaking station; she and her husband have Cuban flags inside their houses and constantly listen to Cuban music; her spiritual leader is Oscar Piñango, a Santero; she dresses in 1940s Americanized Cuban fashion; and she has created a line of "Cuban" body beauty products labeled "Body of Cuba."

Simultaneously, Reina Agüero, who became an adult under the Cuban Revolution, decides to start a new life—without severing her ties—outside Cuba and has no need for home-building: she does not fear losing her Cubanness no matter where she settles. Her most precious possession, which reminds her of her accomplishments and her debt to the Cuban Revolution, is her toolbox: "Reina could be dropped anywhere with her tools, in a faraway galaxy with no water and a fraction of the earth's gravity, and somehow—she grins to think of this—she knows she would survive" (165). Reina's memory of Cuba is from a past that is very close in time so she has no need for nostalgia, even though she does crave homemade Cuban food and cannot help whistling Cuban tunes. She cannot feel at home in Constancia's apartment or in her warehouse factory because everything is so artificial. There is no real Cubanness here, only the construction of a Cuba that no longer exists on the island she came from. The only place where Reina feels alive and in touch with herself is on Heberto's boat. Here she can distance herself from the consumer society that Miami represents; she can board a boat that is functional, that requires her mechanical and boating skills to go out to sea, a space where even Constancia has to stop being the model of the preservation of youth and beauty: "she likes the per-

spective it [the boat] gives her, the ocean's open contempt for desti-
nations. Why hadn't she ever realized before the futility of living on
land?" (165). When Constancia asks Reina what she would do if she
were rich, her answer is not what her sister expected: "[she] would
spend the rest of her life floating around the world, ravishing her
choice of men. Certainly she wouldn't choose to live like this, cheek
by jowl with the pathological rich" (165). Reina also refuses to be
part of the exile community. Home-building and place-making for
her means family, which at this time only includes her sister, and
her wish is to reunite with her daughter Dulcita and future grandchildren. Meanwhile, she adopts Constancia's daughter and grandson, Isabel and newborn Raku. This is the only home she wishes for
except that of lovers and *compañeros* who give her immediate and
unencumbered love.

In spite of her mother being a government outstanding worker
and her father a Revolutionary hero, Dulcita chose the hard road.
She refused to participate in revolutionary activities; she did not take
advantage of the opportunities to have a good education, get a good
job, and continue to develop skills and acquire knowledge that could
later be useful to her. Instead she chose to "be a wild child," getting
pregnant at fourteen, deciding on an abortion, and becoming a *jinetera*:
having sex with tourists who provided her with dollars, consumer
goods, and eventually an exit visa from Cuba. She comes to realize
that her choice of leaving Cuba with the Spanish tourist Abelardo
and settling in Madrid is the worst decision of her life. Even if urban
Madrid is a large and important urban center, it is not a metropolitan
center, not a contact zone, not a place to construct another identity.
Madrid is the equivalent of a Caribbean capital like Havana, San Juan,
and Santo Domingo. It is too familiar, too close to home, with a very
dangerous side for anyone perceived as foreign. Instead of an established order, reality is perceived as chaotic, constantly changing, and
characterized by exclusion. "But it's a place with rules I don't understand. I look for clues in the shredded bullfight posters, in the sepa-
ratist graffiti, in the conversation I overhear in the meat department
of El Corte Inglés. Each word is a map I track toward the same blank
wall, thickly covered with moss" (143).

Once Dulcita is under her husband's rule, she has lost the freedom she fought so hard for in Cuba. She can no longer claim inde-

pendence; quite the contrary, she must submit herself to the man of
the house. When she runs away from "home," she becomes an illegal migrant with no rights at the mercy of exploiting employers.
She describes her job as a nanny as "I'm the woman hired to clean
the mansion and love the lonely two-year-old girl" (141). Still, she
prefers the anonymity of not even using her own name over the
familiarity she was accustomed to in Cuba, "Nobody knows where I
am....But more to try on a fresh identity, plant a tentative new root.
Sometimes I wish everything I wanted could be arranged this
easily....Believe me, it's a relief to be this invisible" (142). As a live-in
nanny, she solves the problem of housing, but she has no freedom
of movement to find a better job or take advantage of living in the
big city. When Dulcita is fired from this job because of obscene
phone calls she receives from strangers, she finds herself on the
street with no money, no one to call and ask for help, spending days
and nights in a revival movie theatre where American films from
the 1950s are projected. Her hunger, after various days of only eat-
ing discarded popcorn and drinking leftover orange soda, tempts
her to go to a Cuban restaurant and perhaps appeal to a waiter's or
client's sympathy. But she has nothing in common "with fat expatri-
ates" (205), and she decides to break into her ex-husband's apartment and steal whatever she can. Dulcita finds a letter from Reina
and decides to leave the strangeness of Madrid she so desired and
move again close to her only family. She sells sex for three days to
get the $700 to buy her ticket to Miami.

Dulcita rejected her homeland, Cuba, and has no intention of
being trapped into home-building and place-making. Abelardo, the
Spaniard she married, can never be her family nor can Madrid ever
be home. Just like Reina, she discovers that location does not determine home, only human affection can provide the familiarity and
security of home. Once in Miami, Dulcita will try to find her own
path; she still rejects her mother's offer to work with her in the auto
restoration garage and cannot see herself working for Constancia in
her factory making useless potions that give her a headache. She
prefers to find a job on her own and live some kind of normality
after, in her short life, doing "the everyday outlawed things" (286).

Even though each sister and their offspring have different agendas, all the women converge in Constancia's apartment, which is

transformed by their presence. The lavish and comfortable place bought by Heberto for his retirement becomes a space for women of diverse interests and ideologies. While he is off playing soldier somewhere in the proximity of Cuba, Constancia has opened the doors to their home to a sister who once proudly worked for the Revolutionary government, a niece who was a *jinetera* in Cuba and homeless in Madrid, and a daughter abandoned in advanced pregnancy in Hawaii by her live-in companion. These women have been able to blur their differences and home-build in a place previously characterized by friction and known for its intolerance of dissidence. The women support each other by soothing Constancia's loss of her husband, Reina's recent and abrupt distance from her island home, Dulcita's very harsh livelihood in Madrid, and Isabel's failure to make a life on her own. They also look out for one another as Reina works with Constancia to turn an old bowling alley into a warehouse and factory, and as she takes care of the daughter and niece who have just come home after attempting to disown their mothers. Even Constancia's childhood and adolescent resentment of Reina because of her mother's open preference for the younger daughter, evaporates when she realizes that Blanca, their mother, is their link and that now Constancia wears her face ("She looks up at the past trapped in Constancia's face and doesn't know what to say." 159).

Constancia, Reina, and Dulcita see the past in entirely different ways. Constancia refuses to live like the exiled community in Miami in their frozen picture of Cuba in the 1950s. Her nostalgic yearning for a past focuses on her childhood, her contact with her grandfather's farm in Camagüey, her father's lessons on nature, and his memorabilia in the Havana apartment. Even though she does not believe in stopping time, she is determined to stay young as long as possible. She has a very frugal diet, rides a bicycle, and walks, and she has invented a line of products that will erase wrinkles, stretch marks, cellulitis, and other bodily imperfections: "My products bring back that feeling. The beauty of scent and sensation, the mingling of memory and imagination" (162). Reina, on the other hand, disdains all this artificiality because she believes that nature must take its course and that there is beauty at every stage of the aging process. She did keep their stuffed birds, instruments, and notes as a way of remembering the parents she lost as an adolescent.

She brings some of these "memories" with her almost as an over-ture to her sister who never hid her preference for their father and disdain for their mother. Reina wonders "if memory is little more than this: a series of erasures and perfected selections" (163). When Reina tells her sister what she misses from Cuba—"the little plazas in every town"— Constancia accuses her of romanticizing the past. But Reina insists that she is remembering and not trying to forget the good things back in Cuba: "I guess it's less painful to forget than to remember" (174). Dulcita is the closest one to a past that contin-ues to be present because there has been no closure to her life in Cuba or Madrid:

> I have no home, no job, no friends or family here. Only a stubborn fear. I've been wondering lately whether fear is necessary for survival, whether it sharpens the senses during storms of uncertainty. Or is it, as I suspect, merely another variant of weakness? Back in Cuba, the certainty was dismal, but it was still a certainty. It was hard to fall between the cracks, to starve outright. I haven't decided yet where I'm the poorest. (204)

Now she starts all over in Miami.

Yet even if Dulcita does not want to be in her mother's shadow and rejects the artificial and the phoniness of Cuban Miami, she realizes that she cannot embark in any adventure without tapping that source. Reina and Constancia are not just mother and aunt but the daughters of grandparents she admires and wishes she had known. This is the legacy she reclaims when she "goes home" to mother, aunt, cousin, and second cousin. She remembers what Reina always told her when Dulcita wanted to sever all her ties: "What we pass on is often as much a burden as a gift" (206).

It is the choice of relocation that makes the women in *Dreaming in Cuban* different in their attitudes, open rebellion, and difficulties forging new identities. When Lourdes arrived in Miami with her husband and daughter, she was immediately immersed in Cuban culture as molded by that city. There was no need to know English to be able to negotiate with government agencies. The Cuban Refu-gee Program provided everything, and the existing Cuban commu-nity there was very supportive. New York, on the contrary, is a con-centrated metropolitan center where many ethnic and racial groups make a living; it is truly a contact zone, even if after work migrants or new arrivals return to the margins. The Del Pino Puente family in García's *Dreaming in Cuban* chooses New York as their new home. Lourdes's entrepreneurial skills seem better suited in a place where she can play at being American without having to cater to the exiled Cuban community that controls Dade County. Besides, "Lourdes couldn't stand Rufino's family, the endless brooding over their lost wealth, the competition for dishwasher jobs" (69). Contrary to Heberto and Gonzalo Cruz in *The Agüero Sisters,* Lourdes never plans to go back to Cuba no matter what political changes take place in the future. For her, Cuba is the past she left behind, while New York is the future where she can construct a new identity as a "true" American: "She wants no part of Cuba, no part of its wretched carnival floats creaking with lies, no part of Cuba at all, which Lourdes claims never possessed her" (*Dreaming,* 73). In *Dreaming in Cuban,* multiple narrators tell the story of the del Pino family. Jorge and Celia's three children and five grandchildren are separated by the political events in Cuba after January 1959. The oldest daughter, Lourdes, moves to the United States with her husband Rufino and two-year-old daughter, Pilar, while Celia's youngest daughter, Felicia, always at the margin of the changes taking place in the country, will stay in Cuba. Her only son, Javier, studies and decides to stay in Czechoslovakia. Lourdes will sever her ties with her mother while affirming her link to her father who moves in with her when he becomes terminally ill. Pilar serves as negotiator between Lourdes and Celia but in the end will make her own connection with her grandmother through whom she redefines the homeland.

Lourdes's life is full of contradictions. While she wants to totally assimilate herself into U.S. culture, her husband re-creates Cuba in his warehouse/home, where he can smoke Cuban cigars, drink Cuban rum, listen to Cuban music, grow flowers, fruits, and vegetables to recall life in the farm, and become immersed in nostalgia for a lost homeland. For Lourdes, this attitude means passivity, regression, and paralysis. She decries this home-building but cannot prevent Rufino's pursuit of it: "Immigration has transformed her, and she is grateful. Unlike her husband, she welcomes her adopted language, its possibilities for reinvention" (73). Her place-making is more creative because she copies and surpasses what she understands being an American means: the use of English, the celebration of all patriotic and cultural holidays—Thanksgiving being the most important family gathering—participation in political events not community/ethnic activities, membership in vigilante volunteer groups, and establishment of businesses that serve the centre—the hegemonic, white, English-speaking society. Even if Lourdes swears she is disembodied from the Cuban culture, her relationship with her husband, who she places as the head of the family and demands his fidelity and function as a sexual partner, her close surveillance of her daughter's social activities and her incursions into her privacy such as reading her diary, her continuous fiery discussions with other exiles about Fidel Castro evidence her attachment to the past she so vehemently denies. When her father comes to live with her in New York, she tries to make him feel at home by providing him with Spanish-speaking radio stations and TV channels, and letting him reminisce about Cuba and his wife Celia in spite of her rejection of anything connected to the island she wishes to forget.

Lourdes's great achievement in this society is her bakery, where she sells virtually every imaginable cake, donut, pie, strudel, creme puff, and éclair to a broad and variable clientele. She does not specialize in Cuban delicacies, quite the contrary, she wants to please customers with made-to-order pastries. She believes that naming her business Yankee Doodle will make people understand that her place of birth—accidental, of course—has no significance. She hires immigrants and Puerto Ricans who are obviously beneath her and watches them like a policeman to make sure they do not steal. Her contempt for blacks, dark-skinned immigrants, and Puerto Ricans is evident in her insistence as an "auxiliary policewoman" on "guarding her neighborhood" to be sure these people do not disturb her way of life with their known criminal behavior. Lourdes suspiciously eyes anyone who looks "different" in her Brooklyn neighborhood. Because she wishes to totally transform herself and sever all ties with her culture, Lourdes has no past to be nostalgic about. It matters little to her that Pilar wants to follow the exact opposite path.

Even at thirteen, Pilar, who left Cuba at two, knows that her home is in Cuba with her grandmother, Celia. Her mother wants to instill her with American values—work hard, study at the best universities, pursue of a career that will bring her stability and wealth, and aspire to have everything that money can buy—as she demands total obedience and respect. Lourdes is not only going to defend and uphold American values, she is also going to improve on them by eliminating the laxity and licentiousness that young people have appropriated. She stalks Pilar, wanting to know her every move and thought. Punishment is both physical and mental: she beats her daughter and grounds her so that she cannot draw or paint—Pilar's passion—and forces her to work in the bakery under her constant supervision:

> ...she beat me in the face and pulled my hair out in big clumps. She called me a *desgraciada* and ground her knuckles into my temples. Then she forced me to work in her bakery every day after school for twenty-five cents an hour. She leaves me nasty notes on the kitchen table reminding me to show up or else. She thinks working with her will teach me responsibility, clear my head of filthy thoughts. (27)

Even though Pilar shares more common ground with her father, especially because he is always recalling Cuba and not following Lourdes's rules, Rufino has also constructed his own world which has little connection with his adolescent daughter ("Dad only looks alive when he talks about the past, about Cuba." 138). When Pilar accidentally sees him with a lover, she makes up her mind to leave Brooklyn and her parents: "That's it. My mind's made up. I'm going back to Cuba. I'm fed up with everything around here" (25). She has always known that Abuela Celia and Cuba are home. She was forced to leave her grandmother's side and then brought to a strange place with relatives she had never met or barely knew and then relocated in a cold and threatening city, in which her mother became defensive, aggressive, and intolerant. When her grandfather came to live with them, he simply exacerbated her desire to be back on the island he had left never to return. It is perhaps Lourdes's denial of a homeland that makes Pilar yearn for one so strongly. At thirteen, she can only think of using her savings to buy a bus ticket to Miami and, from there, somehow get to Cuba.

Pilar does not make this journey, although later on she does make it back. When her mother has to face her own father's death and her daughter's escape, she steps back and gives her daughter enough breath-

ing room to live a nearly normal life. Pilar very seldom has to write
to her grandmother because they communicate telepathically, and
she is willing to pursue normalcy even while making plans to see
Celia once more. Meanwhile, she still cannot consider the United
States or New York or Brooklyn as home. No place-making occurs
because there is no community for her to tap into. Pilar chooses to
play the role of the rebellious adolescent and young adult, never
accepting her parents' rules and values, disdaining her mother's
reactionary politics, playing music that Lourdes considers intoler-
able, dressing in unladylike style, and using street English and foul
language. There are no mother-daughter conversations, just never-
ending battles. After high school, Pilar wins scholarships to study at
the elite colleges Vasaar and Barnard, but she chooses to study at an
art school in Rhode Island, where she only remains for one semes-
ter before going off to Florence and then returning to New York to
study anthropology at Barnard. When she meets Rubén, who seems
to share many of her beliefs and prefers to speak Spanish, Pilar feels
that this is the closest she has been to home since she came to New
York. But this illusion is soon shattered when she discovers that
Rubén's words were just a way to seduce her and fulfill his sexual
needs (180).

Lourdes cares very little whether she fits in the centre or not.
She is convinced that she knows and has followed the formula to
become an American and that nothing and no one can stop her.
She is white (Cuban white), knowledgeable of U.S. history, laws, and
culture, and successful in her business. She has erased her roots and
she expects Americans to take her at face value. Pilar, on the other
hand, refuses to assimilate, rebels against everything her mother
upholds, and asserts her Cuban roots even as they are becoming
more distant over time.

> Most days Cuba is kind of dead to me. But every once in a while a
> wave of longing will hit me and it's all I can do not to hijack a plane
> to Havana or something....Every day Cuba fades a little more inside
> me, my grandmother fades a little more inside me. And there's
> only my imagination where our history should be. (137–138)

As long as she has to stay in Brooklyn, she will rely on her memories
of Celia and complement them by buying old Beny Moré records,

talking to people in Spanish, and visiting the *botánica*. Pilar's nostalgia for a home she has never had is very particular. She is trying to recuperate the home she lost when she was two. That home is both a place and a person, and they will remain in her distant memory until she returns to Cuba.

After nineteen years, Pilar and Lourdes return to Cuba to visit Celia. While Lourdes repeats the same speech, makes the same accusations, demeans everything around her, and wants to leave the moment she arrives, Pilar immediately feels at home. Her grandmother has aged, but Pilar still connects with the woman who gave her unconditional love, protected her from all danger, talked and sang to her in her own language, and established a spiritual link that has made her a better human being. There is no sense of loss because everything can be recovered as long as her grandmother and Cuba signify the only home she has ever believed in. Yet, Pilar realizes that growing up in another country has changed her, that she does not just belong to one place, that homeland might be shards of memory that make a whole: "I'm afraid to lose all this, to lose Abuela Celia again. But sooner or later I'd have to return to New York. I know now it's where I belong—not *instead* of here, but *more* than here" (236).

As in García's *The Agüero Sisters*, class is an essential element in the discussion of Julia Alvarez's *How the García Girls Lost Their Accents* and *¡Yo!*. Everything and everyone in the García-de la Torre family is marked by an upper-class social vision: the father's, Carlos García, profession, the mother's, Laura de la Torre, family name and wealth as land and property owner, their lifestyle in the Dominican Republic, the parents' trips abroad for professional reasons, vacations, and shopping, the composition of the servant quarters, the ability of the entire family to leave their island with visas, money, and acquisitions, and an apartment and job waiting in New York. Yolanda García is the persistent narrator and protagonist of both novels who represents her class, while Sarita, the maid's daughter, in *¡Yo!* characterizes, to a certain extent, the women in the servants' quarters even if it is differently named in New York. These two meet as adolescents—Sarita is thirteen and Yolanda is finishing high school and starting college—but lose track of each other in the United States.

How the García Girls Lost Their Accents, using various time frames and perspectives, and *¡Yo!*, made up of connecting stories of recollection, combine to tell the story of a wealthy Latin American family that has to leave the Dominican Republic in 1960 when the father's life is threatened for conspiring against the Trujillo regime. Upon arriving in the United States, they have to adapt to a differently stratified society, an apparently dissimilar culture, a foreign language, and fewer comforts and commodities than they were accustomed to in Santo Domingo. This apparent rupture is, according to James Clifford, "differentially cushioned by class" ("Diasporas," 257). Although at the beginning the daughters yearned to return to their island and rejected the new culture, after a while they were such models of assimilation that their parents put them in exclusive boarding schools and began sending them back to the Dominican Republic during the summer. Each daughter individually adapts to the American way of life and, at the same time, preserves aspects of Dominican culture at her parents' insistence. They all, and particularly Yolanda, who becomes a writer, find themselves wavering between two homes. The servants back home in the Dominican Republic, Chucha, Gladys, Nivea, Pila, Consuelo, Ruth, and Primi, are never on center stage in these novels. They are the voiceless and invisible women who speak only when spoken to, respond immediately to any order or whim of the *patrones*, and dream of someday making it to the United States, where they can transform themselves into human beings instead of the beasts of burden they have been turned into by the island society.

Even though the García-de la Torre family often cries poverty, for example, when Carlos and Laura first get married and later when they move to the United States, the information provided and the incidents dramatized in their narratives tell another story. During one of their frequent family reunions, Laura introduces a funny anecdote by reminding everyone: "You all know that when we were first married, we were really really poor?" (*Girls*, 43). Yet, in the third section of *How the García Girls Lost Their Accents* 1960–1956, they live in a very large house with all the commodities that distinguish an upper-class family and a chauffeur, a gardener, a nursemaid, a cook, and two additional maids. In the Dominican Republic, in a society structured on a Latin American model, rigid class stratifications very seldom allow people who lack the proper family names to enter the upper and upper-middle classes. Privilege is inherited, married into, acquired through political connections, or all three. In the García-de la Torre marriage, the mother supplies the family name and the money, while the father contributes money and professional distinction. When they left the Dominican Republic they were able to afford an apartment in New York—even if subsidized by Columbia University—and a very short time thereafter to move to a house on Long Island. The daughters are sent to parochial school, then to boarding school, and later to exclusive liberal arts colleges. As teenagers, they also spend their summers in the Dominican Republic. All these expenses are defrayed by the only family income: that of the father-doctor. However, many of these expenses can only be covered because the family is receiving money from their properties on the island, something that is never mentioned. Although the García family had to endure the loss of homeland, the difficulties of relocation, and the acceptance that they would never again be as wealthy or privileged as they were back on the island, their class and the circumstances of their arrival in the United States separate their experience from that of thousands of their compatriots who stand in lines for days and weeks at the U.S. consulate in Santo Domingo to get a visa to enter the United States, or risk their lives in a *yola* to reach Puerto Rico, fly to the United States, and live as illegal migrants.

Because all the members of the García family considered their stay in the United States a temporary arrangement, there was no need for home-building or place-making. Keeping to the family meant protection, security, and preserving their homeland intact. But after residing in New York for a few years and losing hope that the Trujillo regime will fall, they all become U.S. citizens. For the daughters, this is the greatest disappointment since they were forced to leave the Dominican Republic:

> You can believe we sisters wailed and paled, whining to go home. We didn't feel we had the best the United States had to offer. We had only second-hand stuff, rental houses in one redneck Catholic neighborhood after another, clothes at Round Robin, a black and white TV afflicted with wavy lines. Cooped up in those little suburban houses, the rules were so strict as for Island girls, but there was no island to make up the difference. (*Girls,* 107)

Living in neighborhoods where other professionals lived and going to schools where they were the only Spanish-speaking kids never allowed them to have a sense of community. They internalized the rejection they received (spic, greaseballs) and looked for protection within the confines of the family. To further disrupt any possibility of place-making, after a short while the four were sent to an all-girls boarding school where they "would meet and mix with the 'right kind' of Americans" (*Girls,* 108). It is at this stage that the girls who once begged their parents to go back home become so content with the newly discovered American culture that their process of assimilation is accelerated. Of course, what most attracts them to this culture is the freedom to dress, speak, listen to music, dance, and go out with boys without any supervision. They learned the American way quickly and were very lucky not to have their hearts broken or face the complications of teenage pregnancy. Assimilating to the new culture also meant rejecting the "old" one:

> We began to develop a taste for the American teenage good life, and soon, Island was old hat, man. Island was the hair-and-nails crowd, chaperones, and icky boys with all their macho strutting and unbuttoned shirts and hairy chests with gold chains and teensy gold crucifixes. By the end of a couple of years away from home, we had *more* than adjusted. (*Girls,* 108-109)

To bring the girls back to their island culture, the parents decide to send their daughters back to the Dominican Republic every summer—Trujillo is now dead, the United States has invaded and legitimized Balaguer's presidency—so they will not forget where they come from. Of course, they go to their relatives' mansions where they are again served and every wish is satisfied by the voiceless servants who were once part of their life. They never leave this security belt except to go to the countryside residences, where another flock of underpaid *campesinos* takes care of them. Whether in the United States or in the country of origin, they have only one perspective on society: that of the privileged class that has access to the best education, professions, residences, consumer goods, and mobility with very few, if any, restrictions.

Once they grow up and become independent because they marry, get good jobs in other states, or have nervous breakdowns, the daughters always remain in touch with their parents and with their relatives back in the Dominican Republic or in the United States. But to come to terms with their particular notion of identity, they have to battle the burden of patriarchy exemplified by the father. Each sister wants to obliterate this aspect of their culture, but they are stonewalled by a father who believes that he is the head and commander of the family. The four daughters represent the family, and they must be watched over every moment to ensure that they bring no shame to the family name. Once the daughter is married, then the husband is the one in charge of watching over the honor of his new family. The ideal marriage would be to a young man from the Dominican Republic whose family they know and whose wealth and whiteness is assured. Yet, in this case, the parents, who are continuously bragging about their white ancestry ("My great-grandfather married a Swedish girl, you know! So the family has light-colored blood" (*Girls*, 52), are very pleased that three of their daughters married white American or German men. Although mental illness also brings shame to the family, the father has been able to send two of his daughters to expensive private clinics, and they are now near recuperation, ready to readjust to American society. Failed marriages, anti-social behavior, and rejection of parental guidance are considered by the father as mental instability brought on by their residence in the United States.

Yolanda, the narrator and writer daughter, yearns for home, but this relates more to land and not to a particular lifestyle or cultural context. When she returns to the island as an adult, she misinterprets life in the Dominican Republic:

> All around her are the foothills, a dark enormous green, the sky more a brightness than a color. A breeze blows through the palms below, rustling their branches, so they whisper like voices. Here and there a braid of smoke rises up from a hillside—a *campesino* and his family living out their solitary life. This is what she has been missing all these years without really knowing that she has never been missing it. Standing here in the quiet, she believes she has never felt at home in the States, never. (*Girls*, 12)

On one of her trips back to the homeland she decides to go to the countryside to write instead of staying with her family in the city.

William Luis calls this return "a spiritual journey in search of com-
munion not with Dominican culture as it exists during the present
time of the novel, but with a mythical past associated with her childhood" (Dance, 271). Both the house and the land are owned by her
relatives, and she has at least two people making her stay as comfortable as possible. Her attempts to democraticize her surroundings are based on the position she still holds in the island society
because of her class. She wants the peasants to call her by her first
name; she is willing to teach them how to read and write, and she
lectures the women on how to stand up to abusive husbands. But
she never attempts to break away from her class. These underprivileged acquaintances become the subjects of her fiction and private
jokes for the family once she returns to the United States. For the
mother, Laura, home is "the clan," the extended family that always
supported one another and lived close enough to feel each other's
presence (*¡Yo!*, 33). After raising her daughters in the United States,
she has no desire to return home because her children and grandchildren are not there and because she feels that even someone as traditional as she is has more mobility and choices in the United States.
"She did not want to go back to the old country where, de la Torre or
not, she was only a wife and a mother (and a failed one at that, since
she had never provided the required son). Better an independent
nobody than a high-class housewife" *Girls,* 143–144). The García
women, because of their class and relatively seamless racial insertion
in the centre, perceive themselves as having a right to belong to this
version of American society. Much like Lourdes and Constancia in
Cristina García's novels, Laura and her daughters have learned English, received the best education money can buy, pursue careers, or
establish their own profitable businesses, marry men who are also
white, wealthy, and professionals, and keep themselves distanced from
any ethnic community. They feel entitled to have a place that they
can call their past and to be nostalgic about a lifestyle that far ex-
ceeded, in personal comforts, the one they found in the United States.

Woven into the García women's story in *How the García Girls Lost
Their Accents* and *¡Yo!* are the voiceless dark-skinned women ("Indian," "black-black," "Haitian black") who are always there to follow
orders, be treated like unruly children, and please every whim of
the household members no matter how young or old or how ques-

tionable their demands are. These women bring them a drink when they are thirsty, a pillow when tired or sleepy, a blanket when cold, an umbrella when it is too hot. Strangely, they are privileged in the island society because they have a job, a place to live, and receive money they can send their parents and children back home in the countryside. Their special position is based on a very fragile relation, where the *patrones* can, at any time, terminate their stay in the city, move them around to other households, treat them well or abuse them physically or emotionally, and always remind them of their inferior place. Regardless of how generously these women—"the help"—believe they are being paid, they are always exploited. In the luxurious world of the García-de la Torre family, poverty and ignorance are only evident in the servants' quarters. They live not only on the social margins in countryside, shacks, or slums, but when they are employed by the center on the hacienda, or the big house in the city, they disappear into another margin: the servants' quarters. For the crumbs they receive at Christmas and for the privilege of being employed, they are forever grateful to those who hold absolute power over their lives.

In the servants' quarters, the maids create their own hierarchy with Chucha being at the head because of her age and the fact that she is Haitian, which not only implies being black but also having the power of voodoo ("Haiti was synonymous with voodoo" *Girls*, 279.). Pila was mocked for having only one eye and brown skin full of pink patches but is also feared because she is half-Haitian. Although Nivea and Gladys, the younger Dominican maids, are also dark skinned, they are not considered black because they are not Haitians. They are grateful for their jobs, but they also have their own private dreams of one day going to New York: "'I wonder where I'll be in thirty-two years,' Gladys mused. A glazed look came across her face, she smiled. 'New York,' she said dreamily and began to sing the refrain from the popular New York merengue that was on the radio night and day" (*Girls*, 260). These women listen to stories from their compatriots living in or having visited New York; they also admire the gifts that Carlos García brings his wife and daughters every time he goes to New York. Their only value for the Dominican upper and middle classes is to serve and clean; these employers see no need to send them to elementary school or teach

them to read and write. These working-class women have always understood that race in the Dominican Republic automatically places
them in the invisible spaces of the kitchen, the maids' quarters, the
backyard, the sheds, and the slums. New York is then identified as the
space where they can acquire a collective visibility and presence that
will allow them to break away from the stronghold of class and race
on the island. For them it is worth risking savings, small possessions,
and their own lives to just reach the shores of the centre. In *¡Yo!*,
Consuelo is the housekeeper of one of de La Torre's country houses
where Yolanda spends some time writing. Her daughter is one of the
many thousands of Dominican women who make it to New York:

> Ruth had made it to Puerto Rico on a rowboat, then on to Nueva
> York where she worked at a restaurant at night and at a private
> home as a maid during the day. Every month, Ruth sent home
> money along with a letter someone in the village read to
> Consuelo. Every few months the Codetel man came running
> through town, "International call!" Consuelo would be out of
> breath by the time she arrived at the telephone trailer to hear
> her daughter's small voice trapped in the wires. "How are you,
> Mamá? And my baby Wendy?" (*¡Yo!*, 97-98)

Working-class women in Alvarez's novels are "protected" by their
employers who arrange all the paperwork necessary to bring them
to the United States and who continue to "provide" for them as long
as they agree to serve and stay exactly in the same position they
were in back in the Dominican Republic. While Primi in *¡Yo!* is the
perfect servant—forever grateful of having been sent for by Doña
Laura and Don Carlos to serve them in New York—her daughter
Sarita will see this relationship for what it truly is: a class exploitation, where her mother and herself are never seen as human beings
but as inferior creatures because of their race and class. Primi, on
the other hand, whose true name was María Trinidad but had been
renamed by her first *patronas*, is destined to a life of hard work and
no possible change in status whether on the island or in New York.
Sarita describes her thus:

> She had spent her whole life working for the de la Torres, and it
> showed. If you stood them side by side—Mrs. García with her

pale skin kept moist with expensive creams and her hair fixed up in the beauty parlor every week; Mamá with her unraveling gray bun and maid's uniform and mouth still waiting for the winning lottery ticket to get replacement teeth—why Mamá looked ten years older than Mrs. García, though they were both the same age, forty-three. (66)

Primi, who has served the de la Torre family all her life, is the only one that makes it to New York but only as a maid to help Mrs. García, who had "the hard life of being a housewife in the United States" (*¡Yo!*, 54).

Sarita's plight is a very common story in the Dominican Republic. Primi, her mother, like most maids who work for an upper or upper-middle class family, are live-in maids and see very little of their own children, who are usually raised by grandmothers or other relatives, as Isis Duarte points out in her essay on household workers in the Dominican Republic (198). In order to keep Sarita as close as possible to her work and living quarters, Primi puts her in a Catholic boarding school. When Primi moves to New York, Sarita goes to live with her grandmother in the countryside. After five years of living abroad, Primi is able to save enough money to send for Sarita, already thirteen, to live in New York in the García household as the maid's daughter.

Even though her mother is always warning her to never forget her place or they will be sent back (*¡Yo!*, 57), Sarita takes advantage of living in a society whose class structures are more relaxed and where one can seep through the cracks. Marta Caminero-Santangelo argues that while the García girls play at identity, "Sarita understands difference" (62). So she convinces Mrs. García to send her to the same school her daughters had attended before going off to boarding school. While Mrs. García is gratified for having done a good deed by providing a good education for a poor girl who probably won't go too far anyway, Sarita plays on this patriarchal good feeling to get ahead. She will get the highest scores in school and win a full scholarship to a private university, where she will major in science to the astonishment of the entire García family. When she leaves the "benevolent" family without regret and guarded gratefulness, she is acting under the same understanding as Maryse Condé's Reynalda in *Desirada*. They have known poverty and have seen the way the wealthy live; from a very early age they understand that poverty is a stigma on the islands; they learn their ways in the metropole and find the spaces that allow them to turn their lives around by turning their backs on the homeland, which to them means fixity, segregation, and oppression in the defense of a culture of privilege.

While Primi's only dream, after she is no longer useful to the García household, is to go back to her island and spend her remaining days close to her birthplace, Sarita will redefine her homeland. The United States is where she is able to stop being the maid's daughter and become successful on her own merits: complete a professional career and, as a result, achieve economic prosperity and stability. Going back to the island is looking back at her own and her mother's life of poverty and serfdom. She will buy a house back home for her mother and send money but will not return to a country where her merits have no value to the upper classes. She has secured her own place in this new country which has been transformed from foreign to familiar: "...I doubt I am ever going to see any of the García girls again. Mamá has died. The past is over. I don't have to make believe anymore" (*¡Yo!*, 72).

Primi looks back with nostalgia at the countryside where she grew up and skips over her long life as a maid whose own name is changed to the convenience of her *patrones*. In contrast, Sarita erases her own past as "the maid's daughter" both in the Dominican Republic and in New York. She does not yearn for any place or any special time in her life. She chooses to live in the present that she has forged. Instead of being perpetually encased back home as backward, she chooses what to preserve and erase from the homeland, and learns to inscribe her name in this new space. She has transformed the present by choosing to live away from a society that never changes no matter the political parties in power or the influence of liberal ideas from developed countries. The families that owned the land, properties, businesses, then and now, continue to control the lives of those less fortunate.

Loida Martiza Pérez's working-class family in *Geographies of Home* did not have to resort to rickety boats to get to Puerto Rico and then New York. Each family member entered legally under the various government agreements after the U.S. invasion of Santo Domingo in 1965. Rebecca, the oldest daughter, was able to secure a work permit, and was later able to bring her parents, Aurelia and Papito, and thirteen of her siblings through the family reunification program to the United States.

> She remembered how, at the age of twenty-one, she had begged her parents for permission to move to the United States. She had honestly believed that she would be able to pick gold off the streets and send for her parents so they might live as grandly as those who returned to the Dominican Republic claimed was possible. (59)

Her commitment to her family went as far as securing green cards for each one of them even though she was "not eligible for residency" (62). What Rebecca had not been able to do was to raise her family from poverty.

For working-class people, last names have no value. For this particular family that comes from the Dominican countryside and did not live in Santo Domingo as a transitory space before moving to the metropole, family unity is one of the most important values they must preserve. They have willingly traveled to the United States because they honestly believe the family can enjoy a better quality of life in a place where they can secure jobs and steady salaries instead of being at the mercy of nature and landowners in their hometowns. This family unity is sustained by a strict patriarchal rule. If Carlos García in Julia Alvarez's novels berated his daughters because he feared they would have sex before marriage and shame the family name, in this working-class family, the daughters are physically and emotionally abused by a father who is a practicing Seventh Day Adventist and would rather kill his own kin than endure dishonor. This rigid stance is not only upheld by the father's generation but also by younger men such as Pasión, Rebecca's abusive husband. Although Iliana, the youngest and the only daughter to go to college, is the protagonist, the stories of three other women are also told through their own voices and minds: Aurelia, the mother, and the older daughters Rebecca and Marina. By geographically distancing herself from the family, Iliana can be less immersed in the imaginary family her parents have constructed in the metropole. Rebecca should have adapted best because she was the first to arrive and was forced to deal with the daily life of being a foreign migrant in New York, yet she adheres to the most traditional wife-husband relations. Marina, like Yolanda and Sandra García in Alvarez's stories, suffers a nervous breakdown because of her inability to handle the frictions between the two cultures. This analysis of *Geographies of Home* will focus on these three very different characters—Aurelia, Rebecca, and Iliana—who represent distinctive notions of island versus metropolitan life.

In this traditional family, Papito (interestingly the father has no name; he is called "dad" by wife and children), as head of the household, assumes all responsibility for taking care of the sixteen-member family. A wife cannot work outside the home because her sole function is that of housekeeper and mother; the children must be fed, clothed, and have a safe shelter; they must be taught the traditional family values of their island that are endorsed by the church. To accomplish this, Papito sometimes will work three jobs without sick leave or vacation, endure hunger, take advantage of free meals provided by the city, beg for money in the name of God to buy food, ration milk, and live off charity to clothe the children and send them to public school (69–70). To avoid the risk of becoming homeless and separating the family, Papito will save money to buy a rundown house in Brooklyn that they can at last call home.

> ...it had kept them from the streets ...it was the only house in their adopted country which they had been able to call their own....she had expected each family member to feel secure in the knowledge that never again would they be cramped into a three-room apartment like their first or be evicted as they had from their last. (21)

Home-building for this family, as expressed by the only voice recognized with authority, means being fanatically religious, instilling blind respect for parents and other elders, physically punishing any transgression, and keeping close surveillance on daughters. The result of all these preventive measures to preserve family unity is disastrous: the oldest daughter and her children are neglected and abused by another authority figure; a son has an affair with his sister-in-law; two brothers have sworn to kill each other if they ever meet again face to face; another son drops out of graduate school and his wife walks out on him; a suicidal and belligerent daughter has not been able to overcome a severe nervous breakdown; one of the younger daughters leaves home and no one knows her whereabouts; the youngest son rarely leaves his room; and another daughter opts to study as far away from home as possible. However, Papito does not accept the reality of failure and continues to construct the illusion of family life in which they all live in harmony; Marina is not sick, and Rebecca is not abused. The women have absorbed this traditional sense of pride and shame. They comply to Papito's wishes and try to keep alive the lie of family.

Papito believes, and his family accepts, that the only way to survive in the United States is by isolating themselves from the "foreign" new society. The father can enter the centre and work, but the women stay home, go to school, do their shopping, go to church, and socialize only within the ethnic enclave. This false sense of protection is supposed to keep customs intact and re-create their hometown on the margins of the metropole. Brooklyn becomes this "place apart" that they can manage without being harmed, while Manhattan is proclaimed as the seat of all evil and temptation ("Sodom and Gomorrah," 9). During the year and a half that Iliana is away at college, the house changes as their economic condition improves. The "hand-carved statuettes and worn but sturdy wooden rocking chairs and tables brought from the Dominican Republic" (50) that were pivotal in home-building are now replaced by American generic furniture and ornaments. The house's gray-looking façade is painted yellow. On return, Iliana becomes nostalgic for the previous home, the one that so reminded her of her island: "While she had been away, her memory had consisted of images imbued with the warmth of a Caribbean sun magically transported to New York and of a house furnished with objects lovingly carved by the inhabitants of an island she had dreamed of" (30). In a way, each family member is trying his or her own version of home-building by raising chickens inside the house, feeding pigeons, or growing vegetables in the backyard. But what they all have internalized as home-building is the patriarchal structure from the island with even stricter rules. As they grow up and leave to study and work, each son and daughter must break away from this enclosure and deal with the wider society. Place-making has been limited to church activities as a way of protecting the family from the other culture's bad influence. The father does not understand that in the metropole everyone is exposed to American global culture, even if they are not immersed in it because of their self-imposed isolation. Even Aurelia, by watching Spanish-language TV stations, gathers information that goes beyond suffocating Bible studies. Papito is unable to accept that religion has not prepared him to confront his daughter's mental illness or his oldest daughter's battered woman syndrome. Because the father holds such a tight rein on his family, Aurelia does not question his authority until it is almost too late to make amends. Every time Iliana threatens to call Social Services to stop the suffering of Rebecca's neglected children (61), Aurelia tells her to shut up and do nothing. It is only when the children have gone cold and hungry for several weeks that she interferes by removing the children herself and taking them back to her own place. Only when Marina tries to burn down the house and thereby almost succeeds in her latest suicide attempt does Aurelia decide to seek help. A tradition of silence, in which internal problems are not publicized to avoid mockery or dishonor, makes Aurelia wait so long that the problems become unsolvable. When Papito proposes to return to the island now that most of the children have left home, Aurelia dismisses this idea because she never questions the role by which she has been defined: wife, mother, and now grandmother (235). She will not "abandon" her children; she must feel needed to be valued as a person. Within the confinements that she has built, Aurelia has reconstructed her homeland so she can survive in a country she barely knows:

> Throughout more than fifteen years of moving from apartment to apartment, she had dreamed, not of returning, but of going home. Of going home to a place not located on any map but nonetheless preventing her from settling in any other. Only now did she understand that her soul had yearned not for a geographical site but for a frame of mind able to accommodate any place as home. (137)

When Rebecca, at age thirty-two, married Pasión after a very troubled and violent relationship with her former boyfriend, Samuel, she believed that at last she had fulfilled her ultimate role in life. The oldest daughter of parents with very conservative ideas, Rebecca always saw marriage and motherhood as her only goals in life. Yet, in the Dominican Republic, she was not willing just to do house-work, marry at a young age, and bear as many children "as God would give her"—like her mother who bore and raised fourteen chil-dren. The need to marry is so culturally ingrained that she cannot see herself as someone who can live on her own and redirect her life apart from her family. She will accept Pasión as her husband be-cause she is afraid that at her age she will never marry and have children and will be mocked by family and relatives. After she moves in with her husband and discovers the lies he continuously told her family about his house, job, and emotional and economic stability, Rebecca does not move out or let her family interfere in her affairs. Even after the repeated beatings, the humiliation of his affairs and of having to live in a pigsty, she denies her unhappiness.

> Mute with shock, Rebecca had followed him [Pasión] through a corridor lined with stained and gutted mattresses. They climbed a staircase with only inches of cleared space for a person to squeeze through.... Shabby armchairs were clustered in what was to serve as the living room. In the dining room mismatched vinyl chairs circled a green Formica table that collapsed when she leaned against it. (55)

Rebecca attempts to remodel this space so she can begin home-building with her new family. After a while, she is discouraged when her husband continues to bring junk into the house and gives more attention to the chicken coop than to the spaces inhabited by hu-man beings. Accepting that there is something wrong in her mar-riage would be admitting failure, provoking Pasión's anger, and hav-ing to start over again. So home continues to be at her parents' house, where she seeks shelter and protection when Pasión beats her or does not come home for weeks or when she has no food to feed her children or heat to keep them warm.

There is no place-making because, as man of the house, Pasión does not allow Rebecca to have any contact with neighbors and even limits her visits to her parents. Even though she came to New York to work and find employment in a garment factory, Pasión prohib-its her from working outside the home. According to him, "'I may not always provide you with everything you need, but God knows I do my best. And how do you repay me? By shaming me and going out to get yourself a job. By letting the world think I'm not man enough to take care of you myself'" (56). Her father does not interfere because he agrees with these patriarchal postulates that he has imposed on his own family. Only Aurelia questions her daughter's situation, but she does nothing to end the beatings and the neglect until Rebecca's two children have been abused for several years (201). Home-building for Rebecca is also upholding the patriarchal structure and inflicting on her children the same unquestionable values that she was taught. The children must respect their father and obey their mother no matter what awful pain they inflict on them; they cannot complain or criticize anything happening at home; they must be willing to take corporal punishment and never talk back. For Rebecca, being forced to go back to her parents' house is both humiliating and a violation of her belief that a wife must stay with her husband regardless of the consequences. That is why it is so surprising when she does not come to Pasión's aid as he suffocates during an asthma attack. She simply chooses to watch him die. Yet this widowhood will not liberate her. Rebecca has internalized the imposed patriarchal behavior and will continue to submit to male authority, whether represented by her father or by another man formed in the same tradition. Her nostalgia is not for a homeland or a house structure she can call her own; she yearns for an imaginary life where a woman is loved and respected because she is a good wife and mother, even if these traits only serve men.

While the father embellishes stories of his childhood—near fabrications—and dreams of going back to the island frozen in his mind that he left behind so many years ago, Iliana allows herself to dream of a Caribbean island she barely knew as a homeland different from the reality she must face every day. Whether she completes her degree or enters the job market, she has to sort out her memories so they serve as a reminder of home and also a first step in building her own life. This new home can never be the college where they see her as an "arrogant bitch" (5), where she was first welcomed with the word "nigger" posted on her dormitory door (1), and where she is not accepted as either black or Puerto Rican: "With her skin color identifying her as a member of one group and her accent and immigrant status placing her in another, she had fit comfortably in neither and even less in the circles she had found herself in when she finally went away to school" (191). This home she now seeks as an adult cannot be a workplace that is constantly shifting depending on current economic needs. Nevertheless, home cannot be her family's house, where she continuously fights patriarchy and religion, where her crazed sister sexually assaults her, and her parents invoke a code of silence to hide the gravity of her sister's illness. Her parents' home can no longer protect her from violence, abuse, disgrace, insults, physical and emotional injuries, because all these have erupted within the imagined home that they tried to construct for their children to protect them from the dangers of the outside world of English-speaking American culture. Therefore, Iliana has to search for home in her own memories of the dream island she now seldom recalls, of times when the family truly came together to protect and provide for one another, and of the sense of independence and confidence she has achieved living by herself with almost no social contact:

> Everything she had experienced; everything she continued to feel for those whose lives would be inextricably bound with hers; everything she had inherited from her parents and had gleaned from her siblings would aid her in her passage through the world. She would leave no memories behind. All of them were her self. All of them were home. (321)

Iliana is willing to face family, community, and religious rejection, but she will not ignore or devalue what she achieved in the eighteen months she lived alone, fended off racial and cultural attacks, and made friends and allies of total strangers. Just as Gloria Anzaldúa in *Making Faces Making Souls* experienced "ostracism, alienation, isolation and shame" when she did "not live up to the 'image' that the family or community" wanted, Iliana will also "rebel against the engravings of our bodies" (xv) so that she can begin to redefine her culture by the choices she now makes.

Even though entry to the United States is smoothed because Puerto Ricans are U.S. citizens by birth, Bonham Richardson has pointed out that despite the advantage of citizenship, they are treated as Hispanic immigrants alongside Dominicans, Mexicans, and other Latin and Central American people who hold the menial jobs and are placed at the bottom of the ladder (220). According to Grosfoguel and Georas, "to be identified as Puerto Rican in the ethnic/racial hierarchy of New York City is a racist marker for a new Latino immigrant" (98). So even if it might, on occasion, be convenient to be wrongly labeled Puerto Rican when immigrants have entered the United States illegally, this association can be detrimental to finding jobs and acceptable dwellings in non-ghetto areas and can lead to criminal profiling. Grosfoguel also points out that as second-class U.S. citizens, Puerto Ricans "who migrated did not receive the proper state support in bilingual programs, education, health, housing, subsidies, and job training. They ended up in the metropole's urban ghettos as unskilled low wage workers with one of the highest poverty rates in the United States" ("Migration." 110). Puerto Ricans do have the advantage of the *guagua aérea* (the airbus), a term coined by Puerto Rican writer, Luis Rafael Sánchez, and defined as the space of a floating nation between two ports where hopes are smuggled ("El espacio de una nación flotante entre dos puertos de contrabandear esperanzas" 22). Their constant departures and arrivals from San Juan to New York, New Jersey, Chicago, and Orlando make it seem that these U.S. cities are just other extensions of Puerto Rican neighborhoods that can be approached at any time. Vanessa Vilches Norat considers this geographical proximity and ease of mobility as distinctive features of Puerto Rican migration (144). Dennis Conway perceives the island home societies as "the constant hub" (333), even if the circuits change and widen. While citizenship guarantees free entry, Puerto Ricans travel to the United States for similar reasons, encounter the same difficulties with language, weather, jobs, and housing, and are discriminated against and face the same racialized ethnic slurs as other Spanish-speaking groups. Being able to go back to one's island without risking loss of passport, green card, or temporary visa does not necessarily mean that Puerto Ricans fare any better than other immigrant groups in terms of jobs, salaries, or education.

Juan Flores, in a cultural studies approach, divides the Puerto Rican migration and assimilation process in four contested "moments": the here and now, the state of enchantment, the return and reentry, and the branching out (187-191). Only a brief transition separates the first and second moment: the arrival with that first impression of being in an unknown country because of the language, weather, people's behavior, landscape, and architecture. Puerto Ricans are able to face this radical change because they still have "a romanticized and idealized image of Puerto Rico" (187), which they try to re-create in the new location (Castles and Davidson's *Citizenship and Migration*). Flores's other two moments seem to be wishful thinking: he asserts that when facing "the Black versus White polarities of the US," Puerto Ricans "give way to a proud identification with Afro-Caribbean cultural traditions" (190), and connect with the groups they share similarities with such as African Americans and black Caribbeans. Authors of studies in migration and adaptation processes such as Ramón Grosfoguel, Alejandro Portes, Patricia Pessar, José Itzigsohn, Dennis Conway, Jama Adams, and Caroline Brettell assert quite the opposite view: people from the Spanish-speaking Caribbean enclose themselves in a cultural context that isolates them from both English and French/Creole-speaking communities, which they perceive as inferior because of their own whitened racial superiority. Puerto Ricans keep their distance from black Americans in the United States because they are perceived as not achieving progress and advancement—the ability to assimilate—as a group that has been part of this society for centuries. America is understood by these migrant groups as white; everyone else is placed at the margins. In Judith Ortiz Cofer's *The Line of the Sun*, and Esmeralda Santiago's *When I Was Puerto Rican*, *Almost a Woman*, and *América's Dream*, the women characters almost never have contact with dark-skinned young men or women, whether in school, neighborhood, or jobs. There are virtually no cross-cultural encounters; ethnic enclaves serve as protective walls, which these young women will try to penetrate to have contact with white America and thereby ignoring the Other America they have been involuntarily placed in.

The first location in *The Line of the Sun* is the Puerto Rican countryside, isolated from urban cities such as Mayagüez, Ponce, and San Juan. Family unity, even if it involves physical punishment and strict surveillance of young women, is presented as a lifeline along which love and care always flow. Mamá Cielo, the grandmother, is an admirable force responsible for supervising family members and making sure that everyone is well provided for. Marisol, the granddaughter, tells this story of nostalgia for the land left behind on the one hand and the reality of economic stagnation, domestic violence, child abuse, and negative behavior caused by poor education, early marriages and childbearing, superstition, and political helplessness on the other. Marisol continues to trace in her story her mother's and brother's relocation to the United States and their very difficult adaptation process because of her mother Ramona's reluctance to change.

According to Marisol, in the small town of Salud that her family comes from, there were no blacks. The first black Ramona ever encounters is a U.S. soldier, whom she differentiates from more familiar faces: "one man who was black, but not bronze, really black" 158). While Dominicans term "Indian" any dark-skinned Dominican, the characters in the Ortiz Cofer novel use "bronze" for dark-skinned Puerto Ricans to recall their Taíno "ancestry." This town is also a recruiting center for agricultural workers to find jobs in the United States. Men apply through a lottery system and are promised a one-way airline ticket and a job that will make them rich (146). Guzmán, Marisol's uncle, imagines New York as a white carpet of snow, a world "where everyone had television and drove big cars" (148). Ramona has her own vision of the United States as a place where "she saw herself far away from the mountain of diapers, Mamá's constant vigilance, and her gentle father's sermons on virtue" (163). Ramona sees marriage not as a shackle but as a unique opportunity to transform her life simply by being away from the enclosure of home. She marries Rafael at sixteen and leaves for the United States with her two-year-old daughter when her husband sends for her. She does not have to worry about securing a dwelling and a job in this new location. As a good protective provider, Rafael has taken care of every detail so that when his family arrives they can have a place called home. What Rafael sees as a temporary abode "an apartment building inhabited mainly by Puerto Rican families" (169), Ramona considers a place-making venture that will make her less nostalgic for the family she left behind. For her, home-building re-creates what they remember as home and all the apartments in El Building share nearly the same decoration. "Fortified in their illusion that all could be kept the same within the family as it had been on the Island, women decorated their apartments with every artifact that enhanced the fantasy. Religious objects imported from the

Island were favorite wall hangings" (172). Ramona does not agree with her husband's pleas to move out of this neighborhood and live in a house in the suburbs. When, after many years, she is forced to move out because the building has been destroyed, she will be constantly depressed in a white neighborhood where people stare at her, never try to be friendly, and always look at her as the invading other. While she lived in the Puerto Rican neighborhood, she was part of an ethnic enclave that shared the same fears of the new location, and she easily integrated herself into a women's support group to deal with everyday crises. "They went shopping together, patronizing only certain stores; they attended the Spanish mass at ten o'clock on Sundays...; and they visited each other daily, discussing and analyzing their expatriate condition endlessly. But their main topic after husband and children was the Island" (174). Ramona does not have to face harassment, insults, or mistreatment on the job site. She is one of the very lucky women who has a husband—Rafael is in the navy—who can support the family. She learns about these situations from the other women, who mostly work in factories. She is lucky not so much because she deals infrequently with the outside "foreign" world, but because Rafael is away for many months, she does not have to fight patriarchy or justify her actions to him. When he comes home, everyone coexists pleasantly for these short periods. Once he leaves, normality returns, and Ramona can continue to be Puerto Rican without her husband supervising and criticizing her behavior.

While Ramona serves as a link to the island and a family album for her children, Rafael wants to leave the past behind and construct a new life in which the family is integrated into a new and progressive society. Rafael is always described by his daughter as an angel in white: fair skin, blond hair, blue eyes, and white Navy uniform (177). He speaks to his children in English and enrolls them in a Catholic school attended mostly by Irish and Italian American children. Their only contact with black children is on their way to school. But Marisol and her brother know that they are superior to "those black faces" because they are almost white (Ramona and Guzmán are described as darker because of their "Taíno" ancestry, 205). The father attempts to make their apartment in El Building as generic and global as possible by always bringing them presents from foreign places and consumer goods from big U.S. department stores. He attempts to block out every vestige of Puerto Rican culture from the home he has built. But Ramona will always stand out as foreign, different, other. He will be in charge of dealing with the outside white world, especially school matters, so that his children are not embarrassed by Ramona's presence. This father-children conspiracy can only work if Ramona is not visible outside El Building and the rest of the ethnic enclave. When she transgresses the public spaces reserved for English speakers and acceptable American wardrobe and behavior, the illusion of being part of the centre is obliterated.

> Her long black hair loose and wild from the wind, she was wear-ing black spiked shoes and was wrapped in a red coat and black shawl when she showed up outside the school building. The kids stared at her as if she were a circus freak, and the nuns looked doubtful, thinking perhaps they should ask the gypsy to leave the school grounds....My mother looked like no other mother at the school.... (219)

Marisol, the narrator, presents a very ambiguous picture of her mother based on the revision of her own identity on relocating to the United States. Because of this, Ramona is a towering figure be-cause of her beauty, the strength she displays, the internal assur-ance that allows her to move with her two children to this strange and distant place and construct a homeland so that her family can have a sense of belonging. But when her daughter positions her outside this familiar environment that evokes the not-so-distant past, Ramona is sketched as authoritarian, incapable of accepting and even less of adapting to a new environment, reluctant to change her ways, and ready to embrace the fable she has dreamed of her life back home. From this distorted picture, Ramona emerges, in spite of her daughter, as a woman who marries, has children while very young, and moves to a new country where she has no family ties except a husband who resides away from home most of the time. She is able to keep her sanity only by resisting Rafael's attempt to destroy her home-building and place-making. When she moves to the suburbs, she cannot hide her unhappiness ("...a place that threat-ened to imprison her. In this pretty little house, surrounded by si-lence, she would be the proverbial bird in a gilded cage" 285). When her husband dies in a car accident a few years later, she sees no reason to perpetuate her seclusion. There are no emotional ties to keep her in the United States, and, after fifteen years, she returns home to merge, without regrets and knowing exactly where she belongs, the imagined and the real.

Meantime, Marisol is more interested in constructing a new identity. Her father gives her that opportunity by enrolling her in a school where no one can trace her origins to a Caribbean island. The presence of the white parent who deals with all school matters and the absence of Puerto Rican markers give her the chance to be, so she believes, part of the centre. She is getting an education reserved for the white middle-class, and she is excelling to show her father, the nuns, and her classmates how equal she is to everyone else. Yet, she fails to integrate socially because her dwelling—no matter how provisional it may be—will immediately disclose the marginal community to which she belongs. When her mother gives her permission to attend a family dinner at the home of one of her classmates, everything goes well until she is taken back to her "community":

> We were getting close to El Building. I wished I could just ask him to drop me off a block away. I could see there was a crowd of men and boys gathered on the front steps, probably drinking. One of them had a loud radio. It was blaring salsa music....I hated them all. I started walking toward the door as Doctor Roselli's car pulled away from El Building, the wheels screeching in his haste to get away. (189)

Ramona will become the target of her daughter's resentment of being embarrassed by who she is and where she comes from, regardless of how white her father is, how perfectly she speaks English, or how hard she wants to be part of the centre. The burning down of El Building is a blessing for Marisol because it destroys her mother's home-building and place-making, which Castles and Davidson consider important parts of community formation. Now her mother has no choice but to accept Rafael's initial plan of living in the suburbs and beginning a new life with no ties to an inconvenient past in a place where Americanization equals progress. Yet when they do move to the new house, Marisol fears that Ramona will never adapt and that the silence and emptiness she detected in her since moving out of the old neighborhood will grow stronger. This is exactly what happens when she settles in the suburbs: she becomes silent and subdued, almost crushed by the new surroundings. Ramona's sense of unbelonging is in exact contrast to Marisol's "progress" and integration through formal education, non-Puerto Rican and non-Hispanic friends and acquaintances, and moving in circles where her constructed identity is not questioned. Marisol believes "that to live fully in the present your mind has to be always focused on tomorrow; happiness is the ability to imagine something better for yourself" (284–285). Although she continually reminds the reader that she is in no way like her mother, always nostalgic for her island, Marisol does inherit Ramona's letters when her mother moves back to Puerto Rico. Marisol, the future storyteller, will gather her uncle Guzman's, Ramona's, and her own memories to recall the people and everyday life on the island. The home-building she so rejected will now serve as her source for telling stories.

Esmeralda Santiago's hybrid narratives *When I Was Puerto Rican* and *Almost a Woman* are nostalgic accounts of the island she left behind when her mother and siblings moved to New York to start a new life. Her mother's agenda was to find a better living so that her children would not have to go through the almost insurmountable obstacles she encountered in her relations with men and in the meager wage-earning jobs she could get.

Santiago creates a narrator named Negi, the oldest child, who serves as scribe or memory of her mother Monín's and her own story. Both books narrate the experiences of a Latina adolescent who, when arriving in the United States, has to face ethnic profiling and linguistic prejudice for not being a native speaker of English. These are stories of self-realization, where the hardships are only stages in the young woman's assured climb to success as she situates herself and blends into the centre, the dominant culture based on white hegemony.

Even though Negi comes from a poor working-class family and goes to live in the Puerto Rican ghettos of New York, her stories are not about abject poverty or recurring violence. Monín is able to manage the household in Puerto Rico despite having a husband who is an occasional construction worker, taking care of seven children, and working on and off in nearby factories. Poverty is presented in the countryside as precarious dwellings made of wood with zinc roofs, cramped space for such a large family, and lacking running water and electricity. They are all fed, clothed, and sent to school. They are never isolated because neighbors are close by and relatives visit or are visited by the family. Whenever help is needed to take care of the children, the only thing to do is move the children around for a short time. Everyone is always claimed and the family stays together until the father stays behind when Monín decides to move to New York where she has relatives. The father is loving and caring when he is home, but Monín cannot continue to tolerate a man who has multiple affairs with other women, does not want to marry her, and is not willing to assume financial responsibility for his family.

Because this particular case involves children, the migration process is taken in various stages. Based on what Nicholas Van Hear refers to as "migratory cultural capital," there is already a knowledge of how to go about migration from the moment the decision is made until the migrants reach and settle in the metropole. At home, the success stories of relatives and friends who have made the trajectory are common information. They provide names and places that will serve as contacts for housing and jobs plus information on how to apply for government aids such as welfare, food stamps and checks, and unemployment benefits. Puerto Ricans have established their own networks, while Cubans, as pointed out earlier, were provided with aid, training, jobs, housing, bilingual education, and tutorship available through government agencies. Dominicans who entered the United States legally followed the same course as Puerto Ricans, while Dominicans who enter illegally follow the not-so-underground migrant route detailed by Van Hear in his book *New Diasporas*. Threading these bits of information, Monín constructs an imaginary New York ("'It's really called *Nueva Yor*, but it's so big and spread out people sometimes call it *los Nueva Yores*.'" *When,* 57) from where she receives money orders and worn clothes sent by her mother. Remittances give the impression that the metropole is a place where all goods are accessible, even to the working class ("Things like these are not that expensive in New York. Anyone can afford them." *When,* 79). Other acquaintances, like one of her husband's other women with whom he had a child, have also moved to New York and seem to have done very well. Only the father paints another picture of New York where Puerto Ricans are derided for speaking English with an accent and are contemptuously called "spics" (*When*, 71). In the second stage, the mother travels to New York with Raymond, the youngest and injured son, to see a specialist and comes back with assurances that this is the right move to make. Monín's description of the big city now has a tone of enchantment with its tall buildings and fast trains. With each short trip to New York, her looks and behavior seem to change: "But besides her appearance, there was something new about her, a feeling I got from the way she talked, the way she moved. She had always carried herself tall, but now there was pride, determination, and confidence in her posture" (*When*, 189).

In the third stage, Monín first moves with Negi and the two youngest children. Two months later she sends for the other four, who had stayed with their father until she had the money for their airfare.

For Monín, in New York, there is always place-making "a collective and visible process" (Castles and Davidson, 131)—because she only moves into Puerto Rican neighborhoods. But by moving so many times, home-building will be very difficult because they move from place to place: "...we moved from apartment to apartment, in search of heat, of fewer cockroaches, of more rooms, of quieter neighbors, of more privacy, of nearness to the subway or the relatives" (*Almost*, 1). She always has a job, whether in a factory, the garment district, or working from her apartment when laid off or pregnant. She feels belittled when she has to ask for welfare because the odd jobs are not enough to feed the family, but the moment she is back on her feet, she informs the agency so they do not send the inspectors to poke into her private space. Besides the neighborhood, the dance hall is another element of place-making, where Puerto Ricans from all over the city meet to trace their families back home and listen and dance to live music by salsa musicians and singers. The dance hall truly becomes an extension of the island, a protective place where they are situated in their center (*Almost*, 94–100). Here they can speak Spanish, dress as plain or fancy as they like, move to their rhythms, be themselves without having to be accountable to the white authorities.

Home-building for Monín and Negi means family. As long as the siblings are close to their mother, and the mother is close to Tata, her own mother, and the many relatives that pass through their apartments, they feel part of the island they left behind. There is no need for Monín to go back to Puerto Rico because there are always newcomers with fresh news from the island. She learns about births and deaths, coupling and separations, and changes in the old neighborhoods. Because of this constant two-way current of people, according to Mary Powers and John Macisco, there is no rupture between generations (15). The imaginary homeland remains the same for grandparents, parents, and children no matter the time of arrival in the metropole or differences in age and birthplace. The island is always present through the informal reports of the newest immigrant. The youngest family members are exposed to a different culture in school, but at home, their homeland never changes and becomes the only secure place that they can claim, no matter how far or close to the center they find themselves.

For Monín, New York is not a strange or alien place because her family is here, not only her children but her mother and many other relatives. Her carefully planned resettlement immediately inserts her in their everyday life. She has a place to stay, a job, schools for the children, and a support group that will smooth any rough edges. She can go to work because there are trustworthy people taking care of the children. She lives in a neighborhood that speaks Spanish with *bodegas* that carry all necessary ingredients to cook Puerto Rican dishes. Dance halls are there so that people can listen to their music and meet Puerto Ricans from other neighborhoods and towns back home. Still, Monín emphasizes education for her children so they can have other opportunities in life: "'I'm not working this hard so that you kids can end up working in factories all your lives. You study, get good grades, and graduate from high school so that you can have a profession, not just a job'" (*When*, 246). Much like Aurelia in *Geographies of Home* by Loida Maritza Pérez and Laura in Julia Alvarez's novels, there is no reason for Monín to go back to Puerto Rico when her family and most of her relatives are in New York. Conditions for Monín as a working woman are better in New York. Here, she does not have to battle with men who claim her as a possession or deal with their families who constantly remind her of her duties as wife and mother. In this space, even if it is an ethnic enclave, when Tata does not agree with her daughter's relation with Francisco, Monín moves out. When Francisco becomes terminally ill, Tata returns, and even his family, who also disapproved of their living together, becomes part of her support group. No one dictates proper behavior: Monín chooses to mourn her husband for two years wearing solid black clothes, and she decides when to socialize again. Whether right or wrong, she chooses the men she wants in her life, even if their contact with her children is sporadic because they are married, living with other women, or do not want to formalize the relationship. The one thing that Monín never cares to control, whether for religious reasons or distrust of birth-control methods, is pregnancy. She ends up with eleven children by three different men who are not around to help her raise this large family. This constant presence of too many children in an overcrowded space is rejected by her daughter as she becomes a woman (*When*, 260).

Just like Marisol in *The Line of the Sun*, Negi, an endearing term for Negri or Negrita because she is the sibling with the darkest skin (*When*, 13), aspires to overcome tradition and culture, and take advantage of the opportunities that mainstream life offers. To do this, she diminishes the value of her own cultural background. The immediate and extended families are seen as inferior, backward, and unable to become part of her new and enlarged social ambiance. At the same time, the homeland is erased or left frozen in a dreamlike state. The United States is seen as a changing, dynamic, and progressive society, where diversity is an exciting challenge for someone like Negi. Puerto Rico, as represented by her mother, is frozen in time with no hope of ever catching up with real life in the metropole.

Although Negi feels insulted by school officials, teachers, and social services employees who consider her and her family to be inferior because they come from a different society and barely speak English, once she settles in, she becomes a crusader for change and belittles her own people. Similar to Marisol's shame in *The Line of the Sun*, when Ramona appears unexpectedly to pick her up at parochial school, Negi's humiliation is almost unbearable.

> Mami surprised me one day in front of my school....Mami grabbed my arm, dragged me across the street before I could shake off her strong grip. I avoided the eyes of boys who laughed, slapped

each other five, gave Mami the thumbs up and called "Go Mamma" as we passed....I'd been humiliated in front of the school, and I never wanted to go back there. (*Almost*, 28-29)

While Marisol is ashamed of her mother's looks and wardrobe because they are cultural markers that contradict her aspiration to assimilate, Negi's shame comes from having her schoolmates know that her mother is old fashioned, which blocks her aspiration to become an American teenager. However, this is a public neighborhood school with little or no sense of ethnic negation. Most of the students are Puerto Rican, and they also want to escape their parents' traditional ways and take on the new, the hip, the cool American style that the mass media never ceases to promote. Negi's denial of her Puerto Ricanness takes place later, when she is accepted at the High School of Performing Arts in New York City.

Home-building for Ramona has little to do with whatever apartment the family happens to occupy at the time. As long as the family is together, and they gather with other Puerto Rican families, relatives, and friends to cook traditional dishes and engage in conversations about life and people back on the island, the homeland is always present. Ramona's homebuilding in *The Line of the Sun* takes place both in the apartment she has decorated and in her conversations with other women in El Building. Just as her daughter, Marisol, yearns to live in the suburbs to distance herself from her mother's culture, Negi avoids making friends with people in her neighborhood, refuses to date Puerto Rican men, and dreams of one day living on her own in Manhattan, as far away as possible from the Brooklyn ghetto she has known since she was thirteen. "The more time I spent away from home, the more it felt as if I were a visitor in my family. Our house, with its noise and bustle, was like a pause between parts of my real life in Manhattan, in dance studios, in adventures with Shoshana, in college..." (*Almost*, 217).

Once Negi starts attending Performing Arts, and later goes to Manhattan Community College, traveling every morning from Brooklyn to Manhattan, she knowingly blurs the location that marks her as Puerto Rican to become a privileged high school student who is being trained to become a performing artist. She deludes herself into believing that she is in this place because of her poten-

tial talent and not because New York City is a racialized society that
assigns places to marginal groups as long as they do not threaten
the centre ("At Performing Arts, status was determined by talent."
Almost, 69). Negi's new location, even if she still has to go back to
Brooklyn at night, frees her from having to be like her mother and
grandmother. She now sees other models, other possibilities for her
in spite of being limited to play Cleopatra or Hispanic or Indian
roles. Her makeover also includes having friends and dating "Americans"—meaning non-Puerto Ricans—and white foreigners.
Shoshana, her best friend, is Jewish and also wants to liberate herself from her mother's traditional yoke. Both girlfriends are nineteen, both want to leave behind old customs and be American: to
have the freedom to meet and date American boys without the ob-
sessive protection of a mother's supervision. Negi dates an Israeli, a
white American, and a German, and later on has a prolonged affair
with an older foreign-born man. They are all ignorant of her culture, so she is able to construct for them an image of who she pre-
tends to be and, in this way, erase the sordidness of where she comes
from and the family she belongs to and still lives with.

> [Ulvi] needed a disciple; I needed to be led. I felt myself submerge into
> his need like a pebble into a pond, with no resistance, no trace I'd ever
> been anywhere or anyone without him. With Ulvi I wasn't Negi, daughter
> of an absent father, oldest of eleven children, role model for ten siblings,
> translator for my mother. (*Almost,* 306)

While Negi turns her back on her culture and family to become part
of the centre—even if she is cast as an Indian dancer and never as a
"mainstream" American—she constructs an imaginary Puerto Rican
countryside viewed as paradisiacal. While Monín looks back at her
homeland with critical eyes, Negi embellishes a past where poverty
and her father's infidelity and abandonment of them are substituted
by a child's vision of a home that never existed:

> I flew to the warm breeze of a Puerto Rican afternoon, the air scented
> with jasmine, the *coquí* singing in the grass. I placed myself at my father's
> side as he poured cement, his shovel working quickly in the gray mud,
> scraping the edges, mixing them into the gooey center. As he worked,
> he sang a Bobby Capó *chachachá.* (*Almost,* 29–30)

That trajectory changes in *América's Dream*, which tells the story of a woman who is forced to relocate to stop the jealousy and abuse of her former common-law husband. For América, fleeing the island is an opportunity to live a different life, especially when the dwelling and job are already provided, thus avoiding, like other women who enter the United States in similar circumstances, many of the uncertainties of confronting the vastness, anonymity, and indifference of metropolitan society. Yet living in sectors where they stand out because they speak a different language or are not white makes them totally dependent on white employers, open prejudice, and limited job opportunities, América is a native of Vieques, an offshore island near Puerto Rico, where she lives in a small house with her mother Ester and her daughter Rosalinda and works as a maid in a small guest house. She is offered a job in New York after babysitting an American couple's children. Although at the beginning she is simply grateful for the offer, it becomes a viable option for her when her daughter runs away with her boyfriend only to be rescued by Correa, the girl's father, and forced to live with his family instead of returning home to América. Thus América decides to move to the United States, a country she has never visited, but where she does have relatives who have lived in New York for a number of years,

    América lives in a society that upholds an unwritten but accepted male code that men own women. There was no man to stop Correa from taking América from her home, but he is the man who brings Rosalinda back home and scares her boyfriend away. It does not matter that Correa marries another woman or has multiple affairs; no one questions that América belongs to him. He might not live with her or support her and their daughter, still she cannot even speak to another man without his going into a rage in which he slaps her around or, on occasion, beats her unconscious. Witnesses of this abuse do not dare call the police or, even less, interfere themselves. The laws that exist in this island society to protect battered women—restraining orders and injunctions—have no effect if women who ask for protection are persuaded by repentant spouses/ boyfriends and relatives to drop the charges or, in the case of Rebecca in Loida Maritza Pérez's *Geographies at Home*, if the inability to break the syndrome of abuse results in beatings, broken bones, child abuse, and near-starvation. América knows she must walk away from this abusive situation and start her life elsewhere.

To América "home" also means holding a job she likes and is good at as a maid and babysitter at a tourist hotel, sharing her life with her mother and daughter, living close to people who she knows and who care about her, being immersed in the language, music, food, and other traditions that define her roots, and the knowledge that she belongs with her people. She will miss friends and acquaintances and the familiarity of a place called home when she relocates in the United States, but the preservation of life now takes precedence, and by becoming anonymous, she feels like a human being instead of an object of lust and violence.

In this unfamiliar place called Westchester County, América is able to have "a room of her own" for the first time. Her own house in Vieques belonged to her mother, and Correa could enter her room any time he pleased. Here, people knock at her door and respect her space. The first few days she feels lonely, with no sense of belonging. She tells herself that "There is no home other than the one I left behind" (143). She misses her people's spontaneity and unorganized sense of time. At the beginning, she is intimidated by the cold weather and the voices that speak in English. Living in the Otherland also allows her to meet other women who tell of different lives. These other maids and nannies come mostly from Central America, and they tell stories of institutionalized violence, of being illegal immigrants, of being afraid of the *migra*, of being nurses and teachers in their homeland and here just providing services. She discovers that brutality does not only exist in the private space of her home.

The telephone becomes América's link to home. She has her own phone line and calls her mother and daughter back in Vieques and her relatives in the Bronx. Although it does not take her long to familiarize herself with the new location, she still must rely on the Puerto Rican connection to assert her identity. Westchester County serves as a good transition for América before facing the vastness and sense of dislocation of New York City. In this protected space, she has employment, shelter, and even uses the family car for her own enjoyment. By exploring bit by bit these surroundings with a relatively small population and scattered houses, América loses her fear of the unknown and of the predominant English language. To most of her Spanish-speaking acquaintances, she is seen as an exploited worker who, because she is a U.S. citizen, could have any job of her choice ("They've entered the United States illegally, and they are amazed that she, an American citizen, would work as a maid." 219). Because these women truly believe that citizenship is their passport to equality in this society, they cannot see how close América is to their own positions here. In fact, because of their illegal status, these women are often prevented from seeing their children for many years. Their precarious situation virtually enslaves them to their employers, and all the money they earn goes to remittances, lawyers' fees, and the purchase of documents necessary to stay in the country. If América did not work as a maid, she would probably be an underpaid factory worker in the city, or what she eventually becomes—a maid in a tourist hotel, just like back home. She cannot be deported if she does not comply with the requirements of her job, but she is insulted, harassed, fired, and even blacklisted. What the other women fail to see is that América is becoming an independent woman who drives on her own, takes care of a huge house, is the responsible nanny of two children, and slowly calms her fears of Correa finding her.

> I am América González, she tells herself, the same woman who fifteen days ago folded her maid's uniform and put it on the bottom of an empty dresser, in case she needs it again. Just because I am driving around in an almost new Volvo and I live in a big house and I can take a train into the city...she's smiling....For the first time I can remember I'm in control. I couldn't say that two weeks ago. (181–182)

She has been able to overcome her battered woman syndrome by voluntarily moving away from her victimizer, something Rebecca in Pérez's *Geographies of Home* could never do.

América's strongest sense of home-building takes place in her aunt Paulina's home. Similar to *When I was Puerto Rican* and *Almost a Woman*, Puerto Ricanness is defined in *América's Dream* by the predominant use of Spanish ("'Ay,' she sighs, composing herself with a deep breath, 'it's so nice to be speaking Spanish!'" 185), the ritual of cooking home recipes, the reunion of family, relatives, friends, and neighbors to share food, drink, music, and gossip. As expected in the home culture, men play dominoes and drink beer while the women are busy in the kitchen. When Correa does catch up with her and tries to kill her in her employer's house, he is killed instead. América has a place to go in the Bronx where her family will provide protection, shelter, and love.

Even before Correa's appearance in the United States, América had stopped herself from becoming nostalgic for a place that represented physical and emotional danger and her inability to choose a better life for herself and Rosalinda. This realization does not prevent her from becoming homesick for the place instead of the people: "It takes a while to realize she's homesick for the familiar vistas of Vieques, the green hills and yellow light of the warm sun, the salty ocean, breezes, the flat-rooted houses. She turns from the window as if to erase this new world so hard and gray, so cold, devoid of memories" (213). She also gets homesick when she visits her aunt and walks around the neighborhood, with its bodegas that remind her of the meals her mother prepared for her. She resists her daughter's manipulation to make her return home, and when she finds out that Correa is on his way to get her because Rosalinda gave him her address, like Iliana in Pérez's *Geographies of Home*, she makes a vow to disappear so that no one can ever run her life again ("I'll go someplace where no one knows me. A place with no Puerto Ricans, so there's no chance I see anyone I know. I might even change my name." 283).

In Esmeralda Santiago's *América's Dream*, and Loida Maritza Pérez's *Geographies of Home*, opportunities exist through education and exposure to other lifelines in this contested space. However, achieving this proves difficult when the remnants of home that these women cling to carry the weight of patriarchal gender definitions. Once Correa is out of América's life forever, she chooses to stay in New York, close to her relatives, and to send for her mother and daughter. She has transformed the present by choosing to live away from a society that tolerates and inadvertently encourages domestic violence and mental cruelty. Living in an urban center does not guarantee that history will not repeat itself, since the male hierarchy is established nearly everywhere, but one hopes that América has broken the syndrome that paralyzed her and made her tolerate abuse. The imaginary homeland for América is no longer Vieques but the new space she has reconstructed from at least two diverse geographical locations and the possibility of moving back and forth in direction as dictated by a new awareness and respect for herself and other individuals, regardless of gender.

Notwithstanding the changes women undergo or they are willing to defend in their new locations, the hispanophone communities, which establish their particular national-ethnic enclaves, and the franco and anglophone Caribbean ethnic enclaves that share the margins and center of cities remain separated. Race and language are the two crucial issues that militate against unity among these communities. While in the francophone Caribbean, the mulatto and the black bourgeoisie wrestled for power, "whiter" was the general aspiration in the hispanophone islands regardless of class or gender. When these groups move to the metropole, they immediately understand the importance of whiteness as a marker of progress (Adams, 38). This is why instead of negotiating with the center as a powerful group of workers, "each group of national islanders negotiates its economic, political and cultural dependence differently" (Hall, 226). Cubans, Dominicans, and other Hispanic groups do not want to be identified as Puerto Ricans because of racialized overtones. No matter if they are exiles, *marielitos* or *balseros*, Cubans' political clout places them above other immigrant groups, even Puerto Ricans who already have the coveted U.S. citizenship. Puerto Ricans feel that they have struggled for a long time to establish a community that has municipal, state, and national representation and whose links with the island are never broken. They will work on certain issues with Dominicans and African Americans but want to set themselves apart as whiter and better educated and employed. Dominicans, of course, will not work together with the Haitian or African American communities because they believe they are whiter, more educated, and better off economically. These myths continue to reign as more migrants arrive in New York. Lack of English will set Cubans, Dominicans, and Puerto Ricans apart, especially when they first arrive. Their children will be set back a grade or two and their mobility will be limited to Spanish enclaves and economic niches.

In the stories told by these women writers, nostalgia is closely associated with class. García's Constancia Agüero and Alvarez's

García family, owners of land and property back home, miss what they once had during the different stages of their adaptation to this new culture. Those closer to the working class rely on memory to ease the conflicting situations they find themselves in. According to Françoise Lionnet, memory, defined as the oral trace of the past, is the instrument used to access these women's histories (*Autobiographical*, 5). Gayle Greene places nostalgia and remembrance at opposite ends, the first is seen as forgetting and regressive, while "memory may look back in order to move forward and transform disabling fictions to enabling fictions, altering our relation to the present and future" (298). Most women characters from the hispanophone Caribbean are unwilling to return to the island, even those privileged by class. Ortiz Cofer's Ramona is the only one who never accepted that moving to the United States was an advantage and returns the first opportunity she has with no regrets. All the other first-generation women in these novels are reluctant to return "because it will mean giving up some of the advantages they have gained while abroad" (Brettell, *Theorizing*, 110). The women have been able to establish a sense of community—place-making—that allows them to belong somewhere outside the island home. Some, through home-building—defined by language usage, home cooking, decorations, mementos brought or sent for from the island— have retained the cultural traits that have given them the strength to encounter relocation, isolation, and always being seen as other. Ortiz Cofer's Ramona, Santiago's Monín, Pérez's Aurelia, and Alvarez's Laura see family unity as the only way to protect each other from the teeming world they have just entered. All these mothers watch out for their children, supervise them very closely, but allow them to move in the new society of the metropolitan city to get good educations that will facilitate their entrance into the professional world that they could never be part of because of the islands' patriarchal structure. The dwelling they build is their version of home: the family will always have shelter, food, attention, care, and a place where they belong and can return to. Sometimes fathers interfere with this female notion by imposing the same rules that privileged their positions back home (Alvarez's Carlos García, Pérez's Papito), but these wives and daughters rebel, and the men are forced to retreat into their own nostalgia.

Arlene Dávila distinguishes between the traditional anthropological view of community as "uniformity, parochialism, homogeneity, and consensus" and the very important purpose of diasporic space and place as "an important referent for the construction of memories and identities" (xv). In this newly defined space these women from the hispanophone Caribbean "define new social roles for themselves" (Crespo, 149) and sever the imposed ties to these patriarchal societies that hamper their full development "while remaining true to the nurturing values of their native cultures" (Estéves and Paravisini-Gebert, xxv). James Clifford redefines diasporic experience from the perspective of women, where instead of displacement, traveling, and disarticulation, there is always a sense of construction of placement, dwelling, and rearticulation (Diasporas, 259).

Works Cited

Adams, C. Jama. "Contested Space: Psycho-Social Themes Around the Construction of Caribbean American Identities." *Wadabagei* 2. 1 (Winter/Spring 1999): 29-49.

Alvarez, Julia. *How the García Girls Lost Their Accents*. New York: Plume, 1992.

_____. *¡Yo!* New York: Plume, 1997.

Anzaldúa, Gloria. "Haciendo caras una entrada." In *Making Faces Making Soul*. San Francisco: Aunt Lute Books, 1990. xv-xxviii.

Baronov, David and Kevin A. Yelvington. "Ethnicity, Race, Class, and Nationality." In *Understanding the Contemporary Caribbean*. Eds. Richard S. Hillman and Thomas J. D'Agostino. Boulder, Colorado and Kingston, Jamaica: Lynne Rienner and Ian Randle, 2003. 209-238.

Bosch, Juan. *De Cristóbal Colón a Fidel Castro: El Caribe frontera imperial*. Santo Domingo: Alfa y Omega, 1983.

Brettell, Caroline. *Anthropology and Migration: Essays on Transnationalism, Ethnicity, and Identity*. Walnut Creek, CA: AltaMira, 2003.

_____. "Theorizing Migration in Anthropology: The Social Construction of Networks, Identities, Communities, and Globalscapes." In *Migration Theory: Talking Across Disciplines*. Eds. Caroline B. Brettell and James F. Hollifield. New York: Routledge, 2000. 97-135.

Browdy de Hernández, Jennifer. "The Plural Self: The Politicization of Memory and Form in Three American Ethnic Autobiographies." In *Memory and Cultural Politics: New Approaches to American Ethnic Literatures*. Eds. Amritjit Singh, Joseph T. Skerrett, Jr., and Robert G. Hogan. Boston: Northeastern UP, 1996. 41-59.

Castles, Stephen and Alastair Davidson. *Citizenship and Migration: Globalization and the Politics of Belonging*. New York: Routledge, 2000.

Clifford, James. "Diasporas." In *Routes: Travel and Translation in the Late Twentieth Century*. Cambridge: Harvard, 1997. 244-277.

_____. "Traveling Cultures." In *Routes: Travel and Translation in the Late Twentieth Century*. Cambridge: Harvard UP, 1997. 17-46.

Cofer, Judith Ortiz. *The Line of the Sun*. Athens: U Georgia P, 1989.

Conway, Dennis. "The Caribbean Diaspora." In *Understanding the Contemporary Caribbean*. Eds. Richard S. Hillman and Thomas J. D'Agostino. Boulder: Lynne Rienner, 2003. 333-353.

Conway, Dennis, Adrian J. Bailey, and Mark Ellis. "Gendered and Racialized Circulation-Migration: Implications for the Poverty and Work Experience of New York's Puerto Rican Women. In *Migration, Transnationalization, and Race in a Changing New York*. Eds. Héctor R. Cordero-Guzmán et al. Philadelphia: Temple UP, 2001. 146-166.

Crespo, Elizabeth. "Puerto Rican Women: Migration and Changes in Gender Roles." In *International Yearbook of Oral History and Life Stories. Volume 3: Migration and Identity*. Eds. Rina Benmayor and Andor Skotnes. London: Oxford UP, 1994. 137-150.

Dávila, Arlene M. *Sponsored Identities: Cultural Politics in Puerto Rico*. Philadelphia: Temple UP, 1997.

Delgado Pasapera, Germán. *Puerto Rico: Sus luchas emancipadoras*. Río Piedras: Cultural, 1984.

Díaz Quiñones, Arcadio. *La memoria rota*. San Juan: Huracán, 1996.

Duany, Jorge. "Common Threads or Desperate Agendas?: Recent Research on Migration from and to Puerto Rico." *Centro* VII.1 (winter 94-95): 60-77.

_____. " The Creation of a Transnational Caribbean Identity: Dominican Immigrants in San Juan and New York City." In *Ethnicity, Race and Nationality in the Caribbean*. Ed. Juan Manuel Carrión. San Juan: Institute of Caribbean Studies, 1997. 195-232.

_____. *Los dominicanos en Puerto Rico: Migración en la semi-periferia*. Río Piedras: Huracán, 1990.

Duarte, Isis. "Household Workers in the Dominican Republic: A Question for the Feminist Movement." In *Muchahas No More: Household Workers in Latin America and the Caribbean*. Eds. Elsa M. Chaney and Mary García Castro. Philadelphia: Temple UP, 1989. 197-219.

Estéves, Carmen C. and Lizabeth Paravisini-Gebert. "Introduction." In *Green Cane and Juicy Flotsam: Short Stories by Caribbean Women*. New Brunswick: Rutgers UP, 1991. xi-xxvi.

Flores, Juan. "'Qué assimilated, brother, yo soy asimilao':The Structuring of Puerto Rican Identity in the U.S." In *Divided Borders:*

Essays on Puerto Rican Identity. Houston, TX: Arte Público, 1993. 182-195.

Foner, Philip S. *The Spanish-Cuban-American War and the Birth of American Imperialism. Volume I: 1898-1902*. New York: Monthly Review, 1972.

———. *The Spanish-Cuban-American War and the Birth of American Imperialism. Volume II: 1895-1898*. New York: Monthly Review, 1972.

García, Cristina. *The Agüero Sisters*. New York: Alfred A. Knopf, 1997.

———. *Dreaming in Cuban*. New York: Ballantine, 1992.

García, María Cristina. *Havana USA: Cuban Exiles and Cuban Americans in South Florida, 1959-1994*. Berkeley: U California P, 1996.

González, Lydia Milagros and A.G. Quintero Rivera. *La otra cara de la historia: La historia de Puerto Rico desde su cara obrera*. Río Piedras: CEREP, 1984.

Greene, Gayle. "Feminist Fiction and the Uses of Memory." *Journal of Women in Culture and Society* 16.2 (1991): 290-321.

Grosfoguel, Ramón. "Migration and Geopolitics in the Greater Antilles." In *Colonial Subjects: Puerto Ricans in a Global Perspective*. Berkeley: U California P, 2003. 103-127.

———. "Puerto Ricans in the USA: A Comparative Approach." *Journal of Ethnic and Migration Studies* 25. 2 (April 1999): 233-249.

Grosfoguel, Ramón and Chloé S. Georas. "Latino Caribbean Diasporas in New York." In *Mambo Montage: The Latinization of New York*. Eds. Agustín Laó-Montes and Arlene Dávila. New York: Columbia UP, 2001. 97-118.

Hall, Stuart. "Cultural Identity and Cinematic Representation." In *Ex-iles: Essays on Caribbean Cinema*. Ed. Mbye Cham. Trenton, NJ: Africa World P, 1992. 220-236.

Itzigsohn, José and Carlos Dore Cabral. "The Manifold Character of Panethnicity: Latino Identities and Practices Among Dominicans in New York City." In *Mambo Montage: The Latinization of New York*. Eds. Agustín Laó-Montes and Arlene Dávila. New York: Columbia UP, 2001. 319-335.

Lewis, Gordon. *Puerto Rico: libertad y poder en el Caribe*. Río Piedras: Edil, 1969.

Lionnet, Françoise. "Introduction: The Politics and Aesthetics of *Métissage*." In *Autobiographical Voices: Race, Gender, Self-Portraiture*. Ithaca: Cornell UP, 1989. 1-29.

Luis, William. *Dance Between Two Cultures: Latino Caribbean Literature Written in the United States*. Nashville: Vanderbilt UP, 1997.

Martínez-San Miguel, Yolanda. *Caribe Two Ways: Cultura de la migración en el Caribe insular hispánico*. San Juan: Callejón, 2003.

Pérez, Loida Maritza. *Geographies of Home*. New York: Viking, 1999.

Pessar, Patricia. "New Approaches to Caribbean Emigration and Return." In *Caribbean Circuits: New Directions in the Study of Caribbean Migration*. New York: Center for Migration Studies, 1997. 1-11.

Portes, Alejandro. "Conclusion: Towards a New World- the Origins and Effects of Transnational Activities." *Ethnic and Racial Studies* 22. 2 (March 1999): 463-477.

Powers, Mary G. and John J. Macisco, Jr. *Los puertorriqueños en Nueva York: Un análisis de su participación laboral y experiencia migratoria, 1970*. San Juan: Centro de Investigaciones Sociales, 1982.

Pratt, Mary Louise. *Imperial Eyes: Travel Writing and Transculturation*. London: Routledge, 1992.

Richardson, Bonham C. "Caribbean Migrations, 1838-1985." In *The Modern Caribbean*. Eds. Franklin W. Knight and Colin A. Palmer. Chapel Hill: U North Carolina P, 1989. 203-228.

Sánchez, Luis Rafael. ""La guagua aérea." In *La guagua aérea*. Río Piedras: Cultural, 1994. 11-22.

Santiago, Esmeralda. *Almost a Woman*. Reading, MA: Perseus, 1998.

———. *América's Dream*. New York: HarperCollins, 1996.

———. *When I Was Puerto Rican*. New York: Vintage, 1993.

Sassen, Saskia. *The Global City: New York, London, Tokyo*. Princeton: Princeton UP, 1991.

Scarano, Francisco A. *Puerto Rico: Cinco siglos de historia*. Bogotá, Colombia: McGraw-Hill, 1993.

Smith, Robert C., Héctor R. Cordero-Guzmán, and Ramón Grosfoguel. "Introduction: Migration, Transnationalization, and Ethnic and Racial Dynamics in a Changing New York." In *Migration, Transnationalization, and Race in a Changing New York*. Eds. Héctor R. Cordero-Guzmán et al. Philadelphia: Temple UP, 2001. 1-34.

Torres-Saillant, Silvio. "Dominican Literature and Its Criticism: Anatomy of a Troubled Identity." In *A History of Literature in the Caribbean Volume 1: Hispanic and Francophone Regions*. Ed. A. James Arnold. Amsterdam: John Benjamins, 1994. 49-64.

Turner, Faythe. "Introduction." In *Puerto Rican Writers at Home in the USA: An Anthology*. Seattle: Open Hand, 1991. 1-6.

Van Hear, Nicholas. *New Diasporas*. Seattle: U Washington P, 1998.

Vega, Bernardo. *Memoirs of Bernardo Vega: A Contribution to the History of the Puerto Rican Community in New York*. New York: Monthly Review, 1984.

Vilches Norat, Vanessa. "Sólo resta traducir a la lengua materna." In *De(s)madres o el rastro materno en las escrituras del Yo*. Chile: Cuarto Propio, 2003. 139-169.

Williams, Claudette M. *Charcoal and Cinnamon: The Politics of Color in Spanish Caribbean Literature*. Gainesville, FL: UP Florida, 2000.

Williams, Eric. *From Columbus to Castro: The History of the Caribbean, 1402-1969*. New York: Harper & Row, 1973.

CHAPTER 4

Anglophone Caribbean:
The Deceiving Proximity

Practices of representation always implicate the position from which we speak or write—the position of *enunciation*. What recent theories of enunciation suggest is that, though we speak, so to say, "in our own name," of ourselves and from our own experience, nevertheless who speaks, and the subject who is spoken of, are never identical, never exactly in the same place. Identity is not as transparent or unproblematic as we think.... Perhaps instead of thinking of identity as an already accomplished fact, which the new cultural practices then represent, we should think, instead, of identity as a "production" which is never complete, always in process, and always constituted within, not outside, representation.

(Stuart Hall, "Cultural Identity and Diaspora")

Notwithstanding kidnapping, slavery, apprenticeship, emancipation, crown rule, self-government, federation, and independence, England has continued to be the "motherland." The United Kingdom, the center of commonwealth, became a place of possibilities when jobs were offered to West Indians after WWII to reconstruct cities pounded mercilessly by German air power. In the 1960s, the United States and Canada opened other routes for Caribbean peoples seeking employment and wages that would allow them to send remittances to the family left behind and to save enough money for the return home. When migrating to these countries, workers from the anglophone Caribbean felt on familiar ground because they had in common what Stuart Hall calls the pillars of culture: language, history, and literature. Although in the 1940s and early 1950s, mostly men migrated to metropolitan centers, the pattern changed very quickly in subsequent decades and especially for those who followed newly opened routes to Canada and the United States. In their novels, Dionne Brand, Zee Edgell, Michelle Cliff, Joan Riley, Jamaica Kincaid, and Paule Marshall record the individual experiences of the women who migrate to London, Toronto, and New York and who are seen as foreign, underprivileged, and inferior inside these urban centers even though they speak English, attend schools in the metropolitan centers, and never challenge the hegemonic curriculum. Ashcroft, Griffiths, and Tiffin remind us that "even those who possess English as a mother tongue" experience displacement when they move to the "homeland" (391).

Although discussed in Chapter 1, it is essential to review how immigration laws change according to the needs and prejudices of the particular party in power. As colonies of England, no restrictions existed in recruiting West Indians to fight in European wars. Neither were there any restrictions upon bringing to England, especially London, thousands of islanders to help reconstruct the motherland. But this open policy became worrisome when the flow of black Caribbean people continued for over a decade and they settled in England rather than returning to their islands of origin. The Commonwealth Immigration Act of 1962 closed the door to this migration, though it still allowed husbands, wives, and children of those already in the country to join them. Once the ex-colonies were granted independence in 1962, and in subsequent years, the preferential treatment diminished. However, since some islands were members of the Commonwealth or remained colonies, England continued to grant entrance to students and professionals (Richardson, Bolland, Bolles, Gmelch, Welsh). Michelle Cliff's Clare in *No Telephone to Heaven* decides to study in England, even though she could have easily gone to school in New York, where she had lived from age fourteen. Joan Riley's protagonist Hyacinth in *The Unbelonging* is a resident of England, although born in Jamaica, and receives the benefits of social services, college, and university. Of course, she is looked at as foreign and never has a chance to socialize with other students who are not "foreign."

West Indians had been migrating to the United States and settling mostly in Harlem since the beginning of the twentieth century, but in 1924, the government established a quota system that limited the number of immigrants from each country. The McCarran-Walter Act of 1952 reaffirmed the quota system. Paule Marshall's character Silla in *Brown Girl, Brownstones*, and Michelle Cliff's Kitty in *No Telephone to Heaven*, are able to enter the United States under the 1924 and 1952 restrictions and promptly secure jobs. As England closed its doors to its former Caribbean colonies in 1962, the United States put into effect the 1965 Immigration and Nationality Act, which favored family reunification and eliminated the national quota system. Jamaica Kincaid's narrator in *Lucy* enters the United States under this more liberal immigration law that allows her to have a sponsor who provides a stable job that also allows night schooling because of her age. From 1955 to 1967, Canada sponsored the West Indies Domestic Scheme (WIDS), where Caribbean women were recruited as maids (single, 21-35 age group, good physical and mental health, good character, a minimum of five years of formal education, remain one year in the job) and were granted Landed status with the possibility of acquiring Domicile status and eventually Canadian citizenship (Harris, 89-90; Plaza, 5-6). In 1962, Canada adopted the Universal Immigration Policy, which "removed racial discriminatory biases for entry requirements" (Conway, 344), but still gave "preferential entry to persons with the skills and training they require" (Thomas-Hope, 240). This policy still favored women from the Caribbean who entered Canada as nurses, nannies, health and home caretakers. Dionne Brand's Verlia in *In Another Place, Not Here*, as a young woman, is sponsored by relatives who hold jobs and own property. Brand's Elizete, in the same novel, enters Canada on a visiting/tourist visa and disappears in the vastness of Toronto, where she works anywhere she can and for any salary and lives with the fear of being caught and deported.

The cities that the women characters in these novels migrate to have been or were associated with "centres of colonial trade and administration" (Williams, 287), giving them the historical knowledge to deal with a diverse economy and shifting population. It is the space of colonial encounters that Mary Louise Pratt labels "contact zones" (6) and where people from many countries, regions, and islands have entered and exited and sometimes settled in. The vastness and unfamiliarity of the place may seem threatening, but their goal of finding employment that provides for their basic needs and allows them to send remittances back home helps them overcome their initial fears. They are never the first to come, and they always arrive with a name, an address, a telephone number of someone to contact. Like América in Esmeralda Santiago's *América's Dream*, Kincaid's Lucy has her employers to guarantee job, salary, and dwelling. Lucy has no intention of contacting anyone her mother or some relative might know. She does not seek a West Indian community; quite the contrary, she wants to erase her place of origin. Brand's Verlia is welcomed by relatives from whom she will separate after an undetermined time in order to join social and work groups who represent no specific nationality. Cliff's Kitty and her family arrive in Miami and drive all the way to New York to stay with her cousins in Queens. Marshall's Silla enters a solid Barbadian community that quickly responds to her need for a job and housing. Riley's Adella in *Waiting in the Twilight* goes to England to reunite with her husband. These women find jobs in garment factories, war factories, childcare, clerical work, and cleaning. Very seldom, if ever, do they seek government aid when they are laid off or fired. The community link gives them a safe place from which to explore the city. They learn to move around in buses and trains, familiarize themselves with street addresses and landmarks, avoid extremely dangerous and hostile places, and find adequate housing themselves as working women who, most likely, are also head of households. If children join them, they learn to handle paperwork to secure daycare, schools, and health centers. After a while, these women move around more comfortably in the no-longer-strange spaces of metropolitan life and serve as initiators for others yet to come. They have learned the limits of the centre and the various shifting entrances that permit access to the margins.

Toronto would not qualify, according to Saskia Sassen, as a global city. It is closer, in her definition, to a site of production still in the making that attracts diverse groups that respond to a global economy. Toronto is a center of new and changing industries, with multiple incentives for foreign investment that respond to the needs of the industries, factories, offices, and financial markets of the city (Sassen, 5), In that sense, the city has used visa requirements to attract capital and labor to serve the needs of this growing economy; Dwaine Plaza describes Toronto as one of the two major economic hubs in Canada (17). The West Indies Domestic Scheme for recruitment of Caribbean domestic workers supplied the work force needed to partly fill the low-income work stratum of this burgeoning society.

When too many women had taken advantage of the opportunity to work in a metropolitan center with secure wages and the status of "planted immigrants," who in time could request Canadian citizenship, policies were rewritten: women would still have preferential entry because of their skills, but residence and citizenship became more difficult to acquire. Verlia's aunt in Brand's *In Another Place, Not Here* works as a nurse and expects her niece to study nursing and take on a similar job to assure her stay in Canada. But Verlia does not choose this path and prefers to be an unskilled and transitory worker with the proper documents for residency. Elizete, who if she applied would be denied a work visa because her only experience is as a cane cutter, is sought out by employers who want cheap labor. Although often women who care about her advise her to leave and go home, she prefers to roam the streets of Toronto, get money, food, and shelter where she can, and always be on the lookout for immigration agents rather than return to her place of origin.

Compared to older centers such as London and New York, niches have not yet formed in Toronto that give more mobility to migrants, even if they frequently have to accept the same jobs as early generations of immigrants. The illusion of multiculturalism focuses on the acceptance of diversity and attitudes and policies that are more liberal than other metropolitan centers. However, migrants soon discover that race and ethnicity still determine jobs, housing, and salaries. As a more open city, Toronto's goal is to become a metropole through controlled construction, immigration, and the pre-designed architecture of an expanding city and to avoid the mistakes of Chicago with its treasure of architectural design contiguous to a "massive expansion of new high-income stratum alongside growing urban poverty" (Sassen, 337).

In spite of the restrictions instituted in 1924 and 1952, the United States continued to be the preferred port of entry for emigrants from the anglophone Caribbean. Communities of almost all nationalities were formed in New York, and work was abundant for an arriving population not immediately interested in long-term jobs. As indicated in Chapter 1, Harlem was the center of black and Caribbean culture with thousands of migrants coming from Jamaica, Barbados, Monserrat, Antigua, Bermuda, the Bahamas, the Virgin Islands, Martinique, Haiti, Guadeloupe, Puerto Rico, Cuba, Panama,

and Suriname (Watkins-Owens, 2). Most of the time, a place and a
job were waiting for the arriving relative, neighbor, or acquaintance
of someone from back home. Ethnic niches developed very quickly,
both as protection from the hostile white society and as a way to
establish economic enclaves that would promote small neighborhood
businesses. New York developed as a series of ethnically segmented
sections, which came to characterize the city throughout the twentieth century. Harlem had been a first instance of unity among the
peoples excluded by the white majority, but new areas were delin-
eated as more West Indians and Puerto Ricans arrived in New York.
West Indians set themselves apart from black Americans, who they
perceived as being marked by a history of continued enslavement
and segregation, and who, years after emancipation still occupied
the lowest rung in the country's economic ladder. Philip Kasinitz
asserts that "They entered a society far more prosperous than the
one they left, but in so doing they also joined the ranks of America's
most consistently oppressed minority group. This dilemma—economic upward mobility at the price of downward mobility in status—has confronted all cohorts of immigrants" (32–33). West Indians also tended to subdivide as "each group of national islanders
negotiates its economic, political and cultural dependence differently" (Hall, "Cultural," 226). Barbadians did not want to be confused with Jamaicans because, although both were once colonies of
England, their histories and value systems were very different. Although Brooklyn was home to the great majority of West Indians,
the streets and sectors were divided by island of origin. Cliff's Kitty
in *No Telephone to Heaven* visits Bedford-Stuyvesant to buy the ingredients needed to cook Jamaican dishes, and there she can speak in
her own language without playing British and white like her husband Boy. Barbadians moved in to take over the rundown Brooklyn
brownstones abandoned by Jewish and other white ethnicities, and
Brooklyn became the only place, perhaps, where they could own a
home, as illustrated by the Association of Bajan Homeowners in
Marshall's *Brown Girl, Brownstones.*

London, the motherland centre that recruited men to join the
British Armed Forces and later provided jobs for the reconstruction
of the country, has been variously viewed as imperial power, colonial ruler, refuge for dissidents, center of knowledge and wealth.

The best students in the West Indies competed for scholarships to study in England; Caribbean writers went to London and eventually found publishers and an audience; thousands of skilled and unskilled workers answered the call to come to England and work for the London Transport (the first major employer and recruiter of black workers), the British Hotels and Restaurants Association, and the National Health Service as underground station sweepers, pourers of tea in railway cafeteria stations, trainee bus conductors, trainee nurses, and hotel maids, among other jobs. Riley's Adella in *Waiting in the Twilight*, who had been a dressmaker in Kingston, joins her husband in London, where he works in the bus system, and is immediately employed in a garment factory. However, there were very few warning signs that the British only wanted their labor and were not so willing to allow them to share their lives with them. For example, Adella's two youngest daughters were born in England and speak white English. However, when the police come to investigate a mugging, her daughter, Carol, is treated as a resident of England who seems to know a lot about citizen rights but is still looked down on as a black foreigner. Riley's Hyacinth in *The Unbelonging* receives shelter and schooling from Social Services once she becomes a ward of the state after being abused by her father, but she still gets the leftovers and the badmouthing of administrators and foster caretakers. After several major revolts in 1958, the Race Relations Act established a Commission for Racial Equality. Following revolts in 1981 in Brixton and South London, institutional government-funded spaces were provided for media workers such as those of Sankofa Film/Video Collective and Black Audio Collective who secured spots on TV and undertook independent filmmaking projects to enhance the image of black people in Britain. Small presses such as London's The Women's Press were crucial in disseminating the poetry, testimonies, and fiction of black women in England. The centre opened these spaces to assuage the isolation, frustration, and oppression felt, especially during the Thatcher years, by immigrants and their British-born offspring who were still living on the margins of society.

Charlotte Sturgess describes Dionne Brand's writing as distanced "from a unified linear history," which creates "a fundamental migrancy: a shifting of subject positions and of voice, and a crumbling of texture as narrative deals with erasure" (203). Brand's *In*

Another Place, Not Here introduces two women who seemed to be positioned on opposite sides of society. Using a style characterized by a fragmented storyline and confused narrative voices, Brand presents the lives of Elizete and Verlia through first and third person narrators whose realities are always filtrated through biased visions of the world they live in. Elizete, abandoned as a baby and passed around from woman to woman, is left stranded as an adult. A man who picks her up further brutalizes her, while calling her his wife. She barely knows how to read or write, works as a cane cutter for meager wages, and the countryside is the only world she knows. Verlia, on the other hand, left her unnamed island at seventeen with a good education that she later enhanced in the metropole, was exposed to social organizations concerned with the exploitation of workers, and decided to dedicate herself to establish a better society wherever she lived. Both women meet on the island when Verlia goes back home to organize the sugar cane workers and, in a short time, become lovers. Both undergo radical changes in their lives and travel to Grenada to join Maurice Bishop's New Jewel Movement. They never meet again: Elizete remains in Toronto as a "homeless, countryless, landless, nameless" woman (Brand, 48), and Verlia plunges to her death after the U.S. invasion of Grenada.

Elizete is the first character this study addresses who does not have a plan to migrate. At this point in her life, left alone after Verlia leaves and having overcome battered woman syndrome, she knows she does not want to remain on an island where she has no family or friends (as Isaiah's, her husband, property, no one dared to approach her), and the only work she can get is in the cane fields. She decides to travel to Toronto as a way of linking with Verlia's past, the one that made her such a strong and caring woman. By walking the same streets as Verlia and getting close to Abena, Verlia's long-time friend, Elizete believes she can construct a new life in which she can retain some remnants of her friend and lover. But Elizete has nowhere to go and she knows no one, except the names of Abena and Verlia's aunt and uncle. Time becomes so relative and fragmented that a clear notion never arises of how long Elizete has been in Toronto nor how long it took her to at last contact Abena. For Elizete, there is no home-building because she never intends to secure a home here. She has shared rooms with women with transitory names—

used so as not to be tracked by immigration—who work in sweatshops and any job that does not require "papers." In these circumstances, ethnicity does not matter: West Indians, Haitians, Hispanics share the poor wages equally, the exploitation, the insults, and the fear that someone will turn them in and they will be deported. Furthermore, this defensive behavior only breeds further suspicion among themselves.

> Suspicion could make people disappear from a room without a word or a trace. It could empty a building, crush it or melt it like a secret bomb. It seeped into a perfectly sane and friendly house where at first everybody thought that they were friends and in it together, giving tips on jobs and cheap clothes and then hardly with a word spoken one day because things were going too well, suspicion would seduce the doorway. (58)

Jocelyn is the only one woman Elizete lives with that she knows by name, and she shares with her the same island of origin. They tell each other of the hardships they face both at home and in the metropole—the fascination and danger of the city, and the remembrance of food, hissing, songs, and rum drinking. How long this friendship lasts—could be weeks or months—and why Elizete moves on again in search of Abena on the way to the sea that will remind her of a familiar place she does not want to return to is never clear in the narrator's mind.

There is no community even among Third World people because, instead of binding them, illegality makes them suspicious of one another. Verlia's relatives were able to establish a community with a church as its center, but Verlia rejected this enclosure and moved on. Elizete follows the same pattern by moving on every time she gets too comfortable, too familiar in a new place. Staying too long at a job means eventually being tracked by the police; trusting someone can lead to disappointment and heartbreak. Every time Elizete is abused, raped, insulted, and threatened, she moves on because there are no possessions, no dear remembrances, and no one will miss her because no one really knows her. Everything in Toronto strikes her as unrelated snapshots, much like her rides on trains where the outside world seems to move faster than her eye can behold it. The only place where she feels "protected" is in public spaces such as shopping malls. Enclosed spaces come to represent the city with their constantly moving crowds, indifference to individuals, ignorance of the different rows of stores, shops, cafeterias, occupied spaces, bright lights everywhere, abundance of all kinds of consumer goods useful or disposable. The streets are less familiar and more dangerous because people notice her difference and might call the authorities to question her right to be in the country. Elizete learns that the only way to survive is to move constantly; if someone harms her, she will defend herself or accept the abuse knowing she has no legal protection. She accepts the most menial jobs possible to remain faceless, almost invisible, and always replaceable.

When Abena tells her "'Go home, this is not a place for us.'" (109), it is very difficult for Elizete to explain why she has no home, no place where life would be better than in this hostile country. Even when she lived on the island, she continuously ran away from Isaiah without really knowing where to go, but "I suppose I didn't have nowhere in mind except not here" (9). Yet, Elizete does recall certain moments from back home like those she briefly shared with Jocelyn, especially rum drinking that warmed and numbed her tired body and "imagining another place" (51). The only person she remembers from the island is Verlia, who showed her that she could stop being an abused woman and a cane cutter all her life. She does yearn for the warmth of her island of origin and walks the streets always in search of the "smell of the sea" (53). Despite these comforting thoughts, Elizete has erased her past life and is willing to stand anything just as long as she feels unbound in this vastness of space.

Verlia's story is a different one. She arrived in Toronto at seventeen and lived there for fifteen years, but "she only felt things as someone watching but not living" (94). Her decision to leave was prompted by her loss of memory: she no longer remembered where she had come from. Canada had never been home, and place-making meant for her labor organizing for transient Third World peoples she would usually never meet again. For her, home-building means establishing a close relationship with Abena, the woman with whom she shared ideology, organizing strategies, and social commitment. But it is "not enough." She needs a sense of belonging to a community; for Verlia only a revolution would give her a combination of home-building and place-making based on a common goal.

However, this was not the situation when Verlia first arrived in Toronto. Like Elizete many years later, she wanted to leave behind the island that meant fixity, where a young woman had no choices, where change seemed impossible. Toronto meant freedom of movement, choices in constructing one's life, the possibility of meeting people from other places with new ideas: "any city from the earth-bound stillness of her own small town, any city" (159). She was not bothered by people's seeming animosity or indifference; she embraced city noises, especially the constant movement of many cars. She rejects all attempts at home-building, and this is why she moves out of her relatives' neighborhood as soon as she can and goes in search of the "Movement," which means coming into contact with all organizations and peoples who advocated the solidarity of black people and their resistance in the heart of the empire. When she is able to rent her own room, she keeps it as bare as possible, she wants no attachments to things, people, or her own past: "No photographs, no sentiment, no memory" (156). The only pictures she wants around her belong to the present and are linked to revolutionary movements. Her comrades will become family ("The cell has been her life. Holding her together like family, it's the only family she can bear" 192), but as they leave Canada to join other movements or redefine their causes in the metropole, they will move away and she ends up alone. Abena is her friend and lover, but she cannot fill the void in Verlia's life caused by her severing all ties to everyone from her Caribbean past. She will leave behind everything and everyone familiar, join the Movement, become one of its most militant members, lose patience with what she considers to be the slowness of groups to act, and join a small cell that believes in armed revolution. When this cell is dismembered, she has nothing to give meaning to her existence except the "small work" (helping black people get health cards, rides to Buffalo, ID cards, food vouchers, livable rooms, menial jobs) she does with Abena seven days a week. Work becomes family and belonging.

Verlia, the woman who at seventeen had constructed a new life filled with possibilities and totally unattached to a burdensome past, now finds herself remembering and missing the great-tasting fruits and beautiful flora of home. "She was walking from work, leaning against a late November rain when she missed tamarinds, sour and stingy, and then she missed—bright bright, pooled and mountainous pink or yellow at the side of a road—branches of a poui tree hanging over" (193). This happens when Verlia's political group is scattered, when even working long hours every day does not fulfill her yearning to "change the world," when she stops recognizing the places, incidents, and things that were once meaningful to her in the metropole. To fill this void of not having a place in the city she tried to transform and claim as a new space for black people, she now clings to any remembrance of her distant island past, much like Elizete, her nostalgic memories focus on the warmth, taste, and colors of nature; people remain erased from her memories of home. Returning to the island, working with the cane cutters, and later joining the New Jewel Movement in Grenada give Verlia a new definition of home that transforms the stillness she so despised in her people into the valor, courage, and fortitude of Caribbean people from various islands working together to create a new society. In the end, Elizete and Verlia follow different paths that converge in their memories of place, and as a result, roots and routes become two sides of the same coin: "roots signifying identity based on stable cores and continuities; routes suggesting identity based on travel, change, and disruption" (Friedman, 153).

While New York seems simply overwhelming to most of the women characters in hispanophone Caribbean novels—Esmeralda Santiago's Negi, Monín, and América, Julia Alvarez's Yolanda, the "girls" (sisters), and Sarita, and Loida Maritza Pérez's Rebecca—to Brand's Verlia and Jamaica Kincaid's Lucy, moving to the metropole is their one chance to leave a static life behind. They welcome and rejoice in the vastness, confusion, noise, lights, multitudes, and unfamiliarity of the big city. No matter how they are looked at by the white majority, Verlia and Lucy are content to be part of the anonymous people who walk the streets and go virtually unnoticed. But while Verlia is seeking a broader solidarity with black people, Lucy only deals with the white world, the one she aims to enter someday.

New York, or the unnamed city where Lucy arrives one very cold day in January, is described in very general and unastonishing terms:

"there were lights everywhere.... someone would single out to me a famous building, an important street, a park, a bridge that when built was thought to be a spectacle" (3). These thoughts come from an eighteen-year-old who has never left her small island but who had read about places like New York and had imagined what they would look like in real life. Lucy feels disappointed that the view does not conform to her expectations: "Now that I saw these places, they looked ordinary, dirty, worn down by so many people entering and leaving them in real life..." (4). However, she is impressed by the cold and the absence of colors everywhere she looks. This first-person narrative is written as the intimate diary of a young woman discovering a larger world and finding a place for her new self in it, and traces Lucy's life from her arrival in the United States to work as an au pair and to go to night school to study nursing to one year later, when she becomes an independent woman. In that year, she learns to love and despise her employers, blur her mother's impending presence in her life, quit school, take up photography, discover how to use her body to satisfy her sexual needs, and construct a new self that fits in her new homeland.

In the same way that Verlia wants to keep her room as bare as possible with nothing to remind her of her past, Lucy embraces the room provided by her employers because of its barrenness and anonymity: a bed, a dresser, a radio, and a record-player. She has no pictures to put up except those she later takes of moving and unknown people in the city. The unopened letters sent by a mother who does not allow her to simply drift into oblivion once she is away from her are the only reminders of home. Even if Esmeralda Santiago's América in *América's Dream* does not make her maid's room a replica of Puerto Rico, she is able to stand the strangeness of the place and the persistent cold weather by recalling her family back home through snapshots and phone calls. Lucy might dislike the persistence of winter with its cold weather, bare trees, and shut houses, but she accepts this discomfort because it is the best way of distancing herself from her island of origin. To transform herself into a person used to changing seasons is the first step toward constructing her new self.

Lucy only associates with her employers, Lewis and Mariah, and their friends—she goes out with Hugh, Mariah's best friend's brother, all very white people. When she starts discovering her new surroundings, she meets Peggy, an Irish American, who will become her best friend and, later, her roommate. Her new friends and the men she sleeps with share no common cultural traits, yet race never seems an obstacle for Lucy to feel closer to these people than to her island family. In the same way that Maryse Condé's Reynalda in *Desirada* rejects any reminder of her island once she settles in Paris, Lucy wants to be a woman from nowhere, free to choose who she is and what she wants to do with her life. She wants to build a new home made up of pieces that she picks up from the people she meets: the love and friendship Mariah feels for strangers such as herself, Lewis's unfunny games, Peggy's indifference to knowledge and enjoyment of anything intellectually unchallenging, and her lovers' intensity in love-making without any commitments. This new home she now shares with Peggy holds absolutely nothing to remind her of the island home, which is no longer her past because her year with Mariah, Lewis, and the girls is the only past she wishes to recall: "Your past is the person you no longer are, the situations you are no longer in" (137).

Lucy's rejection of her island past is a concerted effort. She will stop writing to the people back home who knew and loved her; in time they will also stop writing. She will not open her mother's letters because she feels that her mother's power over her leaks through the words she uses to warn her of city dangers, scold her for not following her orders, and complain of her neglect. She learns of her father's death, included in one of her mother's unopened letters from a month before, when Mariah receives a call from Lucy's mother to relay this information to her daughter. While Mariah and Maude, the maid, urge Lucy to visit home and spend some days with her grieving mother, Lucy chooses to write her mother and send her money almost as if buying her off because she sees her as an emotional manipulator. The one word that Lucy dreads is "return," which to her means impairment and fixity. Her fear of having to go back makes her write a long letter to her mother accusing her of wasting her life with a man who did not deserve her and then sending her all her savings for a new apartment. Lucy has set her mind on the present, and her focus only includes the immediacy of her surroundings. There are no long-range plans except never to look back not even to the past she has created and is reminded of by the gifts she received from Mariah before leaving her job: a desk, a rug, a notebook.

Even if Lucy's erasure of island memories seems to be succeeding, she can only construct this new world on the basis of comparisons with her known childhood and adolescence: "But almost everything I did now was something I had never done before, and so the new was no longer thrilling to me unless it reminded me of the past" (31-32). Again, all her memories are tied to her mother, and she can only think of all the good times they shared. The island is never recalled as a place of people gathering and sharing; that "old home" is full of childhood memories that she also intends to erase so that no matter how bad things might be in this new location, returning can never be an option for her. She will make it in this city, which she describes as enclosed spaces such as a room, a record shop, or a museum, even if she does not renew her one-year contract with Mariah and needs a job to pay the rent on the apartment she shares with Peggy. Notwithstanding, she decides to make it on her own, erase the place of origin, and write herself a new life.

Marshall's Silla also came from an island village to New York without her mother, but she was received by a Bajan community that helped her to get settled by finding her a place to stay and a job. Although Silla has made up her mind to never return to Barbados, which, much like Brand's Elizete, to her means poverty, hunger, and exploitation, she has no plans like Lucy's to reconstruct herself as a faceless and nationless person in the centre. Silla becomes a proud member of the Bajan community, and in spite of having a husband, Deighton, who does not share her goals of making the United States her home, she will "work night and day to buy house; rent out every room, overcharge if necessary; sacrifice every penny to maintain property; keep strict vigilance on the children so they will enter high-paying professions" (Washington, 312). Silla will clean homes, work in factories—during the war years in ammunition factories—bake delicacies to sell in the neighborhood, divide and re-divide spaces in the brownstone to have more tenants. If anyone gets in her way, she pushes them aside because her goal is to build a different future for her and her family. She insists on being an active participant of this community that has become her new home.

Although Selina is the protagonist of *Brown Girl, Brownstones*, the ten-year-old who will grow into a rebellious adolescent, the story intertwines with Silla's, her mother. Selina, a first-generation "American" with Barbadian-born parents, enjoys a normal childhood with two working parents and an older sister with whom she has the expected rivalry because of the age gap. While the mother is the authority figure, the father, Deighton, is the one who thinks big, studies several quick careers (mechanic, radio repairer, accountant, trumpet player) to make it in the centre, and constructs an imaginary Barbados. Selina grows up in a household where Silla is constantly deflating Deighton's dreams, but after the factory accident, he becomes a follower of a religious sect and neglects his family. He will die on his way to Barbados after being deported, and Silla will continue to push Selina to study and make a better life for herself. At the end of the novel, Selina embarks on a voyage to recover her origins, while Silla remains in Brooklyn, owner of her own brownstone and surrounded by tenants and the Bajan community.

Silla represents the Bajan spirit overseas in her determination to buy a house and make the United States her home. She follows the code of the "American Dream" to work very hard, take whatever and as many jobs as are available, be frugal, save money, and never relinquish your goals. She and her community, although at the margin, will move closer to the centre by imitating the American way of life, including separating themselves from black Americans who they quickly understand occupy the lowest level of U.S. society: "This snapshot of black American poverty reflects precisely what the black immigrant population wishes to avoid" (Denniston, 20). Silla will encourage her daughters to associate with good-standing members of the Bajan community and occupy spaces closer to the centre, which for Selina would be a dance company and college-oriented high schools. Meanwhile Silla feels contented to stay on the margin and continue to clean houses and, work at dangerous jobs, such as munitions, as long as she can secure a home for her family. Homebuilding for her is not having to lease and be at the mercy of the proprietor; "'Taking in' lodgers was yet another unconventional economic activity of West Indians in New York. For them taking in lodgers was often a business, one which brought a steady flow of income" (Holder, 65).

The only decoration Silla brings to the brownstone are family photos, not from the island but of the only past she wishes to remember, her first years in New York—getting acquainted with the strangeness of the metropole, feeling protected because she had a place in the Bajan community, meeting Deighton, and contemplating the possibility of making it in the here and now. Left in the distant past are her family back home, the memory of working in the cane fields, selling fruits early in the morning, and living in abject poverty. This island home has been erased, and similar to Lucy's refusal to open her mother's letters, Silla has severed all ties and sent no remittances. Deighton invests a lot of effort in establishing his urban roots in Bridgetown, the island's capital, and feels superior because he has inherited property in Barbados and so can return there as a wealthy man even if he has no money to build a house. However, Silla sees New York as her permanent home. The brownstone has no traces of her island of origin except in the smells of Bajan cooking coming from the room of Suggie, a tenant, and Silla's kitchens. Everything else in the house is either leftover from the previous white owners or part of the American consumer goods that Deighton buys.

Since Silla had nothing to bring with her to the new location, and Deighton had gone to Cuba first before entering the United States without a work permit, place-making must compensate for the lack of mementos from the island. The only cultural link to the island are Selina's silver bangles, a reminder that she is a Barbadian woman, which, to this American-born adolescent, meant that you had

> Worn those ugly silver bangles since you were born practically. Religiously went to the hairdresser every two weeks. Belonged to the Episcopal Church, a Negro sorority and of course the Association. That you were already looking around for a nice, ambitious West Indian boy, lighter than you preferably, whose life you could order. Dreaming already of the wedding that would end all weddings and settling down to the house, the car, the two clean well-behaved children. And, of course, you were still a virgin. (*Brown*, 234)

A diasporic version of Barbados will be recreated in the tightly knit Bajan community in Brooklyn. The church, the rituals (weddings,

funerals), Bajan talking, cooking, and neighborhood gossip will be
their bond to the selected memories of their island past. To this
they will add the spirit of enterprise—beginning with the purchase
of a house followed by the establishment of an enclave economy
with credit unions, and political involvement in political affairs—
that will place them closer to the centre, where real achievement is
measured. Despite extolling pride in their nationality and race, the
members of the Association of Bajan Homeowners are always thinking white, meaning they look down on anyone inside their community who does not work hard, invest their money, and have commodities to show for their effort. They also look down on black
Americans who they consider non-achievers stigmatized by slavery
and segregation. Dorothy Hamer Denniston, in her analysis of *Brown
Girl, Brownstones*, points out the particularities of Bajans in New York:
"They, like other immigrants, chose to leave their homelands to escape poverty and exploitation. But, unlike other immigrants, they
also left their native land to escape the historical effects of slavery
and colonialism" (10). Even if these Barbadians are treated with the
same contempt by white employers, they are convinced of their difference and they will teach their children to "imitate the Jew and
disregard the black."

Silla and the other women in the community who were poor in
Barbados and came to the United States in the 1930s,

> Each morning they took the train to Flatbush and Sheepshead
> Bay to scrub floors. The lucky ones had their steady madams
> while the others wandered those neat blocks or waited on
> corners–each with her apron and working shoes in a bag under
> her arm until someone offered her a day's work. Sometimes the
> white children on their way to school laughed at their blackness
> and shouted "nigger," but the Barbadian women sucked their
> teeth, dismissing them. Their only thought was of the "few raw-
> mout' pennies" at the end of the day which would eventually
> "buy house." (*Brown*, 11)

Back on the island there was nothing to look forward to and, like
Brand's Elizete, Silla was once part of the cane fields' work ma-
chine—there was no other space for her. In the city she has mobility; she can start earning better wages cleaning houses than she ever

dreamed of. Compared to the work she had done since childhood back home, these tasks are bearable. In time, she finds other jobs that allow her to work more hours and bring in more money. It is also in the city that she meets Deighton, an educated young man from Bridgetown, someone she would probably never have met in the stratified Barbadian society. Silla believes that home is constructed through work, dedication, and the support of the family. Her daughters benefit from her effort while her husband continually undercuts every step she takes to achieve her goals. Silla, then, relies on the Bajan community, which is her substitute home, while she attempts to achieve total integration into U.S. society. Silla has successfully erased her memories of the island once she sells Deighton's land and he is deported. That her daughter plans to go back to Barbados at the end of the novel removes another member of her immediate family. Silla continues to work, now as a nurse, fixes her house, and always has enough rooms to let in her reconstructed home.

Selina, born in the United States, has no need for home-building or place-making because by the age of ten, home is her house and neighborhood. The labyrinthian structure of the house allows her to live various cultural spaces simultaneously. Sugee's room is full of smells and tastes that come from the same island as her silver bangles; in Miss Mary's room she hears about the old order of things when whites were the owners of everything; in Ina's room she sees her own life in a few years as her older sister dresses up, puts on make-up, and talks big; on her father's terrace she listens to stories about the wonderful island they all came from and where he soon plans to return with all his family; in the kitchen she listens to her mother's and her women friends' adult conversations on how hard they work, the sacrifices they make, and how their spirits continue to be intact. Outside, Selina holds conversations with Miss Thompson, the black American who has a nearby beauty salon, and she explores neighborhood limits and confides in her best friend, Beryl. Interestingly, she never severs her ties to these people, as she becomes an adolescent, although she distances herself more and more from her mother. At fifteen, Selina, Beryl, and other friends are daughters of Barbadian parents in name only, because their cultural interests are American. They decorate their rooms in the latest American style; they

talk about the gifts they will receive when they graduate from high
school (trips or cars) and the careers they will study in college. Although Silla urges her daughter to go to college and become a professional, Selina has no special interest in studying for what are the
acceptable careers for the daughters of Barbadian parents: teacher,
social worker, or doctor.

Selina feels culturally coerced by her parents and the neighborhood to become what they have defined as an American of Barbadian ancestry. They want her to follow the traditions from home—
obedience and respect to parents and elders, discipline at school,
devotion to church—and at the same time, integrate herself into the
centre by going to the right colleges and studying for the right careers that will assure her professional success. They conceive of the
centre as a select space in which achievers and hard workers are
admitted, where race, ethnicity, and gender can be blurred. This
imaginary centre contradicts the closely knit ethnic enclave Selina
and her family live in. When Selina tries to be part of the centre by
joining the Modern Dance Club presided over by Rachel Fine from
Flatbush, she feels uneasy about being the only black woman in the
group. After a while, Selina forgets about the race marker and comes
to believe that she can be a part of the group because of her dancing
ability and not because she is black or white, Barbadian or black
American. However, reality slaps her in the face when she goes to a
party at another dancer's home. The presumption that she could
belong anywhere because of her intelligence and dancing talent results in a wake-up call much like the one her father received when
he assumed he could get a high-paying accountant's job in a big
Manhattan firm. The erasure of race that young women such as
Rachel and Margaret experience because of their link to dance disappears when Margaret's mother finds out that Selina's parents are
from the West Indies and starts ranting on reliability and trustwor-
thiness of black maids not from the United States. Selina, taken by
surprise, reacts by running out and going back to Brooklyn.

> Why couldn't the woman *see*, she wondered—even as she
> drowned—that she was simply a girl of twenty with a slender
> body and slight breasts and no power with words, who loved
> spring and then the sere leaves falling and dim, old houses, who
> had tried, foolishly perhaps, to reach beyond herself? But when

she looked up and saw her reflection in those pale eyes, she knew that the woman saw one thing above all else. Those eyes were a well-lighted mirror in which, for the first time, Selina truly saw—with a sharp and shattering clarity—the full meaning of her black skin. (289)

These experiences, unusual in Selina's adolescence because of enclave protection, become more frequent as she moves into the outer world that her family and community have told her she can also excel in. Instead of claiming her ethnic enclave as home, Selina, much like the narrator in Gisèle Pineau's *Exile According to Julia*, claims her parents' and grandparents' homeland as her own. Both young women travel—to Barbados in Selina's case and to Guadeloupe in the case of Julia's granddaughter—as a way to discover who they really are after being been born and raised and lived and studied in the metropole without feeling American or French. However, Selina feels little nostalgia for a place she knows only through her father's grandiose stories and her mother's painful memories. After living all her life in a protective and oppressive U.S.-Bajan community, she must go to their place of origin to discover what these people, especially Silla, were like before coming to the United States and becoming, what she sees as, harsh, insensitive, and materialistic people.

Michelle Cliff's *No Telephone to Heaven* tells the story, in various flashbacks, of Clare Savage, from the time she emigrates to the United States with her family at the age of fourteen to her return to Jamaica and the guerrilla movement she becomes part of. In this fragmented story, other lives cross Clare's life that have lasting influences on her future choices to leave the United States, move to England to study, travel throughout Europe, and decide to return to her grandmother's land and establish a commune where race and class become subjugated to engagement in political activity. One of these lives is Kitty's, Clare's mother, who with her husband Boy and her two daughters flies from Montego Bay to Miami and then travels by car to New York, where they settle and pretend to be white. While Boy lays claim to an ancestry of white plantation owners in Jamaica, Kitty goes in search of people, things, and places that remind her of home. While Boy's project becomes assimilation, Kitty becomes more and more isolated until, to preserve her sanity, she decides to go back to Jamaica even if it means leaving her husband and oldest daughter in the United States.

Kasinitz, in his studies on Caribbean migration, points out that "Once people are displaced from jobs, high unemployment and limited options in these small countries make emigration often the only viable option even for members of the middle class" (29), which is precisely the case of the Savage family. Kitty and Boy belong to the Jamaican middle class, with their life of leisure, investments, fenced houses, and money to travel inside and outside the island. In 1960, Kitty saw no reason to move away from Jamaica, even though they were embarked on the Federation Project that in 1962 would result in independence. Their class was never in danger of losing their privileges, quite the opposite, in fact, since the people involved in the forging of the new government were from the same class. Kitty's strongest link to Jamaica is her mother and her land; when her mother dies, Boy convinces her to get away from painful memories and start a new life in the United States.

Kitty knows she has made a mistake in giving in to her husband's wishes when they start driving north from Miami through racially segregated regions. She notices signs calling for "lynching" next to the abandoned NAACP office. Boy keeps his family in the car while making arrangements to stay at a motel and insists on fewer stops so they can get to New York faster. Boy also lies to hide any trace of blackness in his family. Kitty is constantly aware of this new country and compares it to Jamaica in its poverty, "the mauger children at the roadside," "the rundown outskirts of towns," "the signs advising people of their limits" (59). New York becomes her only hope to once again link to family because they will stay with her cousins who have lived there many years. But the stories she hears from them confirms Kitty's worst fears about living in the metropole. They have a house in Queens and secure jobs as maid and chauffeur in a Long Island residence; that is all they can expect to achieve. They tell about how they are treated differently both by the blacks and whites in America, and they advise them to pass for white so they can partly avoid these inconveniences that can adversely affect their daily lives in this new place. While Boy commits himself to following their advice, Kitty is afraid there is no place for her in this country, not even in New York. After taking an apartment in an Italian neighborhood in Brooklyn, the Savages continue to visit their cousins to relish the "Jamaican evenings" "of rice and peas and curry chicken and fast games of dominoes and playing mento on electric guitars and marimbas and congas and claves" (62).

Kitty's home-building consists of displaying and using the few things they brought with them from Jamaica and cooking familiar dishes. Since Boy insists in living in a place that has no connections with home, her place-making is limited to visits to her cousins and gatherings with other West Indians who worked all day, saved as much money as they could, and planned to buy or build a house back home. When Boy decides that this link is a threat to his passing for white, he never calls on the cousins again nor asks them to visit them. Kitty, who is still tied to the traditional role of wife, looks for other ways to keep Jamaica alive in the cold of New York, which takes her to Bedford-Stuyeysant and its West Indian community, "where in between the high-priced ghetto-specific chain stores she discovered shops from *home*, as if they had been airlifted intact" (64–65). She spends long hours each week there buying the special ingredients for cooking her favorite dishes, speaking Creole, and talking about events back home. However, Boy comes to disapprove of her cooking because the Italian neighbors complain about the strong strange smells coming from their kitchen. Now Kitty has nothing to link her to Jamaica, since her husband has erased the island from his life and is becoming a white American. Her daily life becomes even more limited and meaningless:

> ...she would labor forever as Mrs. White, walking the streets of Brooklyn on her lunch hours, visiting her home away from home in secret, traveling each evening back to the small apartment where she cooked dinner for the girls, waiting for Boy to reappear, now he had traded his paints for the camaraderie he found in the bar. She, watching the infernal television, thinking it would take her mind off her troubles, suffering as she was from a weariness which did not promise to leave her, wishing her life away, as the days got shorter.... (80–81)

Somehow Kitty again finds a connection with her homeland when she wanders through an old Episcopalian cemetery in Brooklyn and reads the words on an ancient gravestone: Marcus, born in Jamaica, faithful servant, a slave to some family who died in 1702 (63). Similar to the way Veronica in Maryse Condé's *Heremakhonon* was never able to erase the memory of the African man sweeping the streets of Paris, Kitty feels trapped in this location and fears her destiny is to end up in an old foreign cemetery never remembered by the family back home.

In spite of the education and skills that a Jamaican woman has, her credentials are frequently erased and she is only seen as maid or nanny when she arrives in New York. When Kitty goes for a job interview at a bank, as on many previous occasions, her "musical voice" and "golden skin" (78) become markers of difference and result in her not being hired. The only job she can secure is office work—meaning anything the boss asks her to do—in a laundry. The owner thinks she is a very agreeable person but will always keep her in the same position; the other workers think she is a kind of supervisor so they do not speak to her. There is nothing challenging about this job, and it offers no opportunity to make friends. Once, on the way home, she stopped at a shop with Spanish signs and was pleasantly surprised at how the owner, a Puerto Rican woman, recreated her homeland in this place away from home, something impossible for her while she lives with a husband resolved on assimilating to a culture that she considered racist from the moment she arrived in Miami. Not being able to express her feelings in her workplace or to her family, and being forced to relinquish her only outlet—her visits to "Bed-Stuy"—lead Kitty to find creative ways to vent her anger. When she helps in the laundry packing section, she writes her own messages on the notes the owner's wife includes with the bags of clean clothes: "Ever try cleansing your mind of hatred?" "We can clean your clothes but not your heart," "America is cruel. Consider kindness for a change," "White people can be black-hearted," "Marcus Garvey was Right." When Kitty cannot even take responsibility for her acts—Mr. White fires two other women and does not believe Kitty's confession—she quits and, without prior consultation, informs Boy of her decision to go back home with her youngest daughter. She had been cut off from her roots when, after her mother's unexpected death, she reluctantly agreed to move to the United States. She was determined not to allow U.S. society to turn her into what she was not; she needed to belong somewhere and her island was still there; her mother's grave was there, her relatives and friends were there. There is little nostalgia for Kitty in this decision because she wants to recover the Jamaica she left just a few months before. Not enough time has passed to distort her memory of her island; she goes back as if she had a troublesome summer vacation and needs to connect again with her land and her people.

Clare Savage's experience as an adolescent in the schools of New York, where she is put behind a year regardless of how solid and superior her education had been in Jamaica ("proficient in Latin and French, was beginning Greek, and had studied algebra and geometry since she was ten...had read many of the classics: Dickens, Shakespeare, Milton." 97) and called white chocolate instead of being accepted as white, makes her decide, after graduation, to go to London to study. Since her father blurs all memories of Jamaica, Clare claims England as her motherland: "This was the mother-country. The country by whose grace her people existed in the first place. Her place could be here" (109). In this new metropole that she feels she belongs in, Clare plays at being white just as her father has done in New York. She settles in Notting Hill, where mostly foreign students find acceptable inexpensive housing, and keeps to herself so that no one notices "her half-American, half-Jamaican intonation" (112). She fills her days with long walks, visits to museums and libraries, and going to see films, all activities that do not require company. Her island-cleansing goes a step further when she decides to enroll in the Classical Program of the University of London "brushing aside a suggestion that she register at the School of Oriental and African Studies" (117), which, of course, the university advisors thought more suited for someone coming from Jamaica with a British passport. As a way of thanking her uncle who pays for her studies and stay in London, Clare accepts an invitation to spend a brief vacation in Kingston. After attending several parties and dinners with acquaintances from her own class, Clare is sure she does not want to live in this "miserable place" (120). She goes back to London convinced that this is the place she wants to call home.

Clare does see the others—even if she does not recognize herself in the mirror—and the margins they inhabit: "the dark women in saris cleaning the toilets at Heathrow" (109), "the colored buyers, native dress partly hidden by shabby winter coats," "another woman, tribal scars cutting diagonally across her cheeks" (112). She does not communicate or attempt to establish any kind of affinity with them. Instead she befriends a British young woman, Liz, who shares the same interests in archeology, medieval architecture, and Greek and Roman mythology. Because Clare looks white, coming from Jamaica seems simply accidental to the others in the group who visit Gravesend, "a town at the mouth of the Thames" (134). Clare can continue being just a very intelligent student who seems to fit perfectly into metropolitan life. It is only some months later, when the right-wing National Front marches through the streets of London chanting "Kaffirs! Niggers! Wogs! Pakis! Get out," and displays a banner stating "Keep Britain White," that Clare realizes that she cannot simply choose a place to belong to. England is not a motherland if you are not of British stock. Her father wanted so much to assimilate to the U.S. centre that he constructed his own version of being white in Jamaica. He was accepted in some groups, but the centre—with its particular jobs, professions, wages, housing, and gathering places—was always reserved for white Americans. Clare comes to understand her position in British society but instead of trying to form alliances to oppose this resurgence of xenophobia, she flees London after admitting to Liz that she might look white but "'I am...by blood...the sort they [the National Front], and she, were ranting on about'" (139). Not really searching for anything in particular, Clare uses her uncle's money to travel throughout Europe until she feels ready to return to her mother's and grandmother's homeland. Having left at age fourteen, she returns after twenty years, to establish a utopian revolutionary project, where she invites people from all classes to work and live off the land while she and her friends become part-time guerrillas to destabilize the government. According to Meryl Schwartz, "Clare can not simply go home; rather she can only create a home by participating in the struggle to forge imagined communities of political allies" (294).

Unlike her mother, Kitty, Clare never wanted to return to Jamaica; her father had taught her that passing for white in the United States guaranteed her a better life. Although her personal experience told her otherwise, she blurred all memory of Jamaica including the mother who left her in her father's care. Living in London did not make her yearn for a place of her own, quite the contrary, it seemed that here she could be part of the big city without needing a national identity. When she at last understands that belonging some-where—the imaginary homeland—is essential to an understanding of self and charting a future, Clare returns to a Jamaica in turmoil, where the possibility of change is a reality. Similar to Verlia, who returned to the Caribbean she had once rejected, because there was a movement she could be part of to effect change, Clare returns to Jamaica to reclaim her identity and to forge a new society.

Zee Edgell's Pavana in *In Times Like These* also goes to London to study, but in her case, her stay is transitory and she is expected to return to her country where a good-paying job awaits her. She knows that she has a privileged condition in the United Kingdom because she is there to earn a degree in journalism, and the government scholarship covers tuition, books, room and board, and a monthly stipend. For some, the award means separating from family and traveling abroad for the first time; for others it is an opportunity to break away from a family that is very eager to see their daughters go to the metropole and come back as professionals. For Pavana, trav-eling away from the familiar becomes a very personal experience where she comes to see her own life and society in a wider context. According to Said, this is one of the great advantages of living in exile: "[you] look at situations as contingent, not as inevitable, look at them as a result of a series of historical choices made by men and women, as facts of society made by human beings, and not as natu-ral or god-given, therefore unchangeable, permanent, irreversible" (*Reader,* 378). Thus Pavana, who was accustomed to following family tradition and to accepting the elders' ideas and opinions on reli-gion, politics, and especially the expected behavior of women in Caribbean society, now questions and challenges imposed concepts. This is the positive side of living in exile; the negative side that can easily become an insurmountable obstacle is the treatment as other by the receiving country.

In Times Like These begins at the crucial moment when Pavana has to make a choice that could turn her very well-planned life around: she decides not to have an abortion, gives birth to twins, and as a consequence, does not return to Belize. She had gone to London to study and intended, in time, to return to her homeland and occupy a favored job. She now has to work while finishing her studies; she then accepts overseas employment in Africa from where she eventually returns with her children to Belize to fill a government post in politically troubled times. Nevertheless, when Pavana arrives in London at age twenty, she enters with a safety net: she has a scholarship, receives money from her parents, knows other Belizeans that are also studying here, lives in a community of foreign students, participates either socially or politically in associations and movements that deal with pressing issues both here and at home. Everyone in her group accepts their stay in the United Kingdom as a stage in their lives. They all see themselves as superior to the rest of the people back home and are totally assured that when they return, the best jobs will be reserved for them: "In the new year, Alex, Helga and, later, Moria would be returning to Belize, with Stoner following not long behind. They were all impatient to begin their careers, which, as most of their friends agreed over countless dinners, in a variety of pubs and at innumerable all-night parties, were bound to be brilliant" (3). It is in this borrowed space—the one used as place-making—that these Belizeans who talk constantly about home stray away from what is acceptable and expected of them back home. They dress in African clothing, plait their hair or cut it very short, decorate their rooms with posters of Fidel Castro and Che Guevara, and organize or attend all-night parties every weekend. They are very vocal on political matters such as the Guatemala-Belize conflict, establish and break relationships, have short– or long-term affairs, indulge in bi– or homosexual encounters, and dream of successful lives based on imaginary situations. While here, Pavana has an affair with Alex, the leader of the student group, without being reprimanded by family and friends. When she gets pregnant, unlike back home, here she can, if she so desires, go to a safe clinic and anonymously have an abortion. In this space, as seen earlier in Maryse Condé's women characters who are sent to Paris to study, women are not closely supervised, and the metropole offers spaces totally unknown back home.

As Caribbean students based in London, they do not, however, think of the thousands of West Indian immigrants who work in the lowest-paying jobs, live in rundown neighborhoods, are treated as the scum of the earth, and remain in England because nothing better awaits them back in Jamaica, Trinidad, Barbados, Guyana, or Belize. Who cleans the university, government offices, banks, and other public buildings? Who drives buses and conducts the trains these students take? Class demarcates difference among these Belizeans who seem not to feel any prejudice during their stay in London. From this position, Pavana can ignore the looks and comments of landlords, university and government officials, and the rest of the British who hold positions of authority or service. Interestingly enough, this white world does not exist in the novel. In Pavana's walks and rides across the city, London is presented as fascinating because of its diversity, although nothing specifically social is ever mentioned: "...she'd settle, like she did yesterday, for sitting in a café somewhere in the West End drinking cups of coffee, mesmerized by the fascinating variety of people in the London streets...there was an exciting world out there and she intended to try and become a part of it all" (99).

There are no economic advantages for Pavana in this city, except the opportunity to study and earn a degree. In this centre, she cannot afford the comforts she is used to back home. When she is shown her room, she is taken aback by the cramped space and bare and unwashed walls and floors. This special status in London quickly changes when she gets pregnant a year after she arrives. Pavana now has to separate herself from the community of Belizean students and find work to support herself while she deals with school and pregnancy. Low-paying jobs are always available, but when she finishes her degree, she knows, even if it is never expressed, that she can never find a job as a journalist in the centre. She then applies to development agencies—those international organizations that pay very little and care for marginal people. When she realizes that her job in "Project Child" cannot provide for her needs as a mother of twins, she applies to other overseas development agencies that offer better pay, even if it means moving to East Africa and finding a support group that includes Julian, a fellow Belizean. As a member of this agency, Pavana again holds a privileged position where she becomes the representative of the centre. After studying, living, and working abroad, Pavana decides to return to Belize when she is offered a position with the Ministry of Community Development. She has fulfilled her destiny of being sent abroad to study and returns to fill a high government position, even if it took her fifteen years to fulfill her commitment.

Belize is always present while Pavana is living in London, and news from home is immediate. However, when she disconnects herself from the Belizean student community and moves abroad, the homeland is frozen in 1967, when she left to study. Home becomes relevant one day in Africa when she is witnessing a refugee child's funeral rites and realizes "that in many ways she herself was a displaced person, her uprootedness disguised by the economic freedom to travel her education had bought" (18). When she decides to return to Belize after securing a good position, which included travel expenses and housing, she becomes nostalgic for the place of her childhood that she wants her children to know. But she stops and forces herself to recall the real Belize with its poverty and violence: "It was only in recent months that she had allowed herself to remember some of the horror, cruelty and sadness she had witnessed as a child on Kiskadee Avenue" (14). Even these memories do not prepare Pavana for the chaotic situation she will face in her country. She is not able to cope with the ever-present political game that she seems totally disconnected from. She has forgotten the conversations, debates, and crises the Belizean student community had during their stay in London. She is at a loss when Alex, the father of her children and now a leading politician, dies, and the country seems intent on recovery without a period of mourning. She can only hold herself together by redefining home not as a geographical location but as a series of memorable instances: life with her parents in Corozal, her children's love giving her a sense of belonging somewhere, the warm memories of being with Alex in London and with Julian in Africa. Pavana understands that these life remembrances can be transferred to another location; physical contact with Belize is not necessary in order to have a home. She never contemplates going back to London, a city fixed in her memory as a location to leave behind and never a place to live or make a living, but she does not reject the possibility of returning to East Africa, where she was always providing comfort and support to very needy people.

According to Isabel Carrera Suárez, Joan Riley's work "combines the recovery of a history (often re-writing it, against official versions) with the task of inscribing a specific group of people into literature: the West Indian community in Britain, and specifically its women" (290). In *The Unbelonging* and *Waiting in the Twilight*,

Riley presents two different women characters who migrate to England, one as a pre-adolescent and the other as an adult married woman, as examples of the thousands of women who made the same pilgrimage. Both enter London societies with ethnic enclaves and very strong undeclared prejudice and discrimination. British agencies respond to the needs of Hyacinth in *The Unbelonging* and Adella in *Waiting in the Twilight* by providing foster homes and schools when the former runs away from home to escape her father's constant abuse and by making government housing available when the latter loses her house to the council. Both women accept and depend on these provisions, but both also understand that the social workers and government employees are responding to laws they must follow and withhold any additional help or special care. These are reserved for authentic British citizens and not West Indians with British passports. Both novels record realities and present the lives of working-class Jamaican women who remain on the margins after living in the metropole most of their lives. In the case of Hyacinth, she is claimed by her father and has to leave her Aunt Joyce and her familiar neighborhood in Kingston to travel to strange and scary England to join a parent she barely knows. Clashes at home with her stepmother, at school with teachers and classmates, and beatings by her father result in her running away from home at fourteen to become a ward of the state. After completing her studies, she is awarded a scholarship that allows her to return to the Jamaica she barely remembers.

The only things that Hyacinth is permitted to bring with her to her father's house are the remembrances of the people she grew to love and the places, food, songs, and games she knew so well. All her dreams go back to Jamaica, whether she is asleep, daydreaming, or assessing her future. She enters a house already occupied with other people's pictures and objects where she has no room for home-building. The here and now consists of domestic work and going to school because it is compulsory. Neither her father nor Maureen, her stepmother, are interested in whether she is doing well at school, if she is getting good grades, making friends, or participating in other school activities. They believe that most of the time school interferes with the daily chores needed to care for father-husband and the male children, her stepbrothers. Hyacinth's worst failing is bedwetting, which means more washing and cleaning. For this she will be punished over and over again and taken to a doctor, only to receive more beatings for shaming her father by making his domestic problems public. Hyacinth is the only black girl in school, and she will be stigmatized as unintelligent, badly dressed, undisciplined, and different. No teacher or classmate will look at her as a person who is crying out for help. When, later on, a kind teacher enters her life, she will not confide in her because she has been taught to distrust all whites.

> "I am aware that you have a far from satisfactory home life....I would like you to feel that you can confide in me, if you need someone to talk to."
> Hyacinth wanted to die of shame. She looked everywhere but at the woman, feeling sick with embarrassment....
> "There is nothing to tell, Mrs. Maxwell,..." (50)

Since there is no environment for place-making, no support group exists for Hyacinth She has to wait until she is picked up by the police after a sexual attack by her father to find a room that she can treat as her own. The bed she sleeps in every night in the reception center becomes the first space she feels safe in. She slowly expands this area as home-building—a friendly shelter to return to, recovering her worth as a human being, while holding on to her place of origin. She has her own room in the foster home and, at eighteen, a room she has a key to in a hostel paid by Social Services. When she goes to Aston College, she can participate in place-making when she has a room she can make her own and has established a close friendship with Perlene, a fellow Jamaican student with whom she shares memories of the island, although frozen in a bygone era.

Instead of confiding in Perlene, Hyacinth erases her British past and constructs a new, albeit fictional, identity in which she lived most of her short life in Kingston, then traveled to the United States, and has been living in England for just a couple of years. In this illusion, she replaces her abusive father with an aunt who loves and provides for her. In effect, each friend talks about a different Jamaica: while Hyacinth elaborates on the harmony of living in Jamaica compared to the speed and violence of England, Perlene discusses the deterioration of the country under Michael Manley's

People's National party. While Hyacinth addresses Kingston as a special place to live in, Perlene points out that its streets are now a battle zone. However, upholding her imaginary Jamaica is of utmost importance for Hyacinth, since her goal in life has been to return to her island and forget the isolation, loneliness, mistreatment, and neglect she has suffered in England during seven critical years.

She survives the violence that surrounds her at every level—family, school, foster home, hostel, marginal neighborhoods, centre hostility—by trusting no one. She creates her own world where she feels protected from people in authority, such as her father, her schoolmates, or government agencies, who hate her and want to harm her. When rescued from the streets by the police at age fourteen, she is placed in a "reception centre" for prompt relocation. Instead, she spends months there until her case is reassigned. Once in a foster home, she is put under the supervision of a blatantly prejudiced woman who wants to evict her as soon as she arrives, and Hyacinth has to appeal personally to Social Services. Even though she has been promised a clean, safe, private room when she turns eighteen, she is moved to a hostel for young offenders in spite of never having committed any delinquent act.

Various discrepancies appear once Hyacinth begins to create a new life based on fantasy. While she fears anyone white and immediately grants them authority, she also rejects non-Caribbean blacks and assumes all the prejudices of white society:

> As she stood in line waiting to register, she couldn't help noticing how many black students there were. She supposed she ought to be glad that she no longer stood out, but she wasn't sure she liked the way they all bunched up together, and were so arrogant and rude to white people, nor the way they insisted on talking in that awful broken English so that the other students kept staring at them. They just seemed so ignorant, and she felt uncomfortable when several of them kept smiling encouragingly at her. She hoped none of them would approach her, hating the thought of being associated with them. (81)

At Keene Fields—the college at which she studies for her A– and O– level exams—Hyacinth encounters for the first time open hostility between ethnic groups. In school, blacks insult Indians by calling them Coolies, and Indians ignore blacks as intellectually inferior. In this tug-of-war, Hyacinth sides with the Indians, who are soft spoken, have the same interests—study hard to pass the qualifying exams—and are closer to whites phenotypically ("They were not white, but they had long hair, and their noses were straight, their lips nice and thin" 81.) Esmeralda Santiago's Negi in *Almost a Woman* also appropriates Indian ethnicity instead of Puerto Ricanness. In Negi's case, she cannot pass for white in the United States, but she can pretend to be an exotic Indian dancer instead of a non-glamorous racialized Puerto Rican. Hyacinth will also reject any link to Africa, a continent she considers uncivilized; Jamaica is the only homeland she recognizes. Having been exposed to a colonial education in Jamaica and to British hegemonic schooling in the United Kingdom, Hyacinth has internalized the prevalent standards of race. In spite of this, she never looks at England as home. Carrera Suárez points out that "For Hyacinth, despite her unconscious absorption of values, Britain is never home. She has not chosen to come, has been deeply unhappy there, and constantly dreams of finishing her education to return to Jamaica" (300).

When Hyacinth finally returns to Jamaica, thus reversing the usual voyage from island to metropole, she comes face to face with reality: her paradise is a purgatory for its residents, and poverty, unemployment, fear, criminality, and violence abound:

> Her mind screamed rejection of the wooden shack, refused the ragged familiarity of the splintered door. She stood hesitant, disappointment a physical blow. It will be better inside, she told herself stoutly, clutching her parcels closer still. She was painfully aware of the eyes peering from the other shacks, the hostility all around her....She thought longingly of the taxi, the hotel, England, all so far away and safe. God, how civilized England seemed now. (137-138)

The distance of both time and space that kept Hyacinth from returning to her place of birth and her childhood memories also fostered her construction of an imaginary homeland different from a reality that she cannot accept. These same factors force her to rush back to England. Both Hyacinth and Pavena in *In Times Like These* need to understand that "it is impossible to re-enter a society at the point of departure" (James, 248). As an adult, Hyacinth is now caught in the in-between-ness of two places that she barely knows. Her plight is to initiate a dialogue with the familiar and create a new representation to determine her place of origin.

Through instances recalled by the protagonist at several stages of her life, both in the Caribbean and Europe, Riley's Adella in *Waiting in the Twilight* traces the life of a young woman from the countryside who dreamt of one day going to Kingston and perhaps even to England. She is sent by her family to the island capital under the care of a cousin and his wife to earn a living as a dressmaker. Rejecting her relatives' religious zeal, Adella is seduced by a married policeman, Beresford, gets pregnant, is asked to leave her relatives' house, rents a shack in one of the slum areas, becomes pregnant a second time, and is helped out by a carpenter, Stanton, who eventually marries her. His project is to go to England and make enough money to buy land on his return. Once in the metropole, after waiting for eighteen months for her husband to send for her, Adella seems to be the only one interested in progressing. Stanton is content with living in one room with several children as long as his needs are met. Adella buys a house after five years in the city, takes in tenants, and brings the children she left in Jamaica to live with her (except the eldest who was already eighteen by the time she had the money for his ticket and papers), has a solid job in embroidery, and gives birth to two more daughters before having a stroke, which hampers all her plans to succeed.

The story begins in the present after Adella's stroke. She is cleaning offices, the only job she can get after half her body is paralyzed. Her thoughts drift back and forth to her childhood in Beaumont and her two years with Stanton in Kingston. Nostalgia sets in every time she sees how much she has lost in England—a good job in embroidery, a husband who asked for a divorce and moved to the United States, and the house she sacrificed so much to buy. Yet her nostalgia is an illusion because she has no intention to go back with nothing to show people back home after such a long stay.

Even though when Adella lived in the countryside and the immigrants' letters and stories assured her that England was the place where dreams came true, moving to Kingston, the island's capital— so modern and full of people—becomes the first important step in her life. She has a dreamlike description of the city when Aunt May tells stories of where she used to live: "Kingston hot, and de man dem dress sharp and de women dem have fashion. Dem ride in tram car, and it have a lot of noise where de Higgla dem come down fram the hills fe sell dem fruit and grun provision. Plenty rich people live dere. Buckra, and high yellow people, wid servant and posh car" (35). Of course, she fails to mention the yards, in which most of the population live in poverty. For five years, Adella lives happily in Kingston, even if she finds too many restrictions and too much surveillance. She is able to develop a clientele among the middle class that allows her to become well regarded as a dressmaker and save money. However, she gets pregnant the very first night she has sex with Beresford, the policeman who had helped her when she once lost her way in the city. She then discovers the real Kingston with its extreme poverty and daily violence without hope of change. After two years of passively accepting Beresford's sexual demands in exchange for food and shelter, two years in which she never contacted her family for fear of shame, Adella is "saved" by Stanton who provides for her and her two sons and, more importantly, marries her. During the next two years she lives in a "little house so like her cousin's" (150) in Kingston, where her family comes to visit. Once she has revived her sewing profession, Adella is content with her life. As a married woman, the church now accepts her; her family is proud of her; she has her own house; economic problems lessen because there are plenty of clients for dressmaking; and she has a maid to help her take care of the children. When Stanton proposes to go to England, "where life will be even better," she does not dare oppose his plans: "Deep in her heart she did not want to start again, not now that she had achieved what she most wanted out of life....Whatever he wanted she would accept. She loved him and she trusted him" (153). The plan was to go to England, stay for two years, earn as much money as they both could, and then return to Jamaica to buy a house and start a small business.

When Adella does not hear from Stanton for a year and a half, she begins to wonder, as Margaret Prescod-Roberts' and Norma Steele's Bajan women do in *Black Women: Bringing It All Back Home*, if he was ever going to come back: "Quite often the men would come over, maybe leave a family in Barbados, but pick up with another woman in London or New York to reproduce them and do the housework—and start another family. So when the men went by themselves, you were taking a chance because you didn't know what you were going to get" (25). Surprisingly, Stanton does send her the money for the trip to England, but what Adella finds there is far from promising: he has a low-paying job on the buses; the room he has rented is small and expensive, and he has no long-range plans. Although Adella had made some friends on her journey to England, especially her best friend, Lisa, it is not until she is able to buy a house that she can begin home-building (Castles and Davidson). The house is in frightening condition, but it is a space where the entire family as well as new additions can fit, a place with a guestroom for relatives and friends who visit from the island and where no landlord can evict her. She is now in a West Indian enclave that serves as a protective wall for place-making—being the only sector they can buy real estate in—with a church and market place, which are meeting points and also serve as links between the island and the diasporic communities. The children do not stand out because of their race or accent in the local schools, and even though the neighbors gossip, they also help out when help is needed. However, house-building and place-making cannot compensate for her other domestic problems. Throughout the novel, Adella centers her life around Stanton, even though proof abounds of his inability and unwillingness to be the family's breadwinner. His wages first go to satisfy his whims: expensive foods for his dinners, new name-brand clothes, drinks for his friends at the local pub, and dancehall expenses. Adella saves the money to buy the house, yet it is Stanton who makes the decisions on tenants, relatives who come to stay with them, purchase of furniture, and house repairs. She abides by his decisions until the household is put in jeopardy by her cousin Gladys, whom Stanton attempts to use as in-house mistress. Yet Adella does allow Stanton to display his masculinity, which is supposed to be threatened by the white man's authority, by never reporting to the police the many times he punches, beats, and tries to suffocate her (Mama). Stuart Hall in "What Is This 'Black' in Black Popular Culture?" labels Caribbean masculinity as a poor excuse to repeat false cultural expressions:

> ...certain ways in which black men continue to live out their counter-identities as black masculinities and replay those fantasies

of black masculinities in the theatres of popular culture are, when viewed along other axes of difference, the very masculine identities that are oppressive to women, that claim visibility for their hardness only at the expense of the vulnerability of black women and the feminization of gay black men. (473)

Back home, Adella was immobilized by being a single mother; in the metropole, she is so ashamed that her husband left her for a younger woman that she distances herself from the community and waits for Stanton's return. This inability to cope with the predatory men in her life, Beresford and Stanton, contrasts with her resolution to find jobs regardless of her physical condition, work long hours, go without food in order to pay the mortgage, stand up for her rights as a citizen of the United Kingdom, and ensure that her children receive the best education possible.

In spite of the advice of her friend Lisa, the letters she receives from home urging her, her children encouraging her to go back to Jamaica, and her own reminiscences of her childhood in Beaumont, Adella refuses to return home because she feels she cannot live there with the shame of not having made it in England. Her husband abandons and later divorces her, and she loses her only possession, her dilapidated house. Living in government housing, Adella has the commodities she needs to survive the damp, cold winters. However, she is also isolated, and only receives sporadic visits from Lisa and her youngest daughters, Carol and Audrey. Adella admits to herself this disturbing seclusion, and when she thinks of death, she remembers Mada Beck: "Everyone had looked up to that woman, loved her for her age. But then she had died in her own place and among her people" (8). Sidonie Smith and Gisela Brinker-Gabler refer to Benedict Anderson to explain these erasures and re-inventions of the past as a play between memory and amnesia: "Memory is founded upon forgetting. An insistent coherence of memory and narrative implies forgetfulness. Yet incoherences and discontinuities make spaces for lost memory traces, with the result that the relationship of memories to amnesias is ever adjustable, fluid, and productive of new meanings and new narratives." (17). Adella's memories recall not only a landscape but the people who meant and still mean so much to her: her sister, Danny, her firstborn, the friends and acquaintances who still remember the young woman who, after many obstacles, found her calling in Kingston, only to lose her way in England. The memories of home, perhaps a bit blurred with the passing of time, alleviate the harsh weather and the decaying health of a woman whose fighting spirit does not allow her to give up at the same time that her pride prevents her from returning to where she belongs.

The women in the novels of Dionne Brand, Jamaica Kincaid, Paule Marshall, Michelle Cliff, Zee Edgell, and Joan Riley move to Toronto, New York, and London thinking of the advantages they have over other immigrants because they already speak the metropolitan language and, thus, share part of its culture. This misperception becomes their first disappointment when, in Toronto, they are treated as cheap labor no different from the women of other Caribbean islands, or in New York, when they are categorized as black Americans, or in London, when they are seen as colonial blacks and not as fellow British subjects. The expectation of a smooth entrance only complicates the difficulties they encounter in the service job market they are forced to compete in, the lack of adequate housing available for immigrant workers, and the prevalent racial and ethnic prejudice they face. Adella in *Waiting in the Twilight* is the only woman who planned to move to England and return home in two years with enough money to buy land, build a house, and set up a business. In her case, there was no need to migrate because she was living comfortably in Kingston. She is the only one who dies after spending thirty years building a new life in the metropole and only succeeding in giving a good education to three of her children. Verlia and Elizete in *In Another Place, Not Here*, Lucy in *Lucy*, and Silla in *Brown Girl, Brownstones* migrate to Toronto and New York with no plans of return. They have left behind what they considered provincial societies, where there was no space for change and few opportunities for a woman to be more than a cane cutter or merely a woman burdened with a husband and children. Anything they find in the metropole will give them more options, even if it means long hours of work, no job security, and mistreatment by employers. While it only takes months for Kitty in *No Telephone to Heaven* to know that she does not belong in New York and to return to her island, it takes seven years for Hyacinth in *The Unbelonging* to go back to Jamaica and face a by-then-unrecognizable society. Selina in *Brown Girl, Brownstones* travels to Barbados to discover the place cherished by her father and despised by her mother. Pavana in *In Times Like These* and Clare in *No Telephone to Heaven* spend fifteen to twenty years traveling and working in Europe and Africa before they realize what they miss and return home.

The women who left their islands with one-way tickets go through a very strenuous period of adjusting to the places they have chosen as their new homes. Lucy is continuously making comparisons with her unnamed island, and she wonders how she can miss a place she so wanted to leave. Once she decides not to open her mother's letters and, after her father's death, to send money and an accusatory farewell letter, Lucy begins to get rid of her island skin. Memories still pursue her, but she intends, in time, to delete them from her mind. Silla can erase her memories of Bimshire, but she always holds on to the cultural interpretation of the diasporic Barbadian community, which gives her the support she needs to carry on her mission of making the United States a home for her and her family. Elizete disregards everyone's advice in Toronto to return to her island and not be lost, homeless, and easy prey in a society she neither knows nor understands. However, she only has to remember what home was like—abused as a child, orphaned and passed from one woman to another, abandoned to slave work in the cane fields, and a marriage based on rape and beatings—to be assured that this is the place she wants to be. Verlia and Clare never wanted to look back at their stratified society where they felt suffocated by race and class divisions. They both travel abroad, witness the unofficial but institutionalized racism of Toronto, New York, and London, observe the discrimination suffered by peoples pushed to the margins, and decide to go elsewhere, Verlia to Grenada and Clare to Jamaica, and become part of a movement that envisioned a new society. Both die in their attempts to achieve change; both follow their ideals and refuse to live abroad and merely watch the deterioration of island life from the sidelines.

The women in the novels by women from the franco-, hispano-, and anglophone Caribbean maintain throughout their lives a tense relationship with the metropole and its insistence on keeping them at the margins, even if at times the center stretches to allow them to occupy specifically assigned positions of privilege. The relationship with the island homeland is also problematic, fluctuating from a nostalgia for a non-existent home to the constructive memory of the place that each carries with her as a code of belonging somewhere. In the global city these women have chosen to live in, they form part of the faceless, nationless army of workers who provide disposable bulk labor either for giant corporations or as domestic service providers. The memory of being from a specific somewhere, having a history, a language, and a culture of their own, restores their humanity and dignity.

Works Cited

Anderson, Benedict. *Imagined Communities*. London: Verso, 1991.

Ashcroft, Bill, Gareth Griffiths, and Helen Tiffin, eds. "Place: Introduction." In *The Post-Colonial Studies Reader*. London: Routledge, 1995, 391-393.

Bolland, O. Nigel. *The Politics of Labour in the British Caribbean: The Social Origins of Authoritarianism and Democracy in the Labour Movement*. Kingston: Ian Randle, 2001.

Bolles, A. Lynn. "'Goin' abroad': Working Class Jamaican Women and Migration." In *Female Immigrants to the United States: Caribbean, Latin American, and African Experiences*. Washington DC: RIIES Smithsonian Institute, 1981. 56-84.

Brand, Dionne. *In Another Place, Not Here*. New York: Grove P, 1996.

Carrera Suárez, Isabel. "About Mother(Land): Joan Riley's Fiction." In *Motherlands: Black Women's Writing from Africa, the Caribbean and South Asia*. Ed. Susheila Nasta. New Brunswick, NJ: Rutgers UP, 1992. 290-309.

Castles, Stephen and Alastair Davidson. *Citizenship and Migration: Globalization and the Politics of Belonging*. New York: Routledge, 2000.

Cliff, Michelle. *No Telephone to Heaven*. New York: Plume, 1987.

Condé, Maryse. *Heremakhonon*. Washington DC: Three Continents P, 1982 (originally published in 1976).

Denniston, Dorothy Hamer. *The Fiction of Paule Marshall: Reconstruction of History, Culture, and Gender*. Knoxville: U Tennessee P, 1995.

Edgell, Zee. *In Times like These*. London: Heinemann, 1991.

Friedman, Susan Stanford. *Mappings: Feminism and the Cultural Geographies of Encounter*. Princeton: Princeton UP, 1998.

Gmelch, George. *Double Passage: The Lives of Caribbean Migrants Abroad and Back Home*. Ann Arbor: U Michigan P, 1992.

Hall, Stuart. "Cultural Identity and Diaspora" In *Colonial Discourse and Post-Colonial Theory: A Reader*. Eds. Patrick Williams and Laura Chrisman. New York: Columbia UP, 1994. 392-403.

_____. "What Is This 'Black'' in Black Popular Culture?" In *Stuart Hall: Critical Dialogues in Cultural Studies*. Eds. David Morley and Kuan-Hsing Chen. Routledge: London and New York, 1996. 465–475.

Harris, Ruth L. "The Transformation of Canadian Policies and Programs to Recruit Foreign Labor: The Case of Caribbean Female Domestic Workers, 1950's–1980's." Diss. Michigan State U, 1988.

Holder, Calvin. "Making Ends Meet: West Indian Economic Adjustment in New York City, 1900–1952." *Wadabagei* 1,1 (Winter/ Spring 1998): 31-81.

James, Winston. "Migration, Racism and Identity Formation: The Caribbean Experience in Britain." In *Inside Babylon: The Caribbean Diaspora in Britain*. London: Verso, 1993, 231-287.

Kasinitz, Philip. *Caribbean New York: Black Immigrants and the Politics of Race*. Ithaca: Cornell UP, 1992.

Kincaid, Jamaica. *Lucy*. New York: Plume, 1991 (originally published 1990).

Mama, Amina. "Women Abuse in London's Black Communities." In *Inside Babylon: The Caribbean Diaspora in Britain*. London: Verso, 1993. 97-134.

Marshall, Paule. *Brown Girl, Brownstones*. London: Virago P, 1982 (originally published in 1959).

Pineau, Gisèle. *Exile According to Julia*. Charlottesville: U Virginia P, 2003 (originally published in 1996).

Plaza, Dwaine. "Migration and Adjustment to Canada: Revising the Mobility Dream 1900–1998." In *The Society for Caribbean Studies Annual Conference Papers* 3 (2002). www.scsonline. freeserve.co.uk/olvol3.html

Pratt, Mary Louise. *Imperial Eyes: Travel Writing and Transculturation*. London: Routledge, 1992.

Prescod-Roberts, Margaret and Norma Steele. *Black Women: Bringing It All Back Home*. Bristol: Falling Wall, 1980.

Richardson, Bonham C. "Caribbean Migrations, 1838–1985." In *The Modern Caribbean*. Eds. Franklin W. Knight and Colin A. Palmer. Chapel Hill: U North Carolina P, 1989. 203-228.

Riley, Joan. "Introduction." In *Leave to Stay: Stories of Exile and Belonging*. Eds. Joan Riley and Briar Wood. London: Virago, 1996. 1-8.

————. *The Unbelonging*. London: Women's Press, 1985.

_____. *Waiting in the Twilight*. London: Women's Press, 1987.

Said, Edward. *The Edward Said Reader*. New York: Vintage, 2000.

Santiago, Esmeralda. *América's Dream*. New York: HarperCollins, 1996.

Sassen, Saskia. *The Global City: New York, London, Tokyo*. Princeton: Princeton UP, 1991.

Schwartz, Meryl F. "Imagined Communities in the Novels of Michelle Cliff." In *Homemaking: Women Writers and the Politics and Poetics of Home*. Eds. Catherine Wiley and Fiona R. Barnes. New York: Garland, 1996. 287-311.

Smith, Sidonie and Gisela Brinker-Gabler. "Introduction: Gender, Nation, and Immigration in the New Europe." In *Writing New Identities: Gender, Nation, and Imigration in Contemporary Europe*. Minneapolis: U Minnesota P, 1997. 1-27.

Sturgess, Charlotte. "Dionne Brand: Writing the Margins." In *Caribbean Women Writers: Fiction in English*. Eds. Mary Condé and Thorunn Lonsdale. New York: St. Martin's, 1999. 202-216.

Thomas-Hope, Elizabeth. "Emigration Dynamics in the Anglophone Caribbean." In *Emigration Dynamics in Developing Countries. Vol. III: Mexico, Central America and the Caribbean*. Ed. Reginald Appleyard. Aldershot: Ashgate, 1999. 232–284.

Washington, Mary Helen. "Afterword." In *Brown Girl, Brownstones*. London: Virago, 1982. 311–324.

Watkins-Owens, Irma. *Blood Relations: Caribbean Immigrants and the Harlem Community, 1900–1930*. Bloomington: Indiana UP, 1996.

Welsh, Sarah Lawson. "(Un)belonging Citizens, Unmapped Territory: Black Immigration and British Identity in the Post-1945 Period." In *Not on Any Map: Essays on Postcoloniality and Cultural Nationalism*. Exeter, Devon: U Exeter P, 1997. 43-66.

Williams, Eric. *From Columbus to Castro: The History of the Caribbean 1402-1969*. New York: Harper & Row, 1973.

AFTERWORD

Caribbean Women Stepping through the Looking Glass of Difference

Women especially need to remember because forgetting is a major obstacle to change

> (Gayle Greene, "Feminist Fiction and the Uses of Memory")

And where is home? Home may be where we hang our hat, or where our heart is...which may be the same place, or maybe not. It may be where we choose to live...or where we belong, whether we like it or not. It may be all of these things or none of them. Whatever and wherever it is, home is always border country, a place that separates and connects us, a place of possibility for both peace and perilous conflict.

> (J. Edward Chamberlin, *If This Is Your Land, Where Are Your Stories? Finding Common Grounds*)

Caribbean women at the end of one century and the beginning of another write about their experiences—the distant and everpresent past—using the mainstream language of the host and, many times, hostile country where they were not born but now reside. Primarily, they address either an audience with limited or distorted information on their homelands or the enclosed marginal communities in exile who speak Caribbean Creole languages and also enough English to read their narratives. They express their concern for a homeland that they reconstruct from the recollected "shards" (using Ruth Prawer Jhabvala's term) of a cultural past that informs their everyday life. In these post-postmodern times, the term "history" has been first deconstructed to examine the many parts that compose it, then reconstructed so that it remains an open, if still unequal, process. The inclusion of testimony, recollections, memoirs, diaries, autobiography and biography, orality, fictional and non-fictional narratives, as well as documented materials are now part of both history and literature. Linda Hutcheon reminds us that this intertextuality is a desire "to close the gap between past and present of the reader and a desire to rewrite the past in a new context" (118). Writers and readers now seem to think historically, which means thinking critically and contextually (Hutcheon, 88). In this way, history is no longer factual documentation but events that are nurtured by everyone and everything.

The Caribbean women writers in this study share a special concern for women migrants from the franco-, hispano- and anglophone Caribbean who relocate for specific or indefinite periods in metropoles—the places of convergence for the dominant or majority population, people from the countryside, original populations from ex-colonies, and workers from everywhere seeking their livelihood. It is this centre that women find places—however temporary or peripheral—to study, work, dwell, extend, or rupture links to a homeland that one might one day return to. It is the place where women can construct new lives and re-create the best of two worlds: the warmth, care, familiarity, language, and history that shaped and defined home, on the one hand, with the opportunity to be well paid for the housework performed for free or sub-human wages back home, get training to apply for other jobs, go to night school, make housing and employment decisions on their own, on the other. Even though some of these women characters never chose to leave their islands but were forced by economic or family reasons, they quickly adapt to new locations and attempt to start new lives. These women migrants may never have a specific home, but they have all imagined new homes, which continuously shift according to their decisions to move from one place to another. Since migration is such a significant component of Caribbean life, place has often been shifting space where home is continuously redefined.

Similar yearnings, relationships, and attitudes are found in the world of Caribbean women writers inside and outside the entire region. Edwidge Danticat, Gisèle Pineau, Maryse Condé, and Myriam Warner-Vieyra in the francophone, Cristina García, Julia Alvarez, Loida Maritza Pérez, Judith Ortiz Cofer, and Esmeralda Santiago in the hispanophone, and Dionne Brand, Jamaica Kincaid, Paule Marshall, Michelle Cliff, Zee Edgell, and Joan Riley in the anglophone

Caribbean have created women characters by tapping into their own imaginations, experiences, remembrances, stories told by elders, and blurred memories of childhood. Those who share the migratory experience are women who travel on their own and find the strength to face the unknown, and at times terrifying, city; daughters who, after spending their childhood in the Caribbean, are reclaimed by migrant parents; mothers and children who travel together and try to replicate the home left behind in a city where the national culture, determined by race and ethnicity, is a drawback; young women sent abroad to study who are transformed by their stay and decide to postpone indefinitely their return; families whose differences are exacerbated by the new conditions they face; and women who do everything possible to sever all ties with the homeland certain that they will find a place in the centre they so desire to be part of.

Women who accept the challenge of traveling alone and staying for an indefinite period of time in an urban center they only know through the distorted pictures drawn by migrants who write letters, send tapes, make telephone calls, or return for shorter or longer periods, are in a vulnerable position. They have to fend for themselves in the city and face prejudice, harassment, mistreatment, sub-employment, dilapidated living quarters, shortages of food, clothing, and money, and isolation from a homeland and, at times, a diasporic community. Edwidge Danticat's Martine in *Breath, Eyes, Memory* was sent to New York by a mother who thought she would lose her mind if she stayed in Haiti after being raped by a Ton Ton Macoute. This separation from family and her young child forced Martine to delegate her past life to nightmares and focus entirely on how to survive in a city whose population was indifferent to her pain. Paule Marshall's Silla in *Brown Girl, Brownstones* worked very hard so that her mother would have enough money to buy her a one-way ticket to New York. Arriving in the metropole, she is willing to work at any job, accept any living conditions as a starting point in her pursuit of a better life. Loida Maritza Pérez's Rebecca in *Geographies of Home* also convinces her parents to send her to New York to find a job that in time would allow her to bring her family from the Dominican Republic to the United States. She finds factory jobs that pay decent wages—many times more than she would ever earn in Santo Domingo, if anyone would hire her—and in the process of keeping her promise to her family, she forgets to secure United States citizenship for herself. Cristina García's Dulcita in *The Agüero Sisters* rejects her mother's advice and marries a Spaniard to buy herself a ticket to Madrid as the easiest way to leave Cuba. Alone in the European city where she supposedly shares language, history, and literature, she is hungry and almost becomes homeless. Maryse Condé's Reynalda in *Desirada* plans secretly to emigrate to Paris, and, once situated in the metropole, she seldom looks back at her place of origin. She blurs the negative experiences that make her yearn for a homeland where she left a daughter she only reclaimed after ten years. Although García's Reina in *The Agüero Sisters* and Esmeralda Santiago's América in *América's Dream* have sponsored entries into the United States with secure housing and employment, they still have to face the furtive looks and the prejudiced, under-the-breath comments of those already positioned in the centre. Dionne Brand's Elizete in *In Another Place, Not Here*, who shares the same language as the majority of the population in Toronto, is a woman with no friends, no shelter, only sporadic jobs, and is always on the move to avoid being harmed, caught, and deported. Both Dulcita and Elizete become homeless in the metropole, but the former has a family in Miami who will rescue her and give her a chance to build a second home, while the latter has no one and nothing to return to. Toronto, the estranged city, becomes the only home she knows.

Daughters left behind with surrogate mothers—grandmothers, aunts, older friends, or foster parents—are prominent in novels by francophone women writers. Edwidge Danticat's Sophie in *Breath, Eyes, Memory* is sent for and relocated in a country and city so unlike Haiti by her mother, Martine, a woman she barely knows. Myriam Warner-Vieyra's Zetou in *As the Sorcerer Said...* pleads with her mother, Rosamond, to take her to Paris with her, trusting that a mother will always protect and never harm her, even if she abandoned the entire family years before. Juletane, in Warner-Vieyra's novel by the same name, is claimed by her godmother in Paris when her only living parent dies. Maryse Condé's Marie-Noëlle in *Desirada* is sent to Paris to live with her mother and Reynalda's second family—a husband and a young son—although she had never received a letter or even a call from this stranger before. Condé's Coco in *Tree of Life*, born in

Paris and put in a foster home, is reclaimed by her wandering mother who has no idea what to do with her. Although not as frequently, the anglo- and hispanophone novels also record this traumatic experience of a child being forced to leave everything that means home and quickly adjust to new faces in a strange place. Julia Alvarez's Sarita in *¡Yo!* is a privileged child in the Dominican Republic because her mother's wages as a maid in New York for the García family pay for boarding school and remittances. When her mother has enough money to pay for her ticket and has secured permission from her employers for her daughter to live with her, Sarita enters a world where no matter how educated and intelligent she may be, she is known as the "maid's daughter." Joan Riley's Hyacinth in *The Unbelonging* enters a more complex situation when her father sends for her and she soon realizes that instead of having a support group to make the transition and adapt to the new place, as was Marie-Noëlle's and Sophie's experience, she finds herself in a hostile household where her stepmother, stepbrothers, and barely recognized father strip her of the security she had back home.

In the hispanophone Caribbean, Santiago's Monín and her seven children born in Puerto Rico in *When I Was Puerto Rican* and *Almost a Woman*, and Judith Ortiz Cofer's Ramona and her two children in *The Line of the Sun*, arrive in New York and New Jersey, respectively, to build homes away from home, after deciding to leave Puerto Rico and settle elsewhere. While these mothers do everything in their means to hold the family together in a closely knit diasporic community, the daughters first resent the separation from the familiar home they knew so well yet, later on, disapprove of the mothers' attempts to hold on to their culture instead of integrating into the dominant society. When they understand their mothers' motives for being so backward and repressive, the daughters are already too immersed in becoming American to acknowledge the sacrifices their mothers have made so that their offspring can have a better life while still retaining the extended family bond with Puerto Rico.

Studying abroad places Caribbean women in a privileged position. Whether they come from the middle or upper classes, government scholarships or family support, these young women find themselves in secure, if transitory, positions. They move to the metropole with enough money to make appropriate arrangements for housing, tuition, and a generous allowance that allows them to study full time and be assured that a secure job awaits them back home once they have completed their studies. The women characters in this study seldom obtain degrees, and they decide to stay abroad rather than to return home without fulfilling the expectations of their family, teachers, community, or politicians. To modify their transitory position to one of permanence requires obtaining a job to pay for basic necessities. At that point, these women face the same uncertainties and discrimination encountered by working-class women when they arrive by themselves with very few resources except the determination to find a job and survive in an unfamiliar and hostile environment. Condé's Thecla in *Tree of Life*, Marie-Hélène in *Season in Rihata* and Veronica in *Heremakhonon* are sent to Paris by their Guadeloupean families to study and then return home as educated women to marry into wealth. The painful experiences they undergo while living beyond the protective mantle of their families back home, make them choose Paris or Africa as "new homes." They remember Guadeloupe as a distant place where they enjoyed a childhood that later turned nightmarish for them as adolescents and young adults. Thecla wanders through Europe and later New York and the Caribbean to finally settle in Paris as the exotic wife of a wealthy doctor. Marie-Hélène never really recovers from her sister's suicide and her lover's abandonment. She makes the decision to marry into a wealthy African family and begin a new life in an African village totally disconnected from her Guadeloupean family. Veronica also travels to Africa, but decides to settle in Paris, rather than force herself on her family back in the Caribbean or tolerate the patriarchal political maneuverings she experiences in Africa. Warner-Vieyra's Helene in *Juletane* obtained her degree but decides to stay in Paris rather than face the shame of being jilted by the young man she had planned to marry after both had finished their studies in Paris. Edgell's Pavana in *In Times Like These* becomes pregnant after being in London for a year. She decides to study part time, takes a low-paying job—the only one she could find in the centre—later accepts employment in Africa, and, after fifteen years, returns to Belize as a professional woman with two teenaged children. Cliff's Clare in *No Telephone to Heaven* begins her studies in London, leaves when she feels singled out as "different," travels through Europe, and, after twenty years, returns to Jamaica to stay. Although Clare faces prejudices in the centre, she never has to work for a living, and can return home because she has family land and money to make a new start. These characters are forced to redefine themselves when their plans to study and to become part of island elites fail, and they must rethink their lives in the centre or elsewhere.

When families integrated by two parents and one or more children migrate, the island culture is often transferred to the metropole and serves immediately in home-building and providing the groundwork for place-making. This cultural safety net serves as a buffer zone in an unfamiliar and hostile new environment. Language, traditions, family unity, and identity issues are less challenged or threatened by the dominant society in which they have relocated. However, this sense of security also serves as a kind of chattel for women who continue to be ruled by the remnants of island patriarchy, and, as James Clifford states, "'Community' can be a site both of support and oppression" ("Diasporas," 260). Julia Alvarez's García family—parents and four daughters—in *How the García Girls Lost Their Accents* move to the United States and, even living outside of an ethnic enclave, maintain the Dominican family structure traditions, even if by class, profession, and intention they move toward the"new" values of the centre. They live in the suburbs instead of an urban center, the daughters attend private schools and later small liberal colleges, they spend summers in the Dominican Republic, and home is always their parents' house until they marry. The father continuously exerts his authority as the patriarch who defends the family honor and whose judgment cannot be challenged by wife or grown-up daughters. Everyone is expected to gather around the celebration of the father's birthday; marriage is a blessing—especially if the groom is a white foreigner—while divorce is a collective embarrassment, and satisfaction comes when the daughters have their own families, even if the patriarchy is looser. Women, like Yolanda, who choose to "dissent" from this oppressive structure are harshly criticized, accused of assimilating into the metropolitan culture, and assured of unhappiness.

Notwithstanding the pronounced class differences and their urban circumstances, Loida Maritza Pérez's family in *Geographies of Home*—father, mother, and fourteen children—share with the García family a common island of origin and the ingrained belief in a patriarchal society. The father rules as absolute authority over wife and children and defends the family honor. Although many times, the family has gone hungry, the father never allows his wife to work outside the home. His oldest daughter, Rebecca, has a husband who also upholds this code of honor and beats his wife every time he finds out she has gone to work in order to feed their two children. Iliana, the youngest daughter, uses every means possible to persuade her father to allow her to accept a college scholarship far away from New York City, so that she will no longer have to live at home. Home is such a repressive place that Iliana's one wish is to get as far away as possible from a family that only sees her as a woman with a fixed role. Years of living in New York have not broken down this patriarchal illusion.

Cristina García's Pilar in *Dreaming in Cuban* is two when she leaves Cuba with her parents. She grows up between a father whose nostalgia for the Cuba of the 1940s and 50s makes him reject any integration into the larger society and a mother who wants to erase the memory of the island that ruined her life. Lourdes, the mother, believes in total assimilation into the dominant culture but refuses to let her daughter behave like an American girl. She wants Pilar to respect her elders, never question her parents' orders and decisions, and as an adolescent behave as if she were in upper-class Cuban society. Since nostalgia paralyzes the father, and the mother is set on becoming an American, Pilar asserts herself by running away from home to travel to Miami, attempting to return to her place of origin, and later, acting as a young rebel while she continues to yearn for her lost culture in Cuba. García's Constancia in *The Agüero Sisters* travels with her family to Miami—her son from her first marriage leaves before them and they are later reunited—and then settles down in New York where her daughter from her second marriage is born. In this case, any attempt to impose the "old ways" is dismissed by her children, who quickly move away from the ethnic margin into a more fluid group that encompasses being gay, moving back to nature, and being a single mother. Even when the daughter returns to her mother's home, Constancia's influence is almost non-existent. The family structure is dismantled, and family has become a community of women coming from a variety of life experiences to learn from but never impose themselves or their ideas on anyone.

Cliff's Savage family in *No Telephone to Heaven* travels to the United States to start a new life: a way for Kitty to heal after her mother's death and for Boy to pass for white in the racist American society of the 1960s. However, in a few months, Kitty realizes that she feels isolated and marginal in a society where so much is determined by race. To preserve her sanity and to relate once more to her own culture, she packs her bags and returns to Jamaica with her youngest daughter. The older daughter, Clare, interprets this separation as abandonment and grows closer to her father, who insists on her becoming a white American. When she can no longer play the role of dutiful daughter, she travels to the "motherland," England, where she plays at being British until she feels included in a manifesto by the National Front that calls for the ouster of black foreigners. Marshall's Selina in *Brown Girl, Brownstones* is closely supervised by working parents in an ethnic neighborhood. As she grows up, like García's Pilar in *Dreaming in Cuban*, Selina is influenced by a father who tells stories about an imaginary Barbados and a mother who, shielded by a mantle of good behavior, pushes her daughter to become as American as possible. Silla, her mother, encourages Selina to study and dance, but she expects her to respect her elders and never shame them by sleeping around or becoming pregnant. In this particular case, Selina is able to turn away from her mother and the house she so loved, and travel unaccompanied to Barbados to explore the place she might call home. Riley's Adella in *Waiting in the Twilight* travels to England to join her husband who moved there a year and a half before in order to secure employment and housing. Adella's frustration in finding inadequate rooms for a family, no savings, and a low-paying job do not stop her from securing enough money to send for the children she left back home. In England, her husband becomes a stranger who behaves like a single man with no family responsibilities. She, in turn, becomes the breadwinner and the binding force for her six children. Although disappointed when two of her daughters get pregnant and marry at a young age, she is extremely proud of the two youngest, Carol and Audrey, who study and become professionals. However, in her own life, Adella continues to wait for her husband's return and blames herself for his abandonment of the family.

Pineau's Julia in *Exile According to Julia*, is rescued by her soldier son and family from her violent husband, who has been traumatized by his experiences in World War I. She is taken from her house, hidden in a friendly but unknown locale, and then accompanied by her son, his wife and children on a long trip that takes her to France. She is given love, attention, and care by each family member, especially the children, so that she can build a new home away from her island. As a traditional and religious woman, she fears that God will punish her for breaking her marriage vows by being separated from her husband. Her new family provides a safety net in France to protect her from white people who look at her strangely and wonder what language she speaks. Julia finds a semblance of home during the summers when she can be outside, plant her garden, and entertain the children with her stories. Nevertheless, home is always Guadeloupe, her place of birth, the land of her ancestors, and the place where she belongs and eventually returns to.

Women who leave their skin behind when they migrate are better equipped to face the unknown metropole. They have promised themselves never to return; whatever problems they encounter must be solved to achieve their goal of integrating themselves into the dynamics of the city. They carry few, if any, objects to remind them of home; they prefer not to write, call, or receive missives; they take advantage of offers of training, employment, and education; they do not look back. All the women have projects to fulfill in the shortest time possible. Brand's Verlia in *In Another Place, Not Here* goes to Toronto to join the black movement. She renounces her nationality to become a defender of the black race and be part of an international brotherhood and sisterhood of Africans. When, after many years, her memories of where she came from have blurred, Verlia decides to create a new home in the Caribbean, where political liberation is still possible.

Kincaid's Lucy severs her ties with her island and mother by never even opening her mother's letters, associating only with white people living in the metropole, and remembering stories from back home only to discard them from her new life. Her past begins with her journey to New York and her relation with her employers. She erases everyone so she can begin to create herself without looking back. In contrast, Cliff's Clare in *No Telephone to Heaven* follows Boy's advice of playing "white," even when she is called "white chocolate" by classmates. In England, passing for white is more successful, and she never associates with anyone marginal. However, after living and studying in London, Clare understands the impossibility of forsaking her past and constructing a new self. She returns to Jamaica to recover her history and Jamaicanness.

Condé's Reynalda in *Desirada* secretly plans her departure from her island home and never regrets leaving her baby behind or not thanking the people who helped her recover from her early pregnancy and attempted suicide. Once in the metropole, she thoughtfully reconstructs herself from an island nanny to a scholarship holder who becomes a successful social worker. According to Reynalda, once her daughter, Marie-Noëlle, becomes independent, all ties with her past will be severed. García's Constancia in *The Agüero Sisters* and Lourdes in *Dreaming in Cuban* and Alvarez's Sarita in *How the García Girls Lost Their Accents* become accomplished business women and professionals in the cities they have chosen to live in. They have gained a place in that centre, which stretches to create borders where money and enterprise are rewarded. None of them contemplates living in an ethnic community or returning home. Ortiz Cofer's Marisol in *In the Line of the Sun* and Santiago's Negi in *Almost a Woman* reinvent themselves in school as individuals more acceptable to the centre: Italian Americans and Indians. According to these girls, and later, young women, these other ethnic groups do not have the Puerto Rican stigma, what Ramón Grosfoguel calls "racialized groups" ("Puerto Ricans," 244). Both young women idolize their fathers who live elsewhere or come to see them only sporadically; both see their mothers as the markers of their Puerto Ricanness. As soon as they are able to, they disassociate themselves from the mother who built a home for them in the metropole. Both want to enter the life of the centre, like what they see, and do everything in their power to secure a place there.

The global city is chosen as a temporary destination by these Caribbean women. This place, described in another context by Burton Pike as "fragmented and transparent rather than tangible and coherent...consisting of bits, pieces, and shifting moods" (72), is indispensable to the transformation of these fictional characters who voice the multiple stories of thousands of Caribbean women who began migrating to metropolitan centers during the twentieth century and now form part of a massive global migration. The vastness, strangeness, and distance of new and unwelcoming spaces challenge these Caribbean women, who speak other languages or the same language differently and whose "racialized" ethnicity forces them to rethink the lives they had taken for granted on the island. They solve never-before-encountered situations and rely on their sometimes desperate positions to demand their rights, even when it means dismissal from jobs, eviction, or inability to go on welfare. They learn to deal with government agencies such as schools, unemployment, Social Services, immigration, and law enforcement and become familiar with public transportation and renting and purchasing dilapidated houses in ethnic enclaves. The idea of someday being part of the centre resides behind each of these new skills and sources of information. At the same time, a sense of belonging somewhere emerges through home-building and place-making. Home is recreated by securing objects, letters, remembrances of an island left behind but always present even if disassociating from the past is the primary object of moving somewhere else. The city allows women to be anonymous in the centre that provides "low-paid jobs both in services and downgraded manufacturing" (Castells, 285), and at the same time feel protected and cared for by living in a supportive ethnic community. Doubtless this community can also be an obstacle to change behavior, but even in extreme cases where men attempt to impose the roles of back home, women are sufficiently mobile so as to vanish temporarily or to seek protection from women's groups and state institutions.

According to the *World Migration Report 2000*, the number of women who migrate from the Caribbean, as well as from the rest of the world, has surpassed that of men in many ports of entry. Even if women stay in London, New York, Paris, or Toronto, the constant flow of other Caribbean women coming to the metropolitan city makes the homeland a continuous presence instead of a distant memory. Thus, home is never static unless one willingly freezes the moment of departure. U.S., U.K., French, and Canadian media usually do not cover news from the Caribbean unless they consider it a major event—the U.S. invasion and occupation of the Dominican Republic in 1965 and of Grenada in 1983, the intervention in Haiti in 1994 and 2004 to mention recent examples—but local radio stations and newspapers that highlight Caribbean events operate in these ethnic communities. As long as these neighborhoods serve as networks, home remains present as a changing place that may or may not provide the flexibility to deal with the shifting roles and behavior of Caribbean women who live elsewhere but consider the Caribbean their home, the place they can look back to and connect with to their national culture through language, history, and literature.

Through education and exposure to other lifelines in the contested space of metropolitan life, women have an opportunity to choose what to preserve and what to erase from their homeland, as well as how to inscribe their own names in this diasporic space. The imaginary homeland for these women characters is no longer Haiti, Guadeloupe, Cuba, the Dominican Republic, Puerto Rico, Trinidad, Antigua, Jamaica, or Belize but a reconstructed space made of at least two different geographical locations with the possibility of coming and going in either direction and the potential to influence both with their new awareness of respect for all human beings, regardless of gender. Inside the continuously shifting conditions of the postcolonial diaspora, they have found secure places that simultaneously contest the frozen image of the community as "extended family" at home and abroad.

Works Cited

Castells, Manuel. "Information Technology, the Restructuring of Capital-Labor Relationships, and the Rise of the Dual City." In *The Castells Reader*. Oxford: Blackwell, 2002. 285-313.

Chamberlin, J. Edward. *If This Is Your Land, Where are Your Stories? Finding Comon Grounds*. Toronto: Alfred A. Knopf, 2003.

Clifford, James. "Diasporas." In *Routes: Travel and Translation in the Late Twentieth Century*. Cambridge: Harvard UP, 1997. 244-277.

"An Era of International Migration." In *World Migration Report 2000*. International Organization for Migration (IOM)-United Nations, 2000. 3–56.

Greene, Gayle. "Feminist Fiction and the Uses of Memory." *Journal of Women in Culture and Society* 16.2 (1991): 290-321.

Grosfoguel, Ramón. "Puerto Ricans in the USA: A Comparative Approach." *Journal of Ethnic and Migration Studies* 25. 2 (April 1999): 233-249.

Hutcheon, Linda. *A Poetics of Postmodernism: History, Theory, Fiction*. New York: Routledge, 1988.

Jhabvala, Ruth Prawer. *Shards of Memory*. New York: Anchor, 1995.

Pike, Burton. *The Image of the City in Modern Literature*. Princeton: Princeton UP, 1981.

REFERENCES

Abenaty, Kenton. "Intergenerational 'Return' Migration to St. Lucia: A Comparative Analysis." (Eastern Caribbean Island Cultures Conference-St. Lucia. November 2001).

Adams, C. Jama. "Contested Space: Psycho-Social Themes Around the Construction of Caribbean American Identities." *Wadabagei* 2. 1 (Winter/Spring 1999): 29-49.

Adjarian, M.M. *Allegories of Desire: Body, Nation, and Empire in Modern Caribbean Literature by Women*, Westport, CT: Praeger, 2004.

Agosto, Noraida. *Michelle Cliff's Novels: Piecing the Tapestry of Memory and History*. New York: Peter Lang, 2000.

Alegría Ortega, Idsa. "Culture, Politics and Self-Determination in Puerto Rico." In *Islands at the Crossroads: Politics in the Non-Independent Caribbean*. Eds. Aarón Gamaliel Ramos and Angel Israel Rivera. Kingston, Jamaica: Ian Randle, 2001. 28-44.

Alvarez, Julia. *How the García Girls Lost Their Accents*. New York: Plume. 1992.

———. *¡Yo!* New York: Plume, 1997.

Anderson, Benedict. *Imagined Communities*. London: Verso, 1991.

Anzaldúa, Gloria. *Borderlands/La frontera: The New Mestiza*. San Francisco: Spinsters/Aunt Lute, 1987.

———. "Haciendo caras una entrada." In *Making Faces Making Soul*. San Francisco: Aunt Lute Books, 1990. xv-xxviii.

Aparicio, Frances. *Listening to Salsa: Gender, Latin Popular Music, and Puerto Rican Cultures*. Hanover: Wesleyan UP, 1998.

———. "Mujer, ritmo y cultura en la diáspora." *Diálogo* marzo 1999: 25.

Ashcroft, Bill, Gareth Griffiths, Helen Tiffin, eds. "Place: Introduction." In *The Post-Colonial Studies Reader*. London: Routledge, 1995, 391-393.

Aub-Buscher, Gertrud, and Beverley Ormerod Noakes, eds. *Francophone Caribbean Today: Literature, Language, Culture*. Mona: U West Indies P, 2003.

Balutansky, Kathleen. "Anglophone and Francophone Fiction by Caribbean Women: Redefining 'Female Identity.'" In *A History of Literature in the Caribbean. Volume 3 Cross-Cultural Studies*. Amsterdam: John Benjamins, 1997. 267-282.

Baronov, David, and Kevin A. Yelvington. "Ethnicity, Race, Class, and Nationality." In *Understanding the Contemporary Caribbean*. Eds. Richard S. Hillman and Thomas J. D'Agostino. Boulder, Colorado and Kingston, Jamaica: Lynne Rienner and Ian Randle, 2003. 209-238.

Barradas, Efraín. "North of the Caribbean: An Outline for a History of Spanish-Caribbean Literature in the United States." In *A History of Literature in the Caribbean Volume 1: Hispanic and Francophone Regions*. Ed. A. James Arnold. Amsterdam: John Benjamins, 1994. 85-94.

Barrow, Christine, ed. *Caribbean Portraits: Essays on Gender Ideologies and Identities*. Kingston: Ian Randle, 1998.

Basch, Linda, Nina Glick Schiller, and Cristina Blanc-Szanton. "There's No Place Like Home." In *Nations Unbound: Transnational Projects, Postcolonial Predicaments, and Deterritorialized Nation-States*. Longhorne: Gordon and Breach, 1994. 267-295.

Bauman, Zygmunt. "The Making and Unmaking of Strangers." In *Debating Cultural Hybridity: Multi-Cultural Identities and the Politics of Anti-Racism*. Eds. Pnina Werbner and Tariq Modood. London: Zed Books, 2000. 46-57.

Benítez-Rojo, Antonio. *The Repeating Island: The Caribbean and the Postmodern Perspective*. Durham: Duke UP, 1996.

Benjamin, Walter. *The Arcades Project*. Cambridge: Harvard UP, 1999.

Berger, John. *Ways of Seeing*. London: BBC and Penguin, 1985.

Berry, Glyn R. "Immigration to Canada-West Indies Relations: An Unwelcome Retrenchment." *Revista'Review Interamericana* VII. 1 (Spring 1977): 87-98.

Birbalsingh, Frank, ed. *Frontiers of Caribbean Literature in English*. London: MacMillan Caribbean, 1996.

Bolland, O. Nigel. *The Politics of Labour in the British Caribbean: The*

Social Origins of Authoritarianism and Democracy in the Labour Movement. Kingston: Ian Randle, 2001.

Bolles, A. Lynn. "'Goin' abroad': Working Class Jamaican Women and Migration." In *Female Immigrants to the United States: Caribbean, Latin American, and African Experiences*. Washington DC: RIIES Smithsonian Institute, 1981. 56-84.

Bosch, Juan. *De Cristóbal Colón a Fidel Castro: El Caribe frontera imperial*. Santo Domingo: Alfa y Omega, 1983.

Brand, Dionne. *In Another Place, Not Here*. New York: Grove P, 1996.

Brereton, Bridget. "Society and Culture in the Caribbean: The British and French West Indies, 1870-1980." In *The Modern Caribbean*. Eds. Franklin W. Knight and Colin A. Palmer. Chapel Hill: U North Carolina P, 1989. 85-110.

Brettell, Caroline. *Anthropology and Migration: Essays on Transnationalism, Ethnicity, and Identity*. Walnut Creek, CA: AltaMira, 2003.

———. "Theorizing Migration in Anthropology: The Social Construction of Networks, Identities, Communities, and Globalscapes." In *Migration Theory: Talking Across Disciplines*. Eds. Caroline B. Brettell and James F. Hollifield. New York: Routledge, 2000. 97-135.

Browdy de Hernández, Jennifer. "The Plural Self: The Politicization of Memory and Form in Three American Ethnic Autobiographies." In *Memory and Cultural Politics: New Approaches to American Ethnic Literatures*. Eds. Amritjit Singh, Joseph T. Skerrett, Jr., and Robert G. Hogan. Boston: Northeastern UP, 1996. 41-59.

Bryce-Laporte, Roy S. "The New Immigration: The Female Majority." In *Female Immigrants to the United States: Caribbean, Latin American, and African Experiences*. Washington D.C.: RIIES Smithsonian Institute, 1981. vii-xxxvii.

Burton, Richard. *French and West Indians: Martinique, Guadeloupe and French Guiana Today*. Charlottesville: UP Virginia, 1995.

Byron, Margaret. *Post-War Caribbean Migration to Britain: The Unfinished Cycle*. Aldershot: Ashgate, 1994.

Caminero-Santangelo, Marta. "Speaking for Others: Problems of Representation in the Novels of Julia Alvarez." *Antípodas* X (1998): 53-66.

Campuzano, Luisa. 'El viaje que se repite': escritura y política del desplazamiento en la narrativa de Julia Alvarez." *Conferencias e interferencias, escribir desde los borde(r)s*. Ed. Rita De Maeseneer. Valencia: Ediciones E Cultura, 2001. 31-37.

Canepa, Gina. "Representatividad y marginalidad literarias y la historiografía de la literatura latinoamericana." In *Literatura más allá de la marinalidad*. Suiza: AELSAL, 1988. 114-129.

Carrera Suárez, Isabel. "About Mother(Land): Joan Riley's Fiction." In *Motherlands: Black Women's Writing from Africa, the Caribbean and South Asia*. Ed. Susheila Nasta. New Brunswick, NJ: Rutgers UP, 1992. 290-309.

Carrión, Juan Manuel, ed. *Ethnicity, Race and Nationality in the Caribbean*. Río Piedras: UPR, Institute of Caribbean Studies, 1997.

Casimir, Jean. *The Caribbean: One and Divisible*. Santiago, Chile: UN Economic Commission for Latin America and the Caribbean, 1992.

Castells, Manuel. "Information Technology, the Restructuring of Capital-Labor Relationships, and the Rise of the Dual City." In *The Castells Reader*. Oxford: Blackwell, 2002. 285-313.

Castillo, Debra A. *Talking Back: Toward a Latin American Feminist Literary Criticism*. Ithaca: Cornell UP, 1992.

Castles, Stephen and Alastair Davidson. *Citizenship and Migration: Globalization and the Politics of Belonging*. New York: Routledge, 2000.

Castor, Suzy. *La ocupación norteamericana de Haití y sus consecuencias (1915-1934)*. México: Siglo XXI, 1971.

Chamberlain, Mary, ed. *Caribbean Migration: Globalised Identities*. London and New York: Routledge, 1998. 1-17.

_____. "The Family as Model and Metaphor in Caribbean Migration to Britain." *Journal of Ethnic and Migration Studies* 25. 2 (April 1999): 251-266.

Chamberlin, J. Edward. *If This Is Your Land, Where are Your Stories? Finding Comon Grounds*. Toronto: Alfred A. Knopf, 2003.

Chambers, Iain. *Migrancy, Culture, Identity*. London: Routledge, 1994.

Chancy, Myriam J.A. "The Heart of Home: Loida Maritza Pérez in Dialogue." *MaComère* 5 (2002): 6-18.

_____. *Searching for Safe Spaces: Afro-Caribbean Women Writers in Exile*. Philadelphia: Temple UP, 1997.

Chaney, Elsa M. and Mary García Castro, eds. *Muchachas No More:*

Household Workers in Latin America and the Caribbean. Philadelphia: Temple UP, 1989.

Clark, Vèvè A. "Developing Diaspora Literacy: Allusion in Maryse Condé's *Hérémakhonon*." In *Out of the Kumbla: Caribbean Women and Literature*. Eds. Carole Boyce Davies and Elaine Savory Fido. Trenton, NJ: Africa World P, 1990. 303-319.

Cliff, Michelle. *No Telephone to Heaven*. New York: Plume, 1987.

Clifford, James. "Diasporas." In *Routes: Travel and Translation in the Late Twentieth Century*. Cambridge: Harvard, 1997. 244-277.

———. "Traveling Cultures." In *Cultural Studies*. New York: Routledge, 1992. 96-116.

———. "Traveling Cultures." In *Routes: Travel and Translation in the Late Twentieth Century*. Cambridge: Harvard UP, 1997. 17-46.

Cofer, Judith Ortiz. *The Line of the Sun*. Athens: U Georgia P, 1989.

Cohen, Robin. "Cultural Diaspora." In *Caribbean Migration: Globalised Identities*. Ed. Mary Chamberlain. London and New York: Routledge, 1998. 21-35.

Colen, Shellee. "'Just a Little Respect': West Indian Domestic Workers in New York City." In *Muchachas No More: Household Workers in Latin America and the Caribbean*. Eds. Elsa M. Chaney and Mary García Castro. Philadelphia: Temple UP, 1989. 171-194.

Condé, Maryse. *Desirada*. New York: Soho P, 2000 (originally published in 1997).

———. *Heremakhonon*. Washington DC: Three Continents P, 1982 (originally published in 1976).

———. *A Season in Rihata*. Oxford: Heinemann, 1988 (originally published in 1981).

———. *Tales from the Heart*. New York: Soho P, 2001 (originally published in 1998).

———. *Tree of Life*. New York: Ballantine Books, 1992 (originally published in 1987).

———. "What About Those Who Don't Have Grandmothers?" In *Contemporary Women Writing in the Other Americas. Vol. II*. Ed. Georgiana M.M. Colvile. Lewiston: Edwin Mellen P, 1996. 307-311.

Condon, Stephanie. "Gender Issues in the Study of Circulation Between the Caribbean and the French Metropole." *Caribbean Studies* 32.1 (January-June 2004): 129-159.

Constant, Fred. "The French Antilles in the 1990s: Between European Unification and Political Territorialisation." In *Islands at the Crossroads: Politics in the Non-Independent Caribbean*. Eds. Aaron Gamaliel Ramos and Angel Israel Rivera. Kingston and Boulder, CO: Ian Randle and Lynne Rienner, 2001. 80-94.

Conway, Dennis. "The Caribbean Diaspora." In *Understanding the Contemporary Caribbean*. Eds. Richard S. Hillman and Thomas J. D'Agostino. Boulder: Lynne Rienner, 2003. 333-353.

Conway, Dennis, Adrian J. Bailey, and Mark Ellis. "Gendered and Racialized Circulation-Migration: Implications for the Poverty and Work Experience of New York's Puerto Rican Women. In *Migration, Transnationalization, and Race in a Changing New York*. Eds. Héctor R. Cordero-Guzmán, et al. Philadelphia: Temple UP, 2001. 146-166.

Coser, Stelamaris. "From the Natives' Point of View: The Ethnographic Novels of Paule Marshall." In *Bridging the Americas: The Literature of Toni Morrison, Paule Marshall, and Gayl Jones*. Philadelphia: Temple UP, 1994. 27-80.

Crespo, Elizabeth. "Puerto Rican Women: Migration and Changes in Gender Roles." In *International Yearbook of Oral History and Life Stories Volume 3: Migration and Identity*. Eds. Rina Benmayor and Andor Skotnes. London: Oxford UP, 1994. 137-150.

Cresswell, Tim. "Introduction: Theorizing Place." In *Mobilizing Place, Placing Mobility: The Politics of Representation in a Globalized World*. Eds. Ginette Verstraete and Tim Cresswell. Amsterdam: Rodopi, 2002. 11-31.

Crosta, Suzanne "Breaking the Silence: Cultural Identities and Narrative Configurations in the French Caribbean Novel." In *An Introduction to Caribbean Francophone Writing: Guadeloupe and Martinique*. Ed. Sam Haigh. Oxford: Berg, 1999. 159-176.

Cudjoe, Selwyn R., ed. *Caribbean Women Writers: Essays from the First International Conference*. Wellesley, MA: Calaloux P. 1990.

———. "Jamaica Kincaid and the Modernist Project: An Interview." In *Caribbean Women Writers: Essays from the First International Conference*. Wellesley: Calaloux, 1990. 215-232.

Dahomay, Jacky. "Cultural Identity versus Political Identity in the French West Indies." In *Modern Political Culture in the Caribbean*. Eds. Holger Henke and Fred Reno, Mona, Jamaica: U West Indies P, 2003. 90-108.

Daniel, Justin. "The Construction of Dependency: Economy and Politics in the French Antilles." In *Islands at the Crossroads: Politics in the Non-Independent Caribbean*. Eds. Aaron Gamaliel Ramos and Angel Israel Rivera. Kingston and Boulder, CO: Ian Randle and Lynne Rienner, 2001. 61-79.

Danticat, Edwidge. *Breath, Eyes, Memory*. New York: Vintage, 1995.

_____. *The Farming of Bones*. New York: Soho, 1998.

_____. *Krik? Krak!*. New York: Vintage, 1996.

Dash, Michael. "Exile and Recent Literature." In *A History of Literature in the Caribbean. Vol. 1 Hispanic and Francophone Regions*. Ed. A. James Arnold. Amsterdam: John Benjamins, 1994. 452-461.

Davies, Carol Boyce. "'Writing Home': Gender, Heritage and Identity in Afro-Caribbean Women's Writing in the United States." In *Black Women, Writing and Identity: Migrations of the Subject*. London: Routledge, 1994. 113-129.

Davies, Carol Boyce and Elaine Savory Fido, eds. *Out of the Kumbla: Caribbean Women and Literature*. Trenton, NJ: Africa World P, 1990.

Dávila, Arlene M. *Sponsored Identities: Cultural Politics in Puerto Rico*. Philadelphia: Temple UP, 1997.

Delamotte, Eugenia C. *Places of Silence, Journeys of Freedom: The Fiction of Paule Marshall*. Philadelphia: U Pennsylvania P, 1998.

Delgado Pasapera, Germán. *Puerto Rico: Sus luchas emancipadoras*. Río Piedras: Cultural, 1984.

Denniston, Dorothy Hamer. *The Fiction of Paule Marshall: Reconstruction of History, Culture, and Gender*. Knoxville: U Tennessee P, 1995.

Duany, Jorge. "Common Threads or Desperate Agendas?: Recent Research on Migration from and to Puerto Rico." *Centro* VII.1 (winter 94-95): 60-77.

_____. " The Creation of a Transnational Caribbean Identity: Dominican Immigrants in San Juan and New York City." In *Ethnicity, Race and Nationality in the Caribbean*. Ed. Juan Manuel Carrión. San Juan: Institute of Caribbean Studies, 1997. 195-232.

_____. *Los dominicanos en Puerto Rico: Migración en la semi-periferia*. Río Piedras: Huracán, 1990.

_____. *The Puerto Rican Nation on the Move: Identities on the Island and in the United States*. Chapel Hill: U North Carolina P, 2002.

Duarte, Isis. "Household Workers in the Dominican Republic: A Question for the Feminist Movement." In *Muchahas No More: Household Workers in Latin America and the Caribbean*. Eds. Elsa M. Chaney and Mary García Castro. Philadelphia: Temple UP, 1989. 197-219.

Edgell, Zee. *In Times Like These*. London: Heinemann, 1991.

Edmondson, Belinda. "Return of the Native: Immigrant Women's Writing and the Narrative of Exile." In *Making Men: Gender, Literary Authority, and Women's Writing in Caribbean Narrative*. Durham: Duke UP, 1999. 137-167.

Egan, Susanna. "Dialogues of Diaspora." In *Mirror Talk: Genres of Crisis in Contemporary Autobiography*. Chapel Hill: U of North Carolina P, 1999. 120-158.

Ellis, Patricia. *Women, Gender and Development in the Caribbean*. London and Kingston: Zed and Ian Randle, 2003.

"An Era of International Migration." In *World Migration Report 2000*. International Organization for Migration (IOM)-United Nations, 2000. 3-56.

Espín, Oliva M. *Women Crossing Boundaries: A Psychology of Immigration and Transformations of Sexuality*. New York: Routledge, 1999.

Estéves, Carmen, and Lizabeth Paravisini-Gebert. "Introduction." In *Green Cane Juicy Flotsam: Short Stories by Caribbean Women*. New Brunswick: Rutgers UP, 1981. xi-xxvi.

Ferguson, Moira, *Jamaica Kincaid: Where the Land Meets the Body*. Charlottesville: UP Virginia, 1994.

Fernández-Retamar, Roberto. *Calibán: Apuntes sobre la cultura en nuestra América*. México: Diógenes, 1971.

Ffolkes, Suzanne. "Violence against Women: Some legal Responses." In *Gender: A Caribbean Multi-Disciplinary Perspective*. Edss. Elsa Leo-Rhynie, Barbara Bailey, Christine Barrow. Kingston: Ian Randle, 1997. 118-127.

Fido, Elaine Savory. "Mother/Lands: Self and Separation in the Works of Buchi Emecheta, Bessie Head and Jean Rhys." In *Motherlands*. New Brunswick: Rutgers UP, 1992. 330-349.

Fischer, Michael M.J. "Ethnicity and the Post-Modern Arts of Memory." In *Writing Culture: The Poetics and Politics of Ethnography*. Berkeley: U California P, 1986. 194-233.

Flores, Juan. "'Qué assimilated, brother, yo soy asimilao':The Structuring of Puerto Rican Identity in the U.S." In *Divided Borders: Essays on Puerto Rican Identity*. Houston, TX: Arte Público, 1993. 182-195.

Foner, Nancy. "Towards a Comparative Perspective on Caribbean Migration." In *Caribbean Migration: Globalised Identities*. Ed. Mary Chamberlain. London and New York: Routledge, 1998. 47-60.

———. "Transnationalism Then and Now: New York Immigrants Today and at the Turn of the Twentieth Century." In *Migration, Transnationalization, and Race in a Changing New York*. Eds. Héctor R. Cordero-Guzmán, et al. Philadelphia: Temple UP, 2001. 35-57.

Foner, Philip S. *The Spanish-Cuban-American War and the Birth of American Imperialism. Volume I: 1898-1902*. New York: Monthly Review, 1972.

———. *The Spanish-Cuban-American War and the Birth of American Imperialism. Volume II: 1895-1898*. New York: Monthly Review, 1972.

Fouron, Georges E. and Nina Glick Schiller. "The Generation of Identity: Redefining the Second Generation within a Transnational Social Field." In *Migration, Transnationalization, and Race in a Changing New York*. Eds. Héctor R. Cordero-Guzmán, et al. Philadelphia: Temple UP, 2001. 58-86.

Friedman, Susan Stanford. *Mappings: Feminism and the Cultural Geographies of Encounter*. Princeton: Princeton UP, 1998.

Furst, Desider and Lilian R. Furst. *Home Is Somewhere Else: Autobiography in Two Voices*. Albany: SUNY P, 1994.

Gallagher, Mary. *Soundings in French Caribbean Writing Since 1950: The Shock of Space and Time*. Oxford: Oxford UP, 2002.

García, Cristina. *The Agüero Sisters*. New York: Alfred A. Knopf, 1997.

———. *Dreaming in Cuban*. New York: Ballantine, 1992.

García, María Cristina. *Havana USA: Cuban Exiles and Cuban Americans in South Florida, 1959-1994*. Berkeley: U California P, 1996.

García Canclini, Néstor. *Consumers: Globalization and Multicultural Conflicts*. Minneapolis: U Minnesota P, 2001.

George, Rosemary Marangoly. *The Politics of Home: Postcolonial Relocations and Twentieth-Century Fiction*. Cambridge: Cambridge UP, 1996.

Gikandi, Simon. *Maps of Englishness: Writing Identity in the Culture of Colonialism*. New York: Columbia UP, 1996.

Gmelch, George. *Double Passage: The Lives of Caribbean Migrants Abroad and Back Home*. Ann Arbor: U Michigan P, 1992.

Godoy, Ricardo, Glenn P. Jenkins, and Karishma Patel. "Puerto Rican Migration: An Assessment of Quantitative Studies." *Centro Journal* XV.2 (Fall 2003): 207-231.

González, Lydia Milagros, and A.G. Quintero Rivera. *La otra cara de la historia: La historia de Puerto Rico desde su cara obrera*. Río Piedras: CEREP, 1984.

Green, Charles. "Identity and Adaptation in the 1990s: Caribbean Immigrant Youth in New York City." *Wadabagei* 1, 1 (Winter/ Spring 1998): 111-139.

Greene, Gayle. "Feminist Fiction and the Uses of Memory." *Journal of Women in Culture and Society* 16.2 (1991): 290-321.

Griffin, Gabriele. "'Writing the Body': Reading Joan Riley, Grace Nichols and Ntozake Shange." In *Black Women's Writing*. Ed. Gina Wisker. New York: St. Martin's P, 1993. 19-42.

Grosfoguel, Ramón. "Colonial Caribbean Migrations to France, The Netherlands, Great Britain and the United States." *Ethnic and Racial Studies* 20. 3 (July 1997): 594-612.

———. "Migration and Geopolitics in the Greater Antilles." In *Colonial Subjects: Puerto Ricans in a Global Perspective*. Berkeley: U California P, 2003. 103-127.

———. "Puerto Ricans in the USA: A Comparative Approach." *Journal of Ethnic and Migration Studies* 25. 2 (April 1999): 233-249.

———. "La racialización de los migrantes coloniales del Caribe en los centros metropolitanos: una introducción a la historia de las diversas colonialidades en cada imperio" *Caribbean Studies* 38,1 (January-June 2004): 3-41.

Grosfoguel, Ramón and Chloé S. Georas. "Latino Caribbean Diasporas in New York." In *Mambo Montage: The Latinization of New York*. Eds. Agustín Laó-Montes and Arlene Dávila. New York: Columbia UP, 2001. 97-118.

Haigh, Sam. *Mapping a Tradition: Francophone Women's Writing from Guadeloupe*. London: Modern Humanities Research Association, 2000.

Hall, Stuart. "Cultural Identity and Diaspora." In *Colonial Discourse and Post-Colonial Theory: A Reader*. Eds. Patrick Williams and Laura Chrisman. New York: Columbia UP, 1994, 392-403.

———. "New Ethnicities." In *Stuart Hall: Critical Dialogues in Cultural Studies*. London: Routledge, 1996. 441-449.

———. "What Is This 'Black' in Black Popular Culture?" In *Stuart Hall: Critical Dialogues in Cultural Studies*." Eds. David Morley and Kuan-Hsing Chen. Routledge: London and New York, 1996. 465-475.

Hargreaves, Alec G. "Perceptions of Ethnic Difference in Post-War France." In *Immigrant Narratives in Contemporary France*. Eds. Susan Ireland and Patrice J. Prouix. Westport: Greenwood P, 2001. 7-22.

Harlow, Barbara. *Resistance Literature*. New York: Methuen, 1987.

Harris, Ruth L. "The Transformation of Canadian Policies and Programs to Recruit Foreign Labor: The Case of Caribbean Female Domestic Workers, 1950s-1980s." Diss. Michigan State U, 1988.

Heilbrun, Carolyn G. *Writing a Woman's Life*. New York: Ballantine, 1988.

Heisler, Barbara Schmitter. "The Sociology of Immigration: From Assimilation to Segmented Integration, from the American Experience to the Global Arena." In *Migration Theory: Talking Across Disciplines*. Eds. Caroline B. Brettell and James F. Hollifield. New York: Routledge, 2000. 77-96.

Hernández, Carmen Dolores. *Puerto Rican Voices in English: Interviews with Writers*. Westport: Praeger, 1997.

Hezekiah, Randolph. "Martinique and Guadeloupe: Time and Space." In *A History of Literature in the Caribbean. Vol. 1. Hispanic and Francophone Regions*. Ed. A. James Arnold. Amsterdam: John Benjamins, 1994. 379-387.

Hill, Donald R. "The Impact of Migration on the Metropolitan and Folk Society of Carriacou, Grenada." *Anthropological Papers of the American Museum of Natural History* 54.2 (1977): 189-391.

Holder, Calvin. "Making Ends Meet: West Indian Economic Adjustment in New York City, 1900-1952." *Wadabagei* 1,1 (Winter/Spring 1998): 31-81.

Hoving, Isabel. *In Praise of New Travelers: Reading Caribbean Migrant Women's Writing.* Stanford: Stanford UP, 2001.

Hutcheon, Linda. *A Poetics of Postmodernism: History, Theory, Fiction.* New York: Routledge, 1988.

Itzigsohn, José, and Carlos Dore Cabral. "The Manifold Character of Panethnicity: Latino Identities and Practices Among Dominicans in New York City." In *Mambo Montage: The Latinization of New York.* Eds. Agustín Laó-Montes and Arlene Dávila. New York: Columbia UP, 2001. 319-335.

James, Winston. "Migration, Racism and Identity Formation: The Caribbean Experience in Britain." In *Inside Babylon: The Caribbean Diaspora in Britain.* Eds. Winstion James and Clive Harris. London: Verso, 1993. 231-287.

Jhabvala, Ruth Prawer. *Shards of Memory.* New York: Anchor, 1995.

"Joan Riley Talks to Aamer Hussein." *Wasafiri* 17 (Spring 1993): 17-19.

Johnston, R.J., Peter J. Taylor, and Michael J. Watts, eds. *Geographies of Global Change.* Oxford: Blackwell, 1995.

Jusdanis, Gregory. *Belated Modernity and Aesthetic Culture.* Minneapolis: Minnesota UP, 1991.

Kakutani, Michiko. "From the Caribbean." *The New York Times* October 12,1990: G-31.

Kaplan, Caren. "Deterritorializations: The Rewrting of Home and Exile in Western Feminist Discourse." In *The Nature and Context of Minority Discourse.* New York: Oxford UP, 1990, 357-368.

Postmodern Discourses of Displacement. Durham: Duke UP, 2000.

———. *Questions of Travel: Postmodern Discourses of Displacement.* Durham: Duke UP, 2000.

Kasinitz, Philip. *Caribbean New York: Black Immigrants and the Politics of Race.* Ithaca: Cornell UP, 1992.

Kelley, Margot Anne. "'Daughter of Invention': Alvarez's Or(igin)ality and the Composite Novel." *Antípodas* X (1998): 41-52.

Kevane, Bridget and Juanita Heredia, eds. *Latina Self-Portraits: Interviews with Contemporary Women Writers.* New Mexico: U New Mexico P, 2000.

Kincaid, Jamaica. "Girl." In *At the Bottom of the River.* New York: Plume, 1992.

————. *Lucy*. New York: Plume, 1991 (originally published 1990).

King, Bruce. *The Internationalization of English Literature. Vol. 13. 1948-2000*. Oxford: Oxford UP, 2004.

Kubayanda, Josaphat B. "Minority Discourse and the African Collective." In *The Nature and Context of Minority Discourse*. New York: Oxford UP, 1990. 246-263.

Labelle, Micheline and Franklin Midy. "Re-reading Citizenship and the Transnatioal Practices of Immigrants." *Journal of Ethnic and Migration Studies* 25. 2 (April 1999): 213-232.

Lamming, George. *The Pleasures of Exile*. London: Allison & Busby, 1984.

Latortue, Régine Altagrâce. "Francophone Caribbean Women Writers and the Diasporic Quest for Identity: Marie Chauvet's *Amour* and Maryse Condé's *Hérémakhonon*." In *Winds of Change: The Transforming Voices of Caribbean Women Writers and Scholars*. New York: Peter Lang, 1998. 55-59.

Lewis, Gordon K. *The Growth of the Modern West Indies*. New York: Monthly Review, 1968.

————. *Puerto Rico: Libertad y poder en el Caribe*. Río Piedras: Edil, 1969.

Lionnet, Françoise. "Geographies of Pain: Captive Bodies and Violent Acts in Myriam Warner-Vieyra, Gayl Jones, and Bessie Head." In *Postcolonial Representations: Women, Literature, Identity*. Ithaca: Cornell UP, 1995. 101-128.

————. "Happiness Deferred: Maryse Condé's *Heremakhonon* and the Failure of Enunciation." In *Autobiographical Voices: Race, Gender, Self-Portraiture*. Ithaca: Cornell UP, 1989. 167-190.

————. "Inscriptions of Exile: The Body's Knowledge and the Myth of Authenticity in Myriam Warner-Vieyra and Suzanne Dracius-Pinalie." In *Postcolonial Representations: Women, Literature, Identity*. Ithaca: Cornell UP, 1995. 87-100.

————. "Introduction *Logiques métisses*: Cultural Appropriation and Postcolonial Representations." In *Postcolonial Representations: Women, Literature, Identity*. Ithaca: Cornell UP, 1995. 1-21.

————. "Introduction: The Politics and Aesthetics of *Métissage*." In *Autobiographical Voices: Race, Gender, Self-Portraiture*. Ithaca: Cornell UP, 1989. 1-29.

Luis, William. *Dance Between Two Cultures: Latino Caribbean Literature Written in the United States*. Nashville: Vanderbilt UP, 1997.

————. "El desplazamiento de los orígenes en la narrativa caribeña de Reinaldo Arenas, Luis Rafael Sánchez y Julia Alvarez". *La Torre* II. 3 (enero-marzo 1997): 39-71.

Macpherson, Heidi Slettedahl. "Perceptions of Place: Geopolitical and Cultural Positioning in Paule Marshall's Novels." In *Caribbean Women Writers: Fiction in English*. Eds. Mary Condé and Thorunn Lonsdale. New York:: St. Martin's, 1999. 75-96.

Majumdar, Margaret A. *Francophone Studies: The Essential Glossary*. London: Arnold, 2002.

Mama, Amina. "Women Abuse in London's Black Communities." In *Inside Babylon: The Caribbean Diaspora in Britain*. London: Verso, 1993. 97-134.

Marshall, Paule. *Brown Girl, Brownstones*. London: Virago P, 1982 (originally published in 1959).

Martínez-San Miguel, Yolanda. *Caribe Two Ways: Cultura de la migración en el Caribe insular hispánico*. San Juan: Callejón, 2003.

Massey, Doreen. *Space, Place, and Gender*. Minneapolis: U Minnesota P, 1994.

Matos-Rodríguez, Félix V. and Pedro Juan Hernández. *Pioneros: Puerto Ricans in New York City 1896-1948*. Charleston, SC: Arcadia, 2001.

Migrations: The Work of Sabastião Salgado. Berkeley, CA: Occasional Papers Series 26, 2004.

Miles, William F.S. "Fifty Years of 'Assimilation': Assessing France's Experience of Caribbean Decolonisation through Administrative Reform." In *Islands at the Crossroads: Politics in the Non-Independent Caribbean*. Eds. Aaron Gamaliel Ramos and Angel Israel Rivera. Kingston and Boulder, CO: Ian Randle and Lynne Rienner, 2001. 45-60.

Mitchell, David T. "Immigration and the Impossible Homeland in Julia Alvarez's *How the García Girls Lost Their Accents*." *Antípodas* X (1998): 25-40.

Mohanty, Chandra Talpade. "Introduction: Cartographies of Struggle." In *Third World Women and the Politics of Feminism*. Bloomington: Indiana UP, 1991. 1-45.

Morales-Díaz. Enrique. "Catching Glimpses: Appropriating the Female Gaze in Esmeralda Santiago's Autobiographical Writing." *Centro* XIV, 2 (Fall 2002): 131-147.

Mordecai, Pamela and Betty Wilson. "Introduction." In *Her True-True Name: An Anthology of Women's Writing from the Caribbean*. Oxford: Heinemann, 1989. ix-xx.

Morrison, Anthea. "Family and Other Trees: The Question of Identity in the Work of Maryse Condé and Simone Schwarz-Bart." In *The Woman, the Writer and Caribbean Society*. Ed. Helen Pyne-Timothy. Los Angeles: Center for Afro-American Studies, 1998. 80-90.

Mudimbe-Boyi, Elisabeth. "The Poetics of Exile and Errancy in *La Baobab fou* by Ken Bugul and *Ti-Jean L'Horizon* by Simone Schwarz-Bart." *Yale French Studies* 83. 2 (1993): 196-212.

Murdoch, H. Adlai. "Divided Desire: Biculturality and the Representation of Identity in *En attendant le bonheur*. *Callaloo* 18. 3 (1995): 579-592.

———. "Negotiating the Metropole: Patterns of Exile and Cultural Survival in Gisèle Pineau and Suzanne Dracius-Pinalie." In *Immigrant Narratives in Contemporary France*. Eds. Susan Ireland and Patrice J. Prouix. Westport: Greenwood P, 2001. 129-139.

Naipaul, V.S. *The Middle Passage*. Middlesex: Penguin, 1962.

———. *The Mimic Men*. Middlesex: Penguin, 1969.

Nair, Supriya. "Homing Instincts: Immigrant Nostalgia and Gender Politics in *Brown Girl, Brownstones*." In *Caribbean Romances: The Politics of Regional Representation*. Ed. Belinda Edmondson. Charlottesville: UP Virginia, 1999. 183-198.

Nasta, Susheila. *Motherlands: Black Women's Writing from Africa, the Caribbean and South Asia*. New Brunswick, NJ: Rutgers UP, 1992.

Newell, Stephanie, ed. *Images of African and Caribbean Women: Migration, Displacement, Diaspora*. Stirling: Centre of Commonwealth Studies, 1996.

Newson, Adele S. "The Fiction of Zee Edgell." In *Caribbean Women Writers: Fiction in English*. Eds. Mary Condé and Thorunn Lonsdale. New York: St. Martin's, 1999. 184-201.

Niesen de Abruna. Laura. "Dreams of Leaving: Mother and Mother Country in Jamaica Kincaid's Fiction." In *The Woman, the Writer & Caribbean Society: Essays on Literature and Culture*. Ed. Helen Pyne-Timothy. Los Angeles: Center for Afro-American Studies, 1998. 164-186.

Nieves Falcón, Luis. *El emigrante puertorriqueño*. Río Piedras: Edil, 1975.

"North America, Central America, and the Caribbean." *World Migration Report 2000*. International Organization for Migration (IOM)-United Nations, 2000. 235-264.

N'Zengo-Tayo, Marie-José. "Children in Haitian Popular Migration as Seen by Maryse Condé and Edwidge Danticat." In *Winds of Change: The Transforming Voices of Caribbean Women Writers and Scholars*. New York: Peter Lang, 1998. 93-100.

O'Callaghan, Evelyn. "Interior Schisms Dramatised: The Treatment of the 'Mad' Woman in the Work of Some Female Caribbean Novelists." In *Out of the Kumbla: Caribbean Women and Literature*. Eds. Carole Boyce Davies and Elaine Savory Fido. Trenton, NJ: Africa World P, 1990. 89-109.

———. *Woman Version: Theoretical Approaches to West Indian Fiction by Women*. London: MacMillan Caribbean, 1993.

Ormerod, Beverley. *An Introduction to the French-Caribbean Novel*. London: Heinemann, 1985.

———. "The Representation of Women in French Caribbean Fiction." In *An Introduction to Caribbean Francophone Writing: Guadeloupe and Martinique*. Ed. Sam Haigh. Oxford: Berg, 1999. 101-117.

Papastergiadis, Nikos. *The Turbulence of Migration: Globalization, Deteritorialization and Hybridity*. Cambridge: Polity P, 2000.

Pérez, Loida Maritza. *Geographies of Home*. New York: Viking, 1999.

Pessar, Patricia. "New Approaches to Caribbean Emigration and Return." In *Caribbean Circuits: New Directions in the Study of Caribbean Migration*. New York: Center for Migration Studies, 1997. 1-11.

———. *A Visa for a Dream: Dominicans in the United States*. Boston: Allyn and Beacon, 1995.

Pfaff, Françoise. *Conversations with Maryse Condé*. Lincoln: U Nebraska P, 1996.

Pike, Burton. *The Image of the City in Modern Literature*. Princeton: Princeton UP, 1981.

Pineau, Gisèle. *Exile According to Julia*. Charlottesville: U Virginia P, 2003 (originally published in 1996).

Plaza, Dwaine. "Migration and Adjustment to Canada: Revising the Mobility Dream 1900-1998." *The Society for Caribbean Studies Annual Conference Papers* 3 (2002). www.scsonline.freeserve.co.uk/olvol3.html

Portes, Alejandro. "Conclusion: Towards a New World—the Origins and Effects of Transnational Activities." *Ethnic and Racial Studies* 22. 2 (March 1999): 463-477.

Powers, Mary G. and John J. Macisco, Jr. *Los puertorriqueños en Nueva York: Un análisis de su participación laboral y experiencia migratoria, 1970.* San Juan: Centro de Investigaciones Sociales, 1982.

Pratt, Mary Louise. *Imperial Eyes: Travel Writing and Transculturation.* London: Routledge, 1992.

Prescod-Roberts, Margaret and Norma Steele. *Black Women: Bringing It All Back Home.* Bristol: Falling Wall, 1980.

Puri, Shalini. "Introduction, Theorizing Diasporic Cultures: The Quiet Migrations." In *Marginal Migrations: The Circulation of Cultures within the Caribbean.* Oxford: Macmillan, 2003. 1-16.

Quintero Rivera, A.G. *Conflictos de clase y política en Puerto Rico.* Río Piedras: Huracán, 1981.

_____. *Patricios y plebeyos: burgueses, hacendados, artesanos y obreros.* Río Piedras: Huracán, 1988.

Ramos, Aarón Gamaliel and Angel Israel Rivera. "Puerto Rico: Regional Transformations and Political Change." In *Islands at the Crossroads: Politics in the Non-Independent Caribbean.* Eds. Aarón Gamaliel Ramos and Angel Israel Rivera. Kingston, Jamaica: Ian Randle, 2001. 1-27.

Richardson, Bonham C. "Caribbean Migrations, 1838-1985." In *The Modern Caribbean.* Eds. Franklin W. Knight and Colin A. Palmer. Chapel Hill: U North Carolina P, 1989, 203-228.

Riley, Joan. "Introduction." In *Leave to Stay: Stories of Exile and Belonging.* Eds. Joan Riley and Briar Wood. London: Virago, 1996. 1-8.

_____. *The Unbelonging.* London: Women's Press, 1985.

_____. *Waiting in the Twilight.* London: Women's Press, 1987.

_____. "Writing Reality in a Hostile Environment." *Kunapipi* XVI.1 (1994): 547-552.

Robinson, Marc, ed. *Altogether Elsewhere: Writers on Exile.* Boston: Faber and Faber, 1994.

Rodríguez, María Cristina. "The Construction of the Imaginary Homeland: Migrating Women in Novels by Caribbean Women Writers." *TEXT: Studies in Comparative Literature* 26 (2000): 307-320.

_____. "Journey, Migration and the Reconstruction of Imaginary Homelands in Novels by Hispanic Caribbean Women." *Journal of West Indian Literature* 8, 2 (April 1999): 100-108.

_____. "Literature from the English-speaking Caribbean." In *Rethinking English in Puerto Rico*. Río Piedras: Universidad de Puerto Rico, 1998. 93-95.

_____. "Locating Caribbean Women in Centre Spaces in the Novels of Maryse Condé." *La Torre* VII. 25 (julio-septiembre 2002): 343-354.

_____. "The Narrative Work of Three West Indian Women: An Attempt to Find a True Self." *Sargasso* 4 (1987): 56-67.

_____. "Women Writers of the Spanish-Speaking Caribbean: An Overview." In *Caribbean Women Writers*. Ed. Selwyn Cudjoe. Wellesley, MA: Calaloux, 1990, 339-345.

Rosello, Mireille. "Caribbean Insularization of Identities in Maryse Condé's Work: From *En attendant le bonheur* to *Les derniers rois mages*." *Calaloo* 18. 3 (1995): 565-578.

_____. "'One More Sea to Cross': Exile and Intertextuality in Aimé Césaire's *Cahier d'un retour au pays natal*." *Yale French Studies* 83. 2 (1993): 176-195.

Rushdie, Salman. *Imaginary Homelands*. London: Granta, 1991.

Safa, Helen I. "República Dominicana: la manufactura de exportación y la crisis económica." In *De mantenidas a proveedoras: Mujeres e industrialización en el Caribe*. Río Piedras: Universidad de Puerto Rico, 1998. 135-167.

Said. Edward. *The Edward Said Reader*. New York: Vintage, 2000.

_____. "Movements and Migrations." In *Culture and Imperialism*. New York: Vintage, 1993, 326-336.

_____. "Reflections on Exile." In *Reflections on Exile and Other Essays*. Cambridge: Harvard UP, 2000. 173-186.

Sánchez, Luis Rafael. "La guagua aérea." In *La guagua aérea*. Río Piedras: Cultural, 1994. 11-22.

Santiago, Esmeralda. *Almost a Woman*. Reading, MA: Perseus, 1998.

_____. *América's Dream*. New York: HarperCollins, 1996.

_____. *When I Was Puerto Rican*. New York: Vintage, 1993.

Sassen, Saskia. *The Global City: New York, London, Tokyo*. Princeton: Princeton UP, 1991.

Scarano, Francisco A. *Puerto Rico: Cinco siglos de historia*. Bogotá, Colombia: McGraw-Hill, 1993.

Scarboro, Ann Armstrong. "(Re)Writing History: Strategies of Telling in Maryse Condé's *Une Saison á Rihata*." In *Contemporary*

Women Writing in the Other Americas. Vol. II. Ed. Georgiana M.M. Colvile. Lewiston: Edwin Mellen P, 1996. 293-306.

Schmidt, Aileen. *Mujeres excéntricas: La escritura autobiográfica femenina en Puerto Rico y Cuba.* San Juan: Callejón, 2003.

Schwartz, Meryl F. "Imagined Communities in the Novels of Michelle Cliff." In *Homemaking: Women Writers and the Politics and Poetics of Home.* Eds. Catherine Wiley and Fiona R. Barnes. New York: Garland, 1996. 287-311.

Selvon, Samuel. *The Lonely Londoners.* Longman: Three Continents P, 1979.

———. *Ways of Sunlight.* Longman: Three Continents P, 1979.

Shea, Renee. "The Dangerous Job of Edwidge Danticat: An Interview." *Callaloo* 19. 2 (1996): 382-389.

Shelton, Marie-Denise. "Condé: The Politics of Gender and Identity." *World Literature Today* 64. 4 (autumn 1993): 717-722.

———. "Haitian Women's Fiction." *Callaloo* 15.3 (1992): 770-777.

———. "Women Writers of the French-Speaking Caribbean: an Overview." In *Caribbean Women Writers.* Wellesley: Calaloux, 1990. 346-356.

Silverman, Maxim. *Deconstructing the Nation: Immigration, Racism and Citizenship in Modern France.* London: Routledge, 1992.

Singh, Amritjit, Joseph T. Skerrett, Jr., and Robert G. Hogan, eds. "Introduction." In *Memory and Cultural Politics: New Approaches to American Ethnic Literatures.* Boston: Northeastern UP, 1996. 3-18.

Smith, Robert C., Héctor R. Cordero-Guzmán, and Ramón Grosfoguel. "Introduction: Migration, Transnationalization, and Ethnic and Racial Dynamics in a Changing New York." In *Migration, Transnationalization, and Race in a Changing New York.* Eds. Héctor R. Cordero-Guzmán, et al. Philadelphia: Temple UP, 2001. 1-34.

Smith, Sidonie and Gisela Brinker-Gabler. "Introduction: Gender, Nation, and Immigration in the New Europe." In *Writing New Identities: Gender, Nation, and Imigration in Contemporary Europe.* Minneapolis: U Minnesota P, 1997. 1-27.

Smyth, Heather. "Sexual Citizenship and Caribbean-Canadian Fiction: Dionne Brand's *In Another Place, Not Here* and Shani Mootoo's *Cereus Blooms at Night.*" *Ariel* 30.2 (April 1999): 141-160.

Sourieau, Marie-Agnès. "Afterword." In *Exile According to Julia.* Charlottesville: U Virginia P, 2003. 171-187.

Spivak, Gayatri Chakravorty. "Reading the World: Literary Studies in the Eighties." In *In Other Worlds: Essays in Cultural Politics.* New York: Routledge, 1988. 95-102.

Sturgess, Charlotte. "Dionne Brand: Writing the Margins." In *Caribbean Women Writers: Fiction in English.* Eds. Mary Condé and Thorunn Lonsdale. New York: St. Martin's: 1999. 202-216

Suárez, Lucía. "Gisèle Pineau: Writing the Dimensions of Migration." *World Literature Today* 75.3 (summer/autumn 2001): 9-21.

Sunshine, Catherine A. and Keith Q. Warner, eds. *Caribbean Connections: Moving North.* Washington DC: Network of Educators on the Americas, 1998.

Thomas, Derrick. "The Social Integration of Immigrants in Canada." In *The Immigration Dilemma.* Ed. Steven Globerman. Vancouver: The Fraser Institute, 1992. 211-260.

Thomas-Hope, Elizabeth. "Emigration Dynamics in the Anglophone Caribbean." In *Emigration Dynamics in Developing Countries. Vol. III: Mexico, Central America and the Caribbean.* Ed. Reginald Appleyard. Aldershot: Ashgate, 1999. 232-284.

Tirman, John. "Nationalism in Exile." *Boston Review* 26 (Summer 2001): 21-3.

Torres-Saillant, Silvio. "Dominican Literature and Its Criticism: Anatomy of a Troubled Identity." In *A History of Literature in the Caribbean Volume 1: Hispanic and Francophone Regions.* Ed. A. James Arnold. Amsterdam: John Benjamins, 1994. 49-64.

———. "La literatura dominicana en los Estados Unidos y la periferia del margen." *Punto y Coma* III. 1 and 2 (1991):139-149.

Traba, Marta. "Hipótesis sobre una escritura diferente." In *La sartén por el mango.* San Juan: Huracán, 1985. 21-26.

Trinh, T. Minh-ha. *Woman, Native Other.* Bloomington: Indiana UP, 1989.

Turner, Faythe. "Introduction." In *Puerto Rican Writers at Home in the USA: An Anthology.* Seattle: Open Hand, 1991. 1-6.

Van Alphen, Ernst. "Imagined Homelands." In *Mobilizing Place, Placing Mobility: The Politics of Representation in a Globalized World.*

Eds. Ginette Verstraete and Tim Cresswell. Amsterdam: Rodopi, 2002. 53-69.

Van Hear, Nicholas. *New Diasporas*. Seattle: U Washington P, 1998.

Vega, Ana Lydia, ed. *El tramo ancla: Ensayos puertorriqueños de hoy*. San Juan: Universidad de Puerto Rico, 1988.

Vega, Bernardo. *Memoirs of Bernardo Vega: A Contribution to the History of the Puerto Rican Community in New York*. New York: Monthly Review, 1984.

Vilches Norat, Vanessa. "Sólo resta traducir a la lengua materna." In *De(s)madres o el rastro materno en las escrituras del Yo*. Chile: Cuarto Propio, 2003. 139-169.

Warner-Vieyra, Myriam. *As the Sorcerer Said...*. Essex: Longman, 1982 (originally published in 1980).

———. *Juletane*. London: Heinemann, 1987 (originally published in 1982).

Washington, Mary Helen. "Afterword." In *Brown Girl, Brownstones*. London: Virago, 1982. 311-324.

Watkins-Owens, Irma. *Blood Relations: Caribbean Immigrants and the Harlem Community, 1900-1930*. Bloomington: Indiana UP, 1996.

Welsh, Sarah Lawson. "(Un)belonging Citizens, Unmapped Territory: Black Immigration and British Identity in the Post-1945 Period." In *Not on Any Map: Essays on Postcoloniality and Cultural Nationalism*. Exeter, Devon: U Exeter P, 1997. 43-66.

Williams, Claudette M. *Charcoal and Cinnamon: The Politics of Color in Spanish Caribbean Literature*. Gainesville, FL: UP Florida, 2000.

Williams, Eric. *From Columbus to Castro: The History of the Caribbean 1402-1969*. New York: Harper & Row, 1973.

Williams, Raymond. "The New Metropolis." In *The Country & the City*. New York: Oxford UP, 1973. 279-288.

Wilson, Betty. "Introduction." In *Juletane*. London: Heinemann, 1987. v-xv.

Wilson, Elizabeth. "'Le voyage et l'espace clos'-Island and Journey as Metaphor: Aspects of Woman's Experience in the Works of Francophone Caribbean Woman's Novelists." In *Out of the Kumbla: Caribbean Women and Literature*. Trenton, NJ: Africa World P, 1990. 45-58.

Wilson-Tagoe, Nana. "Configurations of History in the Writing of West Indian Women." In *Historical Thought and Literary Repre-*

sentation in West Indian Literature. Gainesville and Jamaica: UP Florida and UP West Indies, 1998. 223-252.

Woodhull, Winifred. "Ethnicity on the French Frontier." In *Writing New Identities: Gender, Nation, and Immigration in Contemporary Europe*. Eds. Gisela Brinker-Gabler, and Sidonie Smith. Minneapolis: U Minnesota P, 1997. 31-61.

Wynter, Sylvia. "On Disenchanting Discourse: 'Minority' Literary Criticism and Beyond." In *The Nature and Context of Minority Discourse*. New York: Oxford UP, 1990. 432-469.